D1460058

Brenda Chamberlain

ARTIST AND WRITER

Self Portrait on Garnedd Dafydd, 1938, oil on canvas

Brenda Chamberlain

ARTIST AND WRITER

Jill Piercy

Parthian
The Old Surgery
Napier Street
Cardigan
SA43 1ED

www.parthianbooks.com

First published in 2013
© Jill Piercy 2013
All Rights Reserved

ISBN 9781906998233

Cover design by www.theundercard.co.uk
Typeset by typesetter.org.uk
Printed and bound by Gomer Press, Llandysul, Wales

The publisher acknowledges the financial support of
the Welsh Books Council.

British Library Cataloguing in Publication Data

A cataloguing record for this book is available from
the British Library

Contents

List of Illustrations

COLOUR PLATES

Mountain Cottager 2, 1938, oil on board
The Harvesters, 1939, hand-coloured linocut
Tŷ'r Mynydd, 1940s, watercolour
Figures in a Landscape, 1941, hand-coloured linocut
Fisherman Resting, 1949, oil on canvas
Girl with a Siamese Cat, 1951, oil on canvas
Jeune Fille aux Aubergines, also known as *Dora Maar – Intérieur Provençal*, 1952, oil on canvas
The Red Coffee Pot, 1952, oil on canvas
Girl with head-dress, mural in Carreg, Bardsey Island, now painted over, photo
The Doves, 1953, crayon & gouache on paper
Encounter at Full Moon (Women by the Sea), 1959, oil on canvas
The Eye of the Sea, 1960, oil on canvas
Charles at Ménerbes, 1961, oil on canvas
Fishing Boats at St. Ives (The Night Fishing), 1959, oil on canvas
Love in a Private Garden III, August 1965, wax crayon on card
Untitled, 1965, wax crayon on card

DUST JACKET

Front: Brenda on Hydra, 1966
Back: Brenda in Carreg kitchen, Bardsey Island, 1953

FRONTISPIECE: Self Portrait on Garnedd Dafydd, 1938, oil on canvas

ILLUSTRATIONS IN TEXT

Introduction:
Notes on her family history written by Brenda Chamberlain

Chapter 1:
Map of north Wales
Marriage of Elsie Cooil and Francis Thomas Chamberlain
Family photo, wedding reception

vii

Source material for *The Wounded Torso of the Drowned Fisherman*, from a scientific magazine

The Wounded Torso of the Drowned Fisherman, 1962, ink on paper

Title page of a draft manuscript for *Tide-race*, ink on paper

Flood Tide in West Cave 2, 1960, chalk and gouache on paper

Map of Europe showing route 20 October 1962

Chapter 9:

Map of Hydra

View of the Harbour,

Spiti Cameron and the Good Wells, Kala Pigadia

Brenda at the Good Wells, Kala Pigadia

Aghia Ephraxia, *A Rope of Vines*, p. 87

Brenda [centre wearing a headscarf] with friends at a cafe in Hydra harbour, July 1963

Leonidas' House, *A Rope of Vines*, p. 105

Chapter 10:

A view from the mountains, *A Rope of Vines,* p. 87

Robertos Saragas rehearsing

Drawing of Robertos dancing to *La Cathédrale Engloutie* by Debussy, ink on paper Drawing of Robertos on the wall of Janette Read's house, Kamini, Hydra, 1964,

The Dance 1964, ink on paper, used on programme cover for *Dance Recital*, November 1964

A page from a music notebook showing Byzantine Chant, ink on paper

Untitled, Dec.1965, wax crayon on card

Brenda on Hydra, 1963

Chapter 11:

Brenda's house

The 10 Black Brides as displayed in the Island Artist exhibition at Oriel Mostyn, 1988

The Black Bride No. 7, 1965, gouache, ink and crayon

Cat on the Terrace, *A Rope of Vines,* p. 88

Monks on Muleback, *A Rope of Vines*, p. 26

The Beast, Oct. 1965, wax crayon on card

Preface

Although I never met her, Brenda Chamberlain has been a part of my life for a long time. It was 1972 when I first came across her work while I was searching for a topic for my final year thesis at Aberystwyth University. Shelagh Hourahane, my Fine Art History tutor suggested I do some original research and select a Wales based artist. She gave me a box full of exhibition catalogues to go through and I was immediately drawn by Brenda Chamberlain's 'Self Portrait on Garnedd Dafydd' from the touring exhibition 'Two Painters – Brenda Chamberlain and Ernest Zobole' in 1963.

Over the following years, I found myself continually meeting friends of hers and recognising her paintings in people's houses. The more I discovered about her, the more I became intrigued about her life and work and decided that there was a fascinating story needing to be gathered and shared with others.

In search of the facts, I have found myself in some strange and wonderful places and have met some warm and fascinating people, all of whom in their different ways have willingly shared their memories of Brenda with me. I have travelled to Bardsey Island, Bangor and Llanllechid, all over England and Wales, Germany, Scotland and the Greek island of Ydra. I have based this biography on a vast amount of handwritten material (letters and notebooks), in both public and private hands, on material published and interviews with friends and family.

While some of the chapter headings are descriptive, the rest are taken from Brenda Chamberlain's own writings.

Key to my research has been the archive of her work at the National Library of Wales, Aberystwyth where many of her manuscripts, sketchbooks, paintings and drawings have been deposited by friends and family. For anyone wishing to explore her work further, this is the best place to begin.

Sadly many of the people I interviewed are no longer with us but I would like to publicly thank all the many individuals and institutions who have helped me along my way especially the following:

Gwynne Brown of the Tegfryn Art Gallery, The Revd William Burman, Alan Clodd, Anthony Conran, Maurice and Anne Cooke, The Daniel family, Mr & Mrs Frank Dahn, Halim El-Dabh and David Badagnani, Hywel Ellis, Lindsey Evans, Ernest & Christine Evans, Nellie Evans, Olwen Foreman, Kaye Gimpel of Gimpel Fils Gallery, Mary Grierson, Elis Gwyn Jones, Peter Jones, Kitty Idwal Jones, Richard Griffiths, Raymond Garlick, Margaret Body of Hodder & Stoughton, Douglas B. Hague, Kate Holman, Shelagh Hourahane, Jonah Jones and Judith Maro, Dr Glyn Jones, Mary Elen Jones, Anna Elwyn-Jones, Esmé Kirby, Eileen and Ravinder Jasser, Dr Karl von Laer & Grita Maria,

Otto Justus von Laer, Varvara & Popi Lembessi, Peter Lockyer, Marios Loizides, Peter Lord, Gavrick Losey, Dick Loxton, David Lyn, Gweno Lewis, Roland Matthias, Alan McPherson, Roger Maybank, Prof. Clement & Sheila Mundle, Donald Moore, Susan Mackay, Aidan McFarlane, John Petts, Vasilis Politis, I.D. Powell, Alan Proctor, Janette Read, Joan Rees, Dr. Martin Richards, Dr Michael Senior, Barbara Stafford, Harold Taylor, Jeremy Theopholus, Dafydd Thomas, Dorothy Tutin, Jean Ware, John Webster, Huw Wheldon, Nerys Wheldon, Kyffin Williams, Mr & Mrs Ieuan Williams Hughes.

With especial thanks to the staff of the National Library of Wales, British Library, Bangor University, Gwynedd Archives & Museum Service, the Estate of Brenda Chamberlain, Dr Ceridwen Lloyd Morgan for her encouragement and attention to detail and the staff and editors at Parthian. The author wishes to acknowledge the award of a Writers Bursery from Literature Wales for the purpose of completing this book.

1. *Mountain Cottager 2*, 1938, oil on board

2. *The Harvesters*, 1939, hand-coloured lino-cut

3. *Tŷ'r Mynydd*, 1940s, watercolour

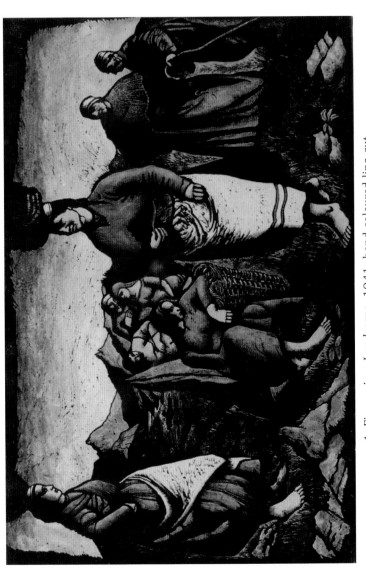

4. *Figures in a Landscape*, 1941, hand-coloured lino-cut

5. *Fisherman Resting*, 1949, oil on canvas

6. *Girl with a Siamese Cat*, 1951, oil on canvas

7. *Jeune Fille aux Aubergines*, also known as *Dora Maar – Intérieur Provençal*, 1952, oil on canvas

8. *The Red Coffee Pot*, 1952, oil on canvas

9. *Girl with head-dress*, mural in Carreg, Bardsey
(now painted over, a study for a figure in *The Doves*)

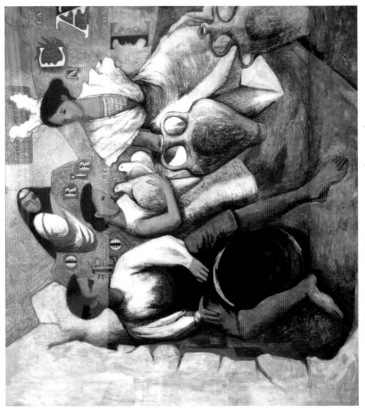

10. *The Doves*, 1953, crayon and gouache on paper

11. *Encounter at Full Moon (Women by the Sea)*, 1959, oil on canvas

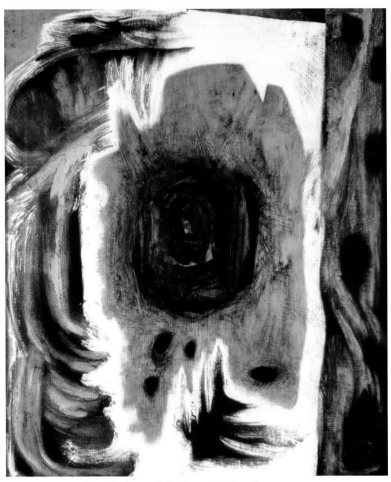

12. *The Eye of the Sea*, 1960, oil on canvas

13. *Charles at Ménerbes*, 1961, oil on canvas

14. *Fishing Boats at St. Ives (The Night Fishing)*, 1959, oil on canvas

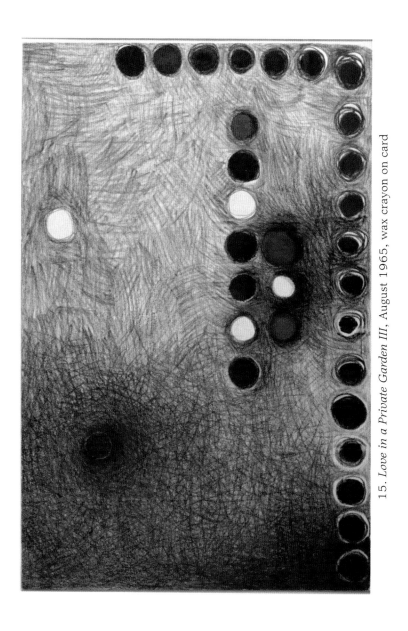

15. *Love in a Private Garden III*, August 1965, wax crayon on card

16. Untitled, 1965, wax crayon on card

Introduction

For Brenda Chamberlain, life was an adventure that she felt impelled to record in minute detail in words and images in a wide variety of styles. She was primarily a writer of prose and poetry, a painter, journal writer and prolific writer of letters. She enjoyed collaborating with others and worked with a dancer, a musician, other poets and performers to produce multimedia work at different times in her life.

Although acknowledged as a successful artist and writer during her lifetime, Brenda Chamberlain's talent has been relatively unrecognised since her death in 1971. Most of her work is now unknown as the majority of her art work is in private collections and much of her written work is still unpublished.

She was born in Bangor, north Wales in 1912 and had a secure and happy childhood. From her mother, she gained the confidence to succeed as a female in a man's world and from her father, the love to explore and travel. Her mother, Elsie, was a dominant force in the household as her husband, Francis, was often abroad with his work – initially importing wood to Britain and later as an inspector of bridges for the railway. Elsie was a committee person, a public speaker and later Mayor of Bangor who encouraged Brenda and her younger brother, Neville, to follow their dreams.

By the age of six, Brenda Chamberlain had decided she wanted to be an artist and a writer and like many strong minded individuals, nothing could dissuade her from her ambition. Aged fifteen, while still at school, she was invited to join three of her friends to work on a hand-written magazine they had been producing. Initially drawn together by a love of hill-walking, the girls took turns in editing the magazine which included accounts of their walks, prose, poetry, handy hints and drawings. It was the first time Brenda had considered combining her interest in writing and drawing together and it was to become a form she explored throughout her life.

At times she kept her writing and visual images separate but she was always seeking to find different ways to combine her words and images together and in three of her books she managed to give the two creative forms equal importance but it was often a struggle:

Emotionally, I was always tempted to drop the writing and concentrate on the painting, because, for some unknown reason, writing has always been for me an unhappy activity; while painting almost invariably makes me happy. But however hard I tried to discipline myself, sooner or later the other form would take over, dominate entirely for a time, and then swing back again.[1]

Although she travelled widely and lived in many places, Brenda's life began and ended in Bangor. It was the centre

2

from which she escaped and the safe anchorage to which she often returned. It meant a great deal to her but she rarely wrote about it or painted it. Her mother and her friends gave her support by buying her work and giving her places to stay when she returned home and she kept in touch with them with frequent conversational letters.

Brenda was always an adventurer and an explorer. She would not hesitate to climb a mountain in plimsoll shoes or walk ten miles to visit a friend and she would leap at opportunities which arose without a second thought. Having decided to apply to study art at the Royal Academy Schools in London, she travelled to Copenhagen where she stayed with a family for six months. There she discovered the work of Gauguin whose paintings would inspire her for many years.

She found the discipline of the Royal Academy stifling but it served her well as she became an excellent draughtsperson and her drawings have a spontaneity that is sometimes lost in her paintings. While in London, she met fellow artist John Petts. Together, they dreamt of an idyllic and romantic life living by their art and, after college, they moved to a cottage in Llanllechid in north Wales. Unusually for the 1930s, they lived together for a few years, before marrying in 1935. Locally they were known as 'Joseph and Mary' as often John would lead the pony with Brenda in the saddle.

Although their relationship ended after the Second World War, many more adventures were to follow. Brenda lived for over fifteen years on Bardsey Island off the Llŷn peninsula in north Wales and for five years on the Greek island of Hydra. She retained a lifelong relationship with her German friend, Karl von Laer who inspired a volume of poetry, *The Green Heart*, and she frequently visited Germany and France to see her friends and create new paintings and writing.

Brenda was continually reinventing herself and her work and would frequently recycle her poems and prose by changing words and titles so she could sell them to different publications. She was often inspired by news cuttings and photographs and would happily base a series of her paintings upon their images. She also took ideas from all manner of literary and visual material and frequently changed the style she worked from figurative to abstract and colourful to monochrome. There was no limit to what would inspire her.

It was a secret joke, never spoken of, that sometime I would write my autobiography, but it should be invented. The opening sentence had been in my mind for years. 'I come from a long line of ladies' maids.'

No, a better construction would be,

'Coming as I do from a long line of ladies' maids it is not surprising that...' What a marvellous springboard onto a fictional life.[2]

This is of course not true as can be seen from her hand-written notes about her family[3] but this sums up Brenda Chamberlain's way of portraying her life in a semi-fictional way. Although she wrote journals, she could not really be described as a keeper of diaries because she rarely kept consistent dated entries. Often she would begin writing one year and go back to the same journal many years later and make more undated entries and corrections. In addition, she used initials for people's names, added fictional accounts to factual ones and left a confused trail of what may or may not have happened.

Sadly, when she returned to Bangor, after the Colonels' Coup in Greece, she found it increasingly difficult to find new inspiration. She returned to earlier journals, writings and drawings and tried to reinvent them in the same fashion she had done throughout her life but she was unable to connect with any passion, became depressed and had a breakdown. Her line drawings in her last series clearly show her despair – figures trapped in jugs, bandaged heads and a woman's head held down by pebbles. In the last few years of her life Brenda's painting had gradually been stripped of colour and her poetry had become sparse and minimal. It was a sad but perhaps a natural end to a life which had overflowed with creativity and brought joy to many people.

1   NLW MS 21501E, f.56.
2   *Rope of Vines* p. 56.
3   Private collection; see pp. 6-7.

Maternal grandfather: Caesar Corlett Cooil born, Castletown,
Isle of Man, schooled at Ballasalla infant, where the 'little
people' lived. His mother was married 4 times, each time to
a farmer. 85 when she died, walking 3 miles a day
till the end, to & fro, the farm. CCC came to Liverpool
in 18●●89, to open engin. dept. of Railway.
Influx of English people to Bangor (formerly purely
Welsh).
Maternal grandmother Her father was a Maddocks of
Portmadoc & of Llangollen. Her mother was one of
the Yardleys, of Cheshire — (My great grandfather)
thought of nothing but horse-riding, skilled riding.
Lived on his wife's money.

Paternal grandmother Elizabeth Derry of County Down.
Her father was head gamekeeper to the Marquess of
Anglesey, in Ireland.
                    (1st cousin of Joseph Chamberlain)
Paternal grandfather with his wife kept a hotel
outside Rugeley in Staffordshire. Died of pneumonia
at 39. horseback riding She was left with 3 children, one daughter,
2 sons. Both sons to Rugeley Grammar school.
21 father went to South Africa & worked in

Notes on her family history written by Brenda Chamberlain

new post office in East Cardon – 8 years there –
returned to North Wales, stayed with brother –
short return, 3 years, in S. Africa. Bought
land on which to build, but remained in Wales.
Brother, architect & surveyor.

Father – chief works inspector, Holyhead to Crewe,
& all branch lines.

Farming on both sides of the family.

Father on his uncle's farm, also coffin-making,
as was the habit in those times.

Chapter 1

The Anchorage 1912-29

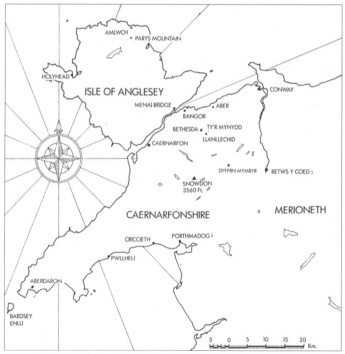

Map of north Wales

On 17 March 1912, Brenda Irene Chamberlain was born in Bangor in the old county of Caernarvonshire (now part of Gwynedd) in north Wales. For centuries, Bangor had been a fairly quiet cathedral city. It remained a comparatively insular community until the end of the eighteenth century, when tours became popular with the English gentry and the wars with France precluded Continental travel. In the nineteenth century Thomas Telford's improved road system along the north Wales coast from London to Holyhead was a major factor in opening up the area. There was a certain amount of industrial growth locally, especially in the commercial quarrying of slate from the hills south of Bangor, and in 1826, the opening of the Menai Suspension Bridge designed by Telford and the subsequent railway link in 1848 from Chester through Bangor to Holyhead allowed much easier access to the region, and much easier communication within it.

Apart from improving the transport of commercial goods to, from and within the area, the railway brought more visitors and tourists to the north Wales coast and the mountains of Snowdonia. Bangor began to gain a reputation as a holiday resort and the richer classes came to spend their summer months by the sea. New hotels were built to encourage them to stay and the newly formed Municipal Borough Council made the decision to construct a pier at Garth Point, sea-water baths and bathing huts, and also to improve the landing facilities at Garth to accommodate the passenger steamers which journeyed along the north Wales coast.

As well as developing its potential as a holiday resort, Bangor was establishing itself as a centre for education as it had been from the Middle Ages onwards. In 1862 Bangor Normal College was set up to train teachers and in

1884 a University College was established. By 1911, specially designed hostels were opened in the Upper Bangor area to house the growing number of students.

Brenda Chamberlain's younger brother, Neville, once described the city of Bangor as 'a snobby place – either you were college or you weren't.'[1] The Chamberlains weren't. It was the railway that had brought Brenda and Neville Chamberlain's grandfather, Caesar Corlett Cooil to the area. He was a Permanent Way Inspector on the railways and had moved to Bangor from Liverpool when his daughter, Elsie, was five years old. Elsie was sent to Glanadda School, then on to Cae Top School and Cynffig Davies School in Menai Bridge. She later gained her teaching certificate at the Pupil Teachers' Centre and taught at Vaynol and Cae Top primary schools. Her father became a member of Bangor Borough Council and Elsie began to take a lively interest in his work with the Council. As a teenager, her ambition was to see her father become Mayor of the city. Sadly this was not to be, as he retired from the council after ten years' service in 1919, shortly after his two sons, Captain C.A. Cooil, a graduate of the University College in Bangor, and Jack, who was in the South Wales Borderers, both tragically died in the Great War.

Although her father's involvement in local government ceased, Elsie's interest grew and from the age of sixteen she began to help with various groups in Bangor. One of the greatest encouragements she had was from Mrs Price-White of a prominent family in Bangor, who told her, 'You have the ability to do public work and it is your duty to serve the citizens of Bangor'. Elsie took this advice to heart and began to help with more committees and groups in the town, becoming a Sunday school teacher and a member of the choir at St. David's church.[2]

11

The Marriage of Elsie Cooil and Francis Thomas Chamberlain on 22 September 1910 at St. David's Church, Glanadda, Bangor

In 1910 she married Francis Thomas Chamberlain at St. David's Church, Bangor. He had been born at Hill Ridware near Lichfield on 7 June 1877, one of two sons. His father, Thomas, was a native of that area while his mother, Elizabeth, came from Ireland. Both Francis and his older brother, Richard, were proficient carpenters and experts in

Family photo at the wedding reception of Elsie Cooil and Francis Thomas Chamberlain

wood turning. During the early years of his marriage to Elsie Cooil, Francis spent a lot of time travelling abroad – to South Africa, the United States and Canada, arranging the import of wood to Britain. By all accounts, Francis Chamberlain was a quiet, intelligent man who enjoyed travelling and a challenging occupation.

The Chamberlains were living in Caernarvon Road, when, after two years of marriage, Brenda was born. Four years later, in 1916, their son Caesar Neville was born. Francis Chamberlain was in the United States when his son was born and on his return he decided to find work which would be based closer to home. He was encouraged by his father-in-law to work for the railways and in fact both Francis and his brother, Richard, became engineers, Richard at Crewe and Francis at Bangor. Although his work was now in Britain, Francis Chamberlain's job still took him away from home a great deal and the dominant force in the children's early life was their mother. As the children grew up they became 'railway children', joining their father on occasional Sundays for examination runs, special journeys and mysterious expeditions to faraway places. But for Brenda, trains were not really necessary; she had found a much easier way to travel – in her imagination. Africa was at the bottom of the garden, in a smelly water tank floating with scum. She boasted to her younger brother and

> ...lied and lied, about the heat, crocodiles, swamps. Alligators turned in strong smooth waters. My brother was sick with envy and admiration.[3]

At an early age, Brenda had discovered how much she enjoyed an audience. Perhaps this trait was inherited from her mother who had become very proficient as a public speaker. As the children grew up, Elsie Chamberlain became more involved with the WVS and was appointed vice-chairman for Wales of the women's section of the British Legion, Secretary of the Citizens Advice Bureau, and also sat on numerous committees. She was developing into a woman of considerable power and energy in Bangor. She was strong and well-built, with a formidable though friendly nature. Although her husband, Francis, was quieter and more reserved, he too was a strong character and had great enthusiasm for his work and his interests in gardening and carpentry. He kept bees in the garden and from the honey Elsie made mead. It was a secure and happy childhood for Brenda and Neville. The stone and brick house in Caernarvon Road where they lived was the end of a terrace and the rear garden backed onto a bracken-covered hillside. As well as bees, they kept rabbits in the garden and they provided endless amusement for the children. Dolls held a transient interest for the young Brenda and soon the rabbits were dressed in the dolls' clothes and taken for walks in the dolls' pram. It was in the garden that Brenda first discovered her enjoyment of drawing. She used fragments of stone and chalk to scratch patterns on the slate fence which enclosed their garden, revelling in the different textures and shapes that she could

Brenda aged 4

create. Her mother encouraged her interest as she herself enjoyed drawing and was adept at embroidery and tapestry. Another of the children's favourite occupations was to play with a toy theatre and they looked forward to the summer holidays when they could go and see plays by Shakespeare at the Memorial Theatre in Stratford-upon-Avon. Their mother's sister, Margaret, lived in the town and the children usually spent a few weeks with her in the summer holidays.

Brenda's first school was, she later wrote

kindergarten under the mothering eye of Bangor University College, where there was freedom to think, and try out one's capacities... From those days, I remember no restraints at all, only encouragement to dress up, dance (it was the time of Rhythmic Movements), paint pictures on a real easel, write essays and poems.[4]

Brenda enjoyed these activities so much so that by the age of six she had decided to be a painter and writer when she grew up.

She was a lively, likeable child with a vivid imagination and loved to dream of faraway lands and people. Even as a child she desperately wanted to be recognised as an individual and she sought attention not by her academic achievements but by her appearance. She took to wearing her long hair with a band around the forehead – an unusual style amongst little girls in the early 1920s. When asked by her school friend, Jean Jones, why she wore it that way, Brenda said that she liked to imagine herself to be a Norwegian princess. Out of doors she begged her father to let her wear his old trilby which she pulled down over her ears. She loved dressing up and enjoyed the extra attention she received when she wore something just a little unusual. But in fact it was her size that really distinguished Brenda easily from her friends. She was not growing as fast as her contemporaries and sometimes this had its drawbacks, as she herself recalled:

There was a dangerous see-saw in the garden [at the school]. I was so much smaller and lighter than my friends that it was inevitable that I should be thrown from this. My arm was broken, and my comrades carried me indoors in an interesting faint. With a sense of high drama they did not speak but presented my body to a mistress while black and white spots swam before my eyes on a fading world.[5]

When Brenda moved on to what she referred to as Miss Mason's School for girls (the local grammar school for girls), she found the discipline much firmer and her idiosyncratic taste in hairstyle and dress was not tolerated.

I suffered as a *madchen* [*sic*] in uniform: drill, prayers, 'shirts must be buttoned to the neck on all occasions', prayers, drill. I hated my shiny gym slip, the seat rubbed mirror-smooth from impatient shuffling. I suffered the indignity of being the most unteachable pupil in mathematics the school had ever known. Latin was an agony, since I longed in vain to be able to read Virgil with ease. Eventually the headmistress capitulated, allowing me to have my own timetable for the last year, English Literature, Art, French, English Language, Latin. The rest

17

of my time was spent in the school library, where I was at peace with books, a thick carpet, and silence.[6]

Despite her application to her work and the help and coaching of her three schoolgirl friends, Jean Jones, Joy Witton Davies and Mary Grierson, Brenda passed only two subjects, Art and English, in the School Leaving Certificate exams.

Brenda aged 15

These four girls were drawn together initially by their interest in fell-walking and they explored the local mountains on Saturdays and in the school holidays. When she was fifteen, Brenda was invited to join Jean, Joy and Mary in their magazine venture *Triod*, which they had begun eight months earlier in April 1927. Jean Jones was the initiator of the magazine. She used to help her father, E.H. Jones, file contributions for *The Welsh Outlook* which he edited, and was inspired to try her own hand as editor of a schoolgirl magazine. The entries were handwritten in covered exercise books and each girl took a turn to edit the magazine and copy out the articles in a neat hand. Amongst the fashion notes, gardening and household hints, puzzle pages, 'Personals', 'Funny paragraphs' and 'Etiquette' there was scope for a serial called 'The Modern Girl', for poems, short stories and drawings. In the third number of *Triod* (Christmas, 1927) the editorial announced:

> The Trefoyle has decided to admit another member into its magazine, by name, Brenda Chamberlain. This has of course upset the name of our magazine which is now called *The Tetralogue*. The contributions to this number of the old *Triod*, are most of them very good, and next number we hope to have more illustrations than ever, and we are much obliged to our new member for her excellent drawings.

In a later section of this issue Brenda was described as 'a budding Royal Academist'. She contributed to the regular features, wrote poems and short stories and illustrated the magazines with coloured line drawings. The authors chose to be identified not by names but by initials: Jean was

19

known as R.H.J.K., Joy as R.L.D., Mary as F.A. and Brenda as A.S.M.J. which stood for Anglo-Saxon-Mary-Jane, for no particular reason except that she liked the way it ran off the tongue.

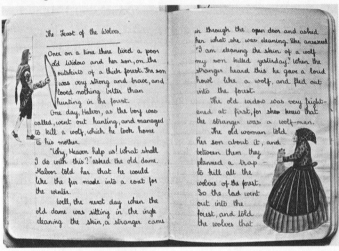

Page of *Tetralogue* written by Brenda

In *Tetralogue* 3, Brenda wrote a poem called 'The Old Witch in the Woods' and an illustrated story called 'The Feast of Wolves'. Her illustrations were well drawn and coloured with fine detail while her writing showed a youthful interest in myths and fairy stories, and although she was three years older than her fellow contributors, there was no obvious difference in maturity in her work at this stage. Brenda was editor of the fourth number of *Tetralogue*, written early in 1928, and again she contributed a poem and some prose. 'The Birth of Song' was a short story about a maiden singing in response to seeing the Sun-god, and her poem, 'The Spirit of Shakespeare' reflected on his presence in the town of

Stratford 'where', wrote Brenda, 'I love to read his plays/In the faint atmosphere of other days'.

The holidays which Brenda and her brother spent in Stratford-upon-Avon with their aunt and uncle were always very special and, as they grew up, they both developed a love of Shakespeare's work. In a later notebook Brenda recalled one of their visits:

> Idyllic afternoons in the backwaters among angry swans and inept punters on the Avon. My aunt walked up and down the punt fore-deck, in a cool lime-green silk and shady straw hat and pipe-clayed plimsoles [sic]. She dropped her pole in at exactly the right angle so as not to get water down her sleeve, so as not to over-run the pole: while we children sat paddling the turgid river, lost half in a haze of Midsummer Night's Dream, half in anticipation of the picnic hamper to be opened on the bank beside a quiet pool of bulrushes and water hens. Home-made scones with home-made butter, cucumber sandwiches, the mouldy smell of the cushions. Brown, thin, damp triangular sandwiches. Anticipation of tennis in the evening on the side of the lawn, the humpy paddock, turkeys, over-emotional dogs.[7]

In her schoolgirl poem in *Tetralogue* 4, Brenda had tried to recapture this dreamlike feeling as she wrote about Shakespeare:

> He haunts the shady lanes of Warwickshire
> For that is where his spirit is most clear.
> He loved these shady paths and stately trees
> Waving their leafy branches in the breeze.

In *Tetralogue* 6 she wrote a poem, 'Day's End' and a lively essay, 'Modern Art and its Reception' which advocated a fresh approach and an open mind when viewing Modern Art:

> When we study a picture of the Modern School we must not only look at the object which the artist has painted, but also attempt to understand what he wishes to express.

It is a well-presented argument which is much more mature and sophisticated than any of her earlier contributions to the magazine. She concludes the article with the statement:

> I suppose the Modern Artists will continue to be persecuted until many people with old-fashioned ideas cease to consider that everything old is good and everything new is bad.

This sixth and last of the *Tetralogue* magazines was completed in the summer holidays of 1928. There is no further written account of the girls' activities until January 1930 when Mary Grierson decided to keep a record of their walks and explorations. Joy, Jean, Mary and Brenda still spent a lot of their time together at weekends and, in the holidays, exploring the local beauty spots. Brenda had still not grown very much and remained much smaller than her younger friends. As Jean Jones (later Jean Ware) recalled,

> In our teens, I fear we all patronised her somewhat and teased her quite a lot, though as one would tease a little

sister. She always seemed younger than us although she was the oldest of the group that went mountain climbing. Her nickname was 'Piglet', as to us she resembled that character in *Winnie the Pooh*. She had very short legs in relation to her long torso and had almost to run to keep up with the rest of us when walking as we were long-legged, but she was a splendid climber.[8]

Mary entitled her notebook 'The Diary of Tramps', and her first entry, on Friday, 10 January 1930 briefly described a short bicycle ride that Mary had taken with her friend, Marie Rowlands. On Saturday, 1 February, the first long walk was recorded, when Jean, Joy, Brenda and Mary went up the Nant Ffrancon Pass. The diary describes twenty walks undertaken between January and July of that year. The walks took the girls deep into Snowdonia and north onto the island of Anglesey. Sometimes choosing a combination of walking and travelling by bus or bicycle, they would travel up to thirty miles a day. Their treks were ambitious, often climbing up to the mountain peaks, and always seemed to incorporate the treat of a picnic lunch. Rain, ice or windy weather did not seem to deter them and Mary's diary gives a delightful account of the girls' love for Snowdonia.

The pattern of Brenda's life was beginning to unfold: her love of walking in the mountains was now well established and already she was taking a serious interest in writing and drawing. She had decided to apply to the Royal Academy Schools to study art and she was drawing and painting as much as she could in order to improve her standard and prepare a portfolio of work. Although Brenda tried her hand at painting landscapes, she much preferred to draw and paint people. Jean Jones's father was the first person Brenda attempted to draw 'in depth', as Jean later recalled:

> She sat opposite him while he was writing an article and produced a good pencil likeness – she would be about fifteen. I was her first nude model, just before Brenda left school. I would be about fifteen and she about eighteen. I think she asked me as I was the only one of her close friends who had begun to grow bosoms. Her mother made her bedroom warm for me with an oil stove and I sat for her several times.[9]

Although Brenda's parents had encouraged both their children to be creative, Brenda's father was not happy to discover that his daughter was showing so much interest in art. He could foresee little prospect of it leading to a secure future career and tried his best to discourage her from applying to go to college to study art further. On the other hand, Brenda's mother gave her every possible encouragement and often sat as a model for Brenda to paint. She was of the opinion that women had the right to follow any career they wished, as she had proved in her own choice of work. Following the success of the women's suffrage movement in the first decade of the twentieth century and new opportunities brought by the Great War, women were now slowly being accepted into previously all-male spheres. Women really had to prove their worth in the male-dominated professions, and Mrs Chamberlain was no exception. When she took her seat on the Bangor Borough Council in 1930 she was only the second woman to have ever been elected. She represented the West Ward, was a staunch Socialist and showed great skills and enthusiasm in her commitment to improving health and living conditions in the area, particularly for those of the poorer classes.

Mrs Chamberlain tried to encourage Brenda to be as determined and single-minded about her own choice of career as she was herself and she was a great source of strength and encouragement to Brenda in these formative years. Brenda was intent on studying art but often Mrs Chamberlain worried how her dreamy and imaginative daughter would cope with the practicalities of life in a city as large as London. Having been brought up in a very secure home, Brenda had never had to fend for herself and had always relied heavily on her mother and friends for support and guidance. Brenda's mother and indeed Bangor were to be her security, the safe anchorage where she sought shelter and support at frequent intervals throughout her life.

[1] In conversation with the author, 3 Sept. 1983.
[2] *North Wales Chronicle*, 14 Nov. 1941, p. 4.
[3] Brenda Chamberlain in Meic Stephens (ed.), *Artists in Wales* (Llandysul: Gomer, 1971), p. 45. [Henceforth *AW*].
[4] *AW*, p. 44.
[5] *AW*, pp. 44-5.
[6] *AW*, p. 45.
[7] Aberystwyth, National Library of Wales, NLW MS 21500E, f. 50.
[8] Jean Ware (*née* Jones, Mrs E.A. Hunt), letter to the author, 16 July 1984.
[9] Ibid.

Chapter 2
Art and Art 1930-34

Brenda's schooldays ended on 30 July 1930. She was given her School Leaving Certificate and left Miss Mason's School for Girls in Bangor. As her close friends were much younger than her, they stayed on, but her sadness at leaving them behind soon gave way to excitement when she heard that she could spend some months abroad before she applied for the Royal Academy Schools. Through a family friend, it was arranged for Brenda to live with a family in Copenhagen for six months. She was thrilled:

> It was marvellous to be for the first time alone in a foreign land. I had so far never visited London. The smell of the sea lured me to the quaysides, where I wandered, sketchbook in hand, among tall wooden warehouses.[1]

Copenhagen provided a great contrast to Bangor architecturally and Brenda found it elegant and stylish. She stayed with two unmarried sisters, whom she would recall vividly forty years later:

The sisters had a brother, Captain Gabe, a sea captain, a sister-in-law who smoked cheroots, and several nephews. They lived at the other end of the town, in a fine house, where they gave majestic dinner parties. At this stretch of time, the dining-room seems to have been endless. It was formally decorated with flowers and silver vases, and Royal Copenhagen porcelain figures. It felt like dining on the high seas, with the bearded captain presiding at the head of the table. The snow and ice of a northern winter was [*sic*] remote behind the double windows. We sat in thin muslins, after dinner, feet on grospoint footstools, the hands of the ladies busy with fine embroidery.[2]

Copenhagen was by far the biggest town that Brenda had visited and she was excited by its open-air theatres, the Charlottenburg Palace and the splendid National-Romantic style Raadhus in the Town Hall Square. But the place that affected her the most was Glyptotek Ny Carlsberg Museum. It was the first modern museum she had visited and the first time she has seen so many twentieth-century paintings. In Wales, there were few public places to see paintings at all, and although exhibitions were occasionally held in one of the University halls, there was no permanent gallery in Bangor.

It was the work of Gauguin that particularly stimulated Brenda: 'I knelt bemused at the feet of Gauguin', she wrote.[3] She was amazed by the colour and vibrancy of his work painted on the roughest of sacking. Gauguin's early work had been inspired by Pissarro and later by Émile Bernard's technique of cloisonnism. This consisted of painting in flat areas of clear, bright colours as used in

Japanese prints. These coloured forms were outlined in darker strong colours to intensify the shapes. The paintings affected her deeply and were to influence her work for the following twenty years.

When Brenda returned to Wales after her visit, she gathered the drawings and watercolours she had made in Copenhagen into a portfolio which she submitted to the Royal Academy Schools in Piccadilly. Much to her delight, in June 1931 she was accepted as a probationer for a three-month period. She moved to London in October of that year, living in a bed-sitting room in South Kensington.

> Life as a probationer was difficult and insecure, second and third year students were autocratic, and one was nervous about making relationships which might have to be broken at the end of the three month period.[4]

To be able to draw all day and every day was a novelty to Brenda and she worked diligently throughout her three-month probation. To her great relief she was accepted as a student and was now able to study at the Royal Academy Schools for the next five years under the tuition of Sir Walter Russell, then Keeper of the Schools, and W.T. Monnington. Living in London in the early 1930s changed Brenda's ideas about art. While the Royal Academy still clung to the classical traditions of Greece and Rome, the more adventurous of the London galleries were exhibiting contemporary painters from all over Europe. Since the First World War, the representational approach to art had been radically shaken up by the vibrant energy of Fauves, Cubists, German Expressionists and many other innovative groups of artists. Brenda found these new movements invigorating and stimulating. In contrast, she was finding the discipline of the formal training at the Royal Academy 'academic to the ninth degree'.[5] Although a serious-minded student, Brenda was extremely unwilling to relinquish her individuality and sometimes her resistance to academic disciplines and teaching made her tutors despair. It was as 'a melting pot for ideas and rebellion against the doctrines of the master' that Brenda would remember the real value of her time at the Royal Academy.

During this period, Brenda's work was being pulled in two directions: under the influence of her Royal Academy training, her current drawing echoed the draughtsmanship of Michelangelo, Leonardo and El Greco, but in spirit, it was Van Gogh and Gauguin who moved her deeply and whose influence was to be lasting. Brenda was also affected by the resurgence of the Neo-Romanticism which was prevalent in the early 1930s. Many artists were beginning to reject the complexity and sophistication of the urban, industrial developments and turn to the less populated countryside in order to lead a more simple and natural life. This philosophy suited Brenda well. At twenty years old, the tiny long-haired provincial girl felt rather overwhelmed by the bustle and competitive energy of London. Although she enjoyed the idea of the stimulus of the city, in reality she was lost in its manner and sophistication, and, like many of her contemporaries, Brenda felt the need to simplify her own living circumstances and return to her roots in Wales. At the end of her first year in London, Brenda looked forward eagerly to the long summer break when she would be able to walk amongst the mountains and see her friends once more.

Her friends, Mary, Jean and Joy, were still in Bangor, spending time between school and college, and so all four had time to meet and walk in the mountains together. However, in the summer of 1932, Brenda met Karl von Laer, a German boy of her own age, and she neglected her friends to spend time in his company. Karl was staying in Bangor for the summer with Jean's family. Her father had arranged an exchange through the German Academic Bureau and Jean was going to stay with Karl's family in Germany the following summer. Karl von Laer was a tall blond boy with bright blue eyes and was a law student at Königsberg. His family home was a small Baroque castle called Schlotheim in Thüringen, East Prussia.

Brenda and Karl instantly became friends. They had a mutual interest in painting and both loved poetry and walking in the mountains. Brenda was fascinated to hear about life in Germany and the other places that Karl had visited, and learned that Karl was 'verloben' – that a betrothal had been arranged with another girl of aristocratic birth. They enjoyed each other's company enormously and soon became inseparable. Standing next to the tall German boy, Brenda, at four feet eleven inches, looked doll-like, which led to a lot of laughter and good-natured teasing from her friends. Brenda did not care at all. She felt as though she had found an older brother, a special friend with whom to share her love of Snowdonia. There was plenty of opportunity for Karl to see the mountains and on most days a group of the young people would go walking or climbing.

Twenty years later, Brenda wrote down her memories of the first of her many walks on the mountains with Karl. They were in a large group of school friends but soon Brenda and Karl were walking ahead engrossed in conversation.

Brenda with lambs

Of what we were speaking I cannot now recall, only that we were absorbed by an exchange of ideas ... we had just climbed a peak covered with huge pillars of rock. Where we now walked, the ground was level and covered with a resilient turf. K and I were brought to a standstill by a shout from the girls. 'Look where you are walking. What a smell! Can't you smell carrion?' Our feet were among the half-rotted bones of a large skull: in places, the bones were white-bleached, the eye sockets were clean and empty, but traces of sun-baked flesh clung along the jaws.[6]

On many of their later walks the two were equally oblivious to all else around them. Brenda's friend Jean recalled that Brenda and Karl

> ... often preferred to stay in a sheltered corner with their easels than go mountain climbing with the crowd of us with our brothers and friends. Once she invited him to go along with her up the mountains as she wanted to show him various things but they were not back till long after dark and my father had to tell her that she must not do that to him again as the German boy was his responsibility – she must be home by dark. He would not accept her excuse that she could see in the dark. Brenda could seldom see other people's points of view if they did not coincide with her own, and she could not understand why he should worry.[7]

Brenda's own memory of that walk with Karl was quite different:

> There was one wonderful day when we escaped the others and went for a long walk to a mountain lake. I saw that day one of the most memorable sunsets of my life. Ah, it comes back to me slowly, the sunset over the lake. The memory is fresh and beautiful as if it had been taken out of tissue paper. We had looked at it upside down to get its full effect.[8]

She remembered nothing of upsetting Jean's father or causing her own family worry. Although a kind person, Brenda could often be self-centred and oblivious to other people's feelings. Frequently that summer, Brenda spent her evenings at Jean's house where she would talk and read poetry out loud to Karl:

> And every evening he always took me home, walking slowly... As we strolled, he talked of student life in East Prussia, of beer drinking, singing, duels. He had a duel to fight as soon as he got back to University. He would let me know the outcome. He told me of foreign countries, described the sensation of looking down into the crater of Etna ...[9]

At the end of the summer Brenda had to return to London to continue her studies. Karl did not have to go back to Germany for another few weeks and promised to visit Brenda in London on his way home. One morning a few weeks later he arrived unexpectedly and they spent the day sightseeing and visiting galleries. In the evening they went to see a play at the Old Vic and afterwards, Brenda recalled, 'we walked through half the night ... we walked to prolong the time together. Next morning, we visited the Tower before going to Red Lion Wharf.'[10]

Karl was sailing to Amsterdam on a small Dutch cargo ship. It was a sad parting although Brenda remembered that they were shy with one another and neither of them showed any emotion. She stayed on the wharf until the ship started down river and passed under London Bridge. A week later, the first of many letters arrived from Karl von Laer. 'It was only after he had gone back to Germany, in his

33

first letter, that he had shown anything of what he had come to feel for me during the days of that student summer', wrote Brenda in retrospect.[11]

After an exhilarating and happy summer, Brenda had to settle back into her studies at the Royal Academy. She enjoyed drawing and soon became immersed in her work. Many months were spent in dusty overheated life-drawing rooms and many more were spent drawing in the academic traditions from the casts of classical busts and statues. Apart from her studies, Brenda had a full social life in London, made regular visits to museums and art galleries and went to the theatre as often as she could afford. Money was scarce, though, and much of her spare time was spent in long discussions with her contemporaries, who came from all walks of life and included an ex-miner from the Durham coalfield and the debutante niece of a Prime Minister. Amongst her fellow students were William Scott, Mervyn Peake and Peter Scott.

During her time in the painting Schools Brenda met another fellow student, John Petts. He was two years younger than Brenda and had already studied at Hornsey College of Art and the Central School of Arts and Crafts before becoming a student at the Royal Academy Schools. Although born and brought up in North London, he had developed a love for Wales after his first visit as a twelve-year-old to a Boy Scout camp at Manorbier near Tenby. On that trip he had found the contrast to London quite startling, as he later recalled:

Here was land to rejoice in: castles reared on high mounds, mighty cliffs with the Atlantic rollers all a-thunder at their feet, St. Govan's tiny prayer-cell wedged between the rocks, deep caves to explore, the cliff-top Hunter's Leap to ogle at, the rock bastion of the Bridge of Wales, that mighty buttress rising from the depths of the frothing sea, and always the beauty of the many-tinted, tide-rolled stones smooth on the beaches, a harmony of soft colours never to be forgotten, and everywhere the majesty of rock.[12]

Perhaps coloured by his strong feelings for Wales, John found himself drawn to its countrymen too. Already at the Royal Academy he had made friends with a lively group from Wales:

There was tall Fred Janes from Swansea, his head full of theories. Bromfield Rees, his lean and studious friend from Llanelli, trying to paint like Braque, and the ubiquitous South Wales bonhomie was heightened by the frequent calling of black-bearded Mervyn Levy from the Royal College of Art, and a podgy, fag-ended young journalist in a cocky pork-pie hat and a dyed green shirt whose name was Dylan Thomas.[13]

But it was Brenda Chamberlain who really captured John's attention.

I first became aware of Brenda as a rare and special person in the autumn of 1933, when I first became a student in the Painting School of the Royal Academy Schools. Down the long, dark corridor, under the galleries of Burlington House, peopled by lines of dusty 'antiques' – busts of classical sculpture – she walked lightly, like a small angel in a dream. In that murk she seemed to carry her own delicate light, a smile on her long face, her hair parted each side of the high forehead, falling in long fair waves to shoulder length. Hardly more than five feet high, she was also slight in build. Wearing a long white smock, belted at the waist, with a deep cape-collar, and walking softly in sandals along the stone flags of the corridor outside the studios, she seemed a special sort of dedicated nun.[14]

Their friendship quickly blossomed. In the summer of 1934 John and Brenda decided to spend their summer holidays together in north Wales and they rented a tiny shepherd's cottage above Abergwyngregyn, about five miles from Bangor, in the mountains of Snowdonia. At the time, it was unheard of for an unmarried couple to live together openly and it was frowned upon by both the local community and Chamberlain's family. Although Brenda's father was totally against it, however, her mother helped her to make the arrangements to rent the cottage.

The cottage was called Hafod-y-Gelyn – 'Summer Shelter from the Enemy' – a name they both found full of portents. Brenda travelled on ahead and John joined her from London a few days later. His impressions of north Wales were vivid:

Truly, I shall never forget the first impact of that landscape. The train from Euston dropped me at Aber station, on the flatlands by the sea. Across the water rested the whaleback of Puffin Island, off the point of the wide Isle of Anglesey... The road led up into the hills above the wooded valley through which the river tumbled from the silver falls. Steadily I climbed up a steep side-track, leaving the trees behind, climbing to the

Brenda & John at Hafod-y-Gelyn

open mountain with its tussocks of gorse and fine, sheep-bitten turf. The hills unfolded beyond: all was magically soaked in subtle greens and duns, patterned with grey rocks and screes, and all sang with the splendour of the clear light, and its voice was the cry of the distant sheep and the fall of water. My city eyes were astounded, and my heart was singing. Along the hill and there was the cottage, tucked under the slope like a lamb under her dam. Above it spread a wide poplar tree, surprising to see in such a tree-less place and there was Brenda smiling at the door. 'The kettle's boiling...' she said. Sharing life with her was participating in a special sacrament.[15]

Life in the tiny shepherd's cottage could not have been simpler: they slept on hay and cooked simple food on a fire fed by gorse twigs collected from the mountain hills. By day they walked the mountain ridges, sketching and painting and swimming in the rivers and lakes, completely absorbed in the land, in all the stones, rocks and crags. Through their art they struggled to express this vigour of the mountains. They walked so much on the mountain turf that it felt strange to them if their hobnàiled boots touched the unyielding surface of the tarmac roads. That summer, life at Hafod-y-Gelyn was so very far removed from the glittering and complex world of the Bond Street galleries. For them both it was an idyll.

'As I grew to know her', wrote John, 'it seemed that her whole small being was lit with pure delight, delight in the beauty and mystery of those aspects of the created world she loved, most especially the mountains of Eryri, the dramatic landscape of Snowdonia ...'[16] Brenda was in the landscape she had known and loved since childhood, while for John it was a totally new experience. Unlike Brenda, he had spent much of his childhood indoors or in the environment of London and for the most part without the companionship of his contemporaries. As a child, he had a distorted spine and spent his early years lying flat either in bed or with his back strapped in the steel and leather of a spinal carriage. His body had strengthened by his teens, but by then he was used to his own company and spent a lot of time alone. Now, he found a great deal of pleasure in being out in the fresh mountain air, feeling fit and healthy, being able to paint and share his days in Brenda's company.

John's younger brother, Peter, came to stay with them while they were at Hafod-y-Gelyn. He was only eight, a late fourth child, small for his age and rather lonely. Like Brenda and John he was delighted to spend his holiday there and ran wild in the hillsides. He would happily disappear for hours exploring his secret worlds and favourite places. Often dressed only in a ceremonial loin cloth hung with tassels, he would run around the fields on his hands and knees, whistling and barking as he rounded up the sheep. He was full of wonder at all forms of nature: how plants grew, how animals moved, the way the sunlight fell on the mountains and he would stay silent, listen and observe. Brenda often sat with him. She found it easy to identify with children, as there was a part of her that did not want to grow up and face the harsher realities of the world. She yearned to have a child but according to her friends and John she was infertile and unable to have any of her own. Instead, she would always be delighted to have other people's children to stay with her during holidays, although sad when they inevitably returned home. Brenda was a dreamer, a weaver of images inside her head. Although a happy, smiling person, enjoying laughter and life, she, like many artists, would withdraw to an inner world for a great part of her life, to draw upon her imagination, upon myths, memories and symbols for inspiration.

Brenda described Peter as 'a strange child, quiet, unnaturally thin, intensely imaginative, and with beautiful eyes. They were so large, that one felt that he must be all eyes behind the flesh of his face'. It is conceivable that it was from her close observation of him that summer that she drew two of the characteristic features which were to recur in all the portrait painting she ever did. They were the dark almond-shaped eyes and the still, quiescent figure. The large dark eyes haunted Brenda long beyond Peter's lifetime and were to appear over and over again in her portraits of both children and adults. Peter's ability to be still and contemplative also moved Brenda deeply and her

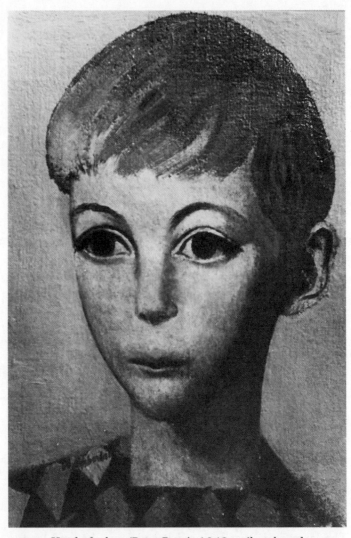
Head of a boy (Peter Petts), 1940s, oil on board

paintings and drawings try to express this mood. It was a theme that would run throughout her work. None of Brenda's characters smile; they have a timeless, almost sad look, and are always composed in their surrounding and almost statuesque in their posture. It is their inner lives that she wants us to glimpse: the land of dreams and contemplation.

Later in that summer, a fellow student from London, Elizabeth Ouston, known as Betsan, also came to stay. Together they all enjoyed an idyllic summer, sleeping outdoors, bathing in the river and walking in the hills. Brenda was reluctant to leave, and as she needed to work on her entries to a number of competitions, she decided to stay on when John and Betsan returned to London in September. As winter approached and she had little money, she was forced to move back to her parents' house in Bangor. She wrote frequently to 'Johnny' signing her letters 'Swci'. She was not very happy there as she found it difficult to be in the same house as her father who hardly spoke to her.

Mother is a martyr. I would have simply walked out one afternoon and never come back. I could not say in the same house as a man who did not SEE me. He wants shaking & ducking and kicking in the pants.

I asked Mother the other day when she was posing for me, didn't Daddy ever say she had lovely hair even when they were young? Good Heavens no, she said, he never said anything like that – But he did tell her a year after they were married that he had only married her to have someone look after his Mother.[17]

41

By the middle of October her paintings were crated up and sent on to London and Brenda travelled down soon after.

1 *AW*, p. 45.
2 *AW*, pp. 45-6.
3 *AW*, p. 45.
4 *AW*, p. 46.
5 *AW*, p. 46.
6 NLW MS 22493C, f. 213.
7 Jean Ware, letter to the author, 16 July 1984.
8 NLW MS 22493C, f. 214.
9 Ibid., f. 213.
10 Ibid., f. 215.
11 Brenda Chamberlain, *The Water Castle* (London: Hodder & Stoughton, 1964), p. 15. [Henceforth *WC*].
12 John Petts, *Welsh Horizons* (1983 Radio Wales Lecture, London: BBC Publications, 1984), p. 5.
13 Petts, *Welsh Horizons*, p. 5.
14 John Petts, letter to the author, Sept. 1983.
15 Petts, *Welsh Horizons*, pp. 6-7.
16 John Petts, letter to the author, Sept. 1983.
17 Letter, Tues., 16 Oct. 1934, from Brenda Chamberlain to John Petts, NLW MS 23207F, f. 21.

Chapter 3

The House on the Mountain,
Tŷ'r Mynydd 1935-38

Back in London Brenda and John discussed their future. They both decided that they wanted to live and work in north Wales and they tried to work out how this might be achieved. In the spring of 1935, they married. As John Petts recalls, 'this was a brief legal ceremony in a Register Office in Kensington. It was an awkward action, a concession to the conventions of the strictly Non-conformist community in which we were setting up home in Gwynedd.'[1] There were no close family members present and it was witnessed by their fellow student, Betsan, and John's cousin Freda. For the rest of the academic year, Brenda found it hard to concentrate on her studies. Although she passed her annual examinations, she had been to many fewer classes than usual and could not wait for the summer holidays.

At the end of the summer term in 1935, Brenda and John went straight to north Wales. Having decided to settle there, they began to search for a base. With the help of Mrs Chamberlain they were fortunate to find, for the grand sum of £68, a pair of old cottages called Tŷ'r

Mynydd (the House on the Mountain) and a sloping field of about a quarter acre. They managed to buy these with loans from the bank, Betsan and Brenda's mother. The cottages were in Llanllechid, north-west of Bethesda and five miles south of Bangor, and situated high up in the village where the steep street petered out onto the rough mountainside. The village lay below them and Tŷ'r Mynydd nestled against the high slate walls left by the quarrymen who had previously worked and lived there. The cottages were simply constructed and quite primitive; there was no electricity, water had to be carried from the well and wood collected from the mountainsides for the fires. Each cottage had a main room with a high ceiling and a big chimney open to the stars. Adjoining the main room was a two-storey area consisting of a downstairs room with a *croglofft* (loft bedroom) tucked into the roof space above.

Tŷ'r Mynydd, ink on paper, by John Petts

Both cottages were in a very poor state of repair and, that summer, they set to work to make them habitable. They both still had a year left of their studies but neither really felt like leaving Wales. John resigned his studentship and managed to transfer his student registration to Chester School of Art. This enabled him to continue to receive his British Institution Scholar's award which he could hold for three years. He received £1.10s a week which John recalls 'kept us from hunger'.[2] He travelled to Chester by train once a week to draw from the life model and for the rest of the week drew and painted at home as well as working on repairs to Tŷ'r Mynydd. Brenda, however, was still officially a student in London, although her attendance was very poor; she went to only three sessions at the college out of a possible three hundred and seventy-nine. Despite the distance from their respective colleges, Brenda and John worked diligently that year and both passed their final examinations.

After making all the necessary repairs, Brenda and John lived in one cottage and used the other as a studio and workshop. They took great pride in their new home and every spring, in time for Easter, John would whitewash the outside and from its high position it could be seen for miles around. Below Tŷ'r Mynydd lay the straggling lines of the terraced houses of Llanllechid and the neighbouring village of Rachub, the distant outlines of the north Wales coast and the Isle of Anglesey sometimes clear but often shrouded under sea-mist. Behind the house were the mountains and a five-minute climb to the brow of the first hill offered a view of Snowdonia's magnificent peaks. The ground was rough with outcrops of dark purple slate and the hills were grazed by wild ponies.

Up in their hillside retreat, the outside world and its realities seemed far away. It was now the late 1930s and

> We knew in our bones that a world war was bound to break out at any moment, so we lived the more intensely in our dreams of a primitive mountain life... Under the influence of D.H. Lawrence, we hated the machine, we outlawed ourselves, though we had never heard of 'beat' or 'offbeat'. We never drank alcohol, and had never heard of narcotics. Free love was our creed and password, though we married towards the end of our student days at the Royal Academy Schools.[3]

The inhabitants of this somewhat conservative and close-knit community were certainly intrigued by the arrival of the young couple with their artistic ways and bohemian appearance. Some called them 'Mary and Joseph' because Brenda, with her long flowing hair, her flowery hats and her ankle-length full skirts would ride side-saddle on her pony mare led by John with his patriarchal beard and sandals. Some said that John also wore long robes but he has since denied this, declaring a cotton shirt and corduroy trousers to be more accurate.

These were full days. Time not spent on art was spent either on the land or entertaining the many visitors who found their way to the fireside of the small cottage. To the young couple, life seemed like a period of transition. John Petts described it as 'a time to try and shed one's "over-education" in art. One was really "egg-bound" for a while, then concentrated on life confronting one, and trying to express it naturally away from London's art sophistication'.[4]

Self Portrait, 1936, pencil on paper

In these early years at Tŷ'r Mynydd Brenda produced an abundance of sketches but very few completed paintings. The sketches were in pen and ink, ink wash and pencil, interspersed with her writing in a lined black notebook. Alongside drawings of chairs, tables and other household objects were sketches of the cats, rocks, portraits and copies of drawings by Michelangelo and Leonardo da Vinci. Still the influence of her Royal Academy years haunted her work. She quoted a passage from Leonardo in the front of one notebook:

Thy strength, O painter, is in solitude!

When you are alone you belong wholly to yourself, but if you have one companion then you are only half your own... But if you must have company, let it be that of the painters and scholars in your studies; all other friendships will be to your detriment – Remember, O painters, that your strength is in solitude.[5]

Already Brenda was facing the struggle which troubled her throughout her days: she was an artist yearning to be alone to create and she was a woman wanting company for the inspiration and comfort. Most times full of happiness and joy, Brenda also had moments of despair. She wrote in her notebook:

Oh God I write in bitterness and agony, wherefore should I be bitter and sad, the people will ask – when my back is against the purple rock and the birds cry spring in the valley. The shepherd tends the ewe with the lamb down the field beneath my feet, the thin wind takes my hair and the mountain seeds [sic] in a chill whistle. Spring is around me, in me and I am bowed with sorrow. It is not my sorrow but the world's. We are so poor in love in boldness and in thought that our souls die and we hate. I long for the love of man and woman, of bird and beast. The beast and bird give me of their love but the others – there are no men and women. The cat nestles with soft aloof movements into my lap, the dog seeks marvels in my face. God knows if he finds them there. I weep when the first lamb staggers and cries in the field – why? He is only mutton – he will soon be dead, something to eat. And yet I watch with pained compassion his first steps on long awkward legs, his tiny body still stained with his mother's blood.

The land is rich – the soil is broken and living things burst forth. Flies and beetles hover over the ploughed field. The air is full of birds with wings rustling like silk. The slate is purple dazzling my eyes, all the hedges are green – surely they never were so green before? – and the plum trees show their blossom to the sky.

But the world is full of bitterness. I know it. Do not people stare at me with so much hate that I almost burst into tears before their eyes? They do not know that they hate me. It is just that they have never watched a bee inside a flower or heard the snipe wheeling in a dim valley. I know these things and am blessed but I draw no joy from my knowledge.[6]

But she would not stay depressed too long: life was too full, there was work to be done and John's company soon brightened her mood. Looking back, almost fifty years later, John reflected on his fond memories of Brenda. He saw her as a

… unique person having special gifts of mind, spirit and creative talent of rare quality. In those days, when quite truly, I felt it a privilege to share her life, she rose so frequently on a wave of happiness and joy in the wonders of creation that all who met her were touched and lifted and warmed and always remembered her smile.[7]

There was a darker side that he experienced too – the need for attention, 'the egotism, the selfishness and the fact that her work was so subjective that she could never lose herself'.[8] Other, female, friends described Brenda as having a wonderful sense of humour but being very demanding and always wanting their full attention. She had an intense interest in every small detail and ordinary events were often dramatised into major events.

They led a hardworking life and apart from their creative output, there was plenty of work to be done on the land. They would help neighbouring farmers with haymaking, sheep-dipping and shearing, there were wild ponies to be rounded up from the hills and logs to be carried from the clearance above Parc Mine in the Gwydyr Forest. John grew some vegetables but most of their land was used to graze a white goat and Brenda's pony, Polly, who had been bought from the greengrocer for £4.10s.0d. She rode Polly down the steep streets of the village to collect shopping, to explore the wild mountainsides and occasionally to visit her mother in Bangor.

To this respectable public figure, the appearance of her tiny daughter, hair and skirts flowing as she rode into Bangor, represented all Elsie did not really want her daughter to be. Through all her hard work with the various committees in the town, Mrs Chamberlain championed better living and working conditions for the poor. It was with a certain degree of sadness and frustration that she viewed the frugal way in which Brenda lived, but with no amount of persuasion could she cajole her to upgrade her own way of life. But despite her difficulties in understanding her daughter's needs, Elsie Chamberlain was always supportive of Brenda and was always there for Brenda to turn to – which she frequently did. As Brenda's old school friend, Jean Ware, observed:

Everyone said how strange that Brenda had such a different mother, a committee woman and an artist as mother and daughter! – but in fact they were very alike. They shared a complete dedication to what they wanted to do – Mrs Chamberlain her committees and Brenda her art ... And they were both ego-centrics.[9]

Brenda was working on her painting now and her first work of real quality was *Self Portrait on Garnedd Dafydd*, painted in 1938 in oil on a small canvas of 12 x 12 in. (about 30.5 x 30.5 cm). She was still struggling to break free of the strict disciplines of her formal art training to find her own natural style and she worked for many months on this painting. Brenda was exploring the technique of chiaroscuro to control the light and shade in her work although this proved to be a short-term exploration, as in most of her later pictures she was to prefer the manipulation of flat planes and blocks of colour.

Brenda worked on this self-portrait under the skylight in the one of the attic bedrooms. As Tŷ'r Mynydd was dark and without electricity, all Brenda's painting had to be done in the hours of daylight, either beneath this skylight or out of doors. In the self-portrait Brenda uses the Renaissance convention of painting a distant landscape behind the head and shoulders to give emphasis to the subject and depth to the composition. She portrays her long, mysterious face with a formal aloofness against the distant Ogwen valley. To John Petts, writing later, this early self-portrait showed 'the proportion of man there was in Brenda and the child who wouldn't grow up'.[10]

In the painting she wears a long maroon dress, yet as John Petts also recalled, her appearance in such formal attire was restricted to those rare occasions when they both attended concerts at the University College in Bangor. Brenda's usual attire (acquired mainly from friends) was a strange medley of clothes which she would wear with a certain flair but also with a disregard for contemporary fashion.

Following her own portrait, Brenda progressed to paint her neighbour, Mrs Margaret Rowlands. This painting, *Mountain Cottager*, also of 1938, clearly shows the development of her style, and the areas of colour are broader and more confident. Again, it was painted in oil and only 17 x 17 in. (about 43.2 x 43.2 cm). This painting was notable as it was the first she was to sell. Mrs Kitty Idwal Jones had heard of Brenda Chamberlain in Swansea and journeyed to Llanllechid to meet her and see her work and asked to buy the picture. For Brenda, this was a new and unsettling experience as she had no idea what to charge. In panic, she and John retreated to the attic where they settled on the price of 10 guineas (£10.10s or £10.50 today).

During this period, Brenda painted very little but kept prolific notebooks which bulge with rough sketches, poems and her observations and journal writing. Her style was natural and fluent as she recorded her experiences of country life with all its pleasures and hardships. In one of the notebooks, she compiled writings about each month of the year. Some of the sections appear in earlier notebooks and here they are written in a revised form. Brenda wrote and rewrote many times, adding an alliterative adjective, removing a phrase, changing a title. She found it very difficult to decide when her writing was finished. These records of the country year give an indication of her

Mountain Cottager, 1938, oil on board

sensitivity to the moods of nature and her interest in local folklore. In this austere environment winter was particularly harsh and she wrote in her notebook:

> It seems now as if there had never been any green fields and flowers and summer trees. The whole earth is given up to whiteness for as far as we can see and that is a great distance. Wind tortures the cottage walls and sends the snow like flung sand against the windows. It was as if we were surrounded by flickering fires of blue flames.
>
> When all the water has frozen hard, we have to fill the kettle with snow, a long task, for a kettleful only produces a little water and to constantly handle hard frozen lumps makes the hands sore.[11]

The back of their cottage was level with the wall which enclosed the mountain, and although it was almost 1000 feet (about 300 metres) above sea level, it was the lowest point where the animals could seek shelter.

> On January nights of bitter wind and snow, mountain ponies run behind our cottage on the open land, up and down they go, hollow sounding through the darkness. They are thin and hungry, but they will not eat hay that we leave outside for them. They are tenacious of life, lying asleep on the snow on days when men are glad to hurry home to the comfort of hot stew and a wood-fire.[12]

Brenda and John would venture onto the mountain in all weathers.

Lakes are frozen to a great depth with polished black ice,

Brenda and John on Y Gribin

and in the clear under water fishes swim among rigid weeds. Crags encircle the lake, their sheer sides glazed with waterfalls. There is a great fear of ice among the shepherds. They will not venture near it. I took a child up a nearby tarn. He said that there was something there that would drag me down under the water and drown me, but when he saw ice covering all the water, he laughed saying it was alright, nothing could get at us. The ice would hold up out of the reach of bogies.[13]

When Shrove Tuesday came the air was 'heavy with the warm smell of pancakes' and loud with the singing of the children who travelled from house to house demanding pancakes in response to their songs. The Chapel Preaching Festival fell in February too and almost everyone from the village dressed up in new clothes to attend.

But at last the end of winter was in sight:

When the yellow smoke of the gorse fires rolls up from the mountain then we feel that it is Spring. Children go past the gate, matches in pocket, newspapers under their arms, happy in the thought of fire-making. With mysterious regularity, like the migration of birds the fires begin flaming and smoking every hillside. The children of our village vie with the boys across the valley to see who can make the most splendid glow. In the cold Spring dusk, black figures run through the smoke, darting here and there, kindling the young shoots of dwarf gorse so that there should be tender new grasses for the sheep.[14]

March brought new experiences:

At the beginning of the month we hear curlews calling in
the dark night as they pass up to the moors. The grey
wag-tail and the water ouzel flit in the cold spray of
mountain streams, seeming incredibly fragile and lovely
in the wild bravery of spring. It is a time of renewal of
old sounds and scents coming like a wave over the land.
Earth can be smelt again. Fields are dunged and a sudden
puff of white dust across a field shows where lime
spreading has begun.[15]

There was a time for each task to be done and Brenda
recorded with deference each occasion in the farming
calendar.

At Easter, potatoes and other vegetables are planted
while the moon is waxing. It is believed that Good Friday
is an auspicious day for seed-planting.[16]

With the coming of April,

The yearling sheep are brought back from the lowlands
on April 5th but they are not driven to the mountain until
April 13th. The days from the first of the month to the
13th are known as Pasg Bach, the little Easter, and the
sheep are kept in a sheltered place until this time is over
so that if March went out like a lion the weather would
have time to settle somewhat.[17]

Because Tŷ'r Mynydd was by the gate to the mountain,
Brenda and John were always in the middle of the local

Brenda climbing on
Tryfan

farming activity. All animals either going up or down the
mountain were herded past their door and they would often
work a few days with a farmer.

In the Spring, foals are earmarked in our lane on their
way back to the mountain then the men's hands stream
in blood from punctured ears, when the young things
scream in intolerable fear and pain. It takes three strong
men to hold an animal as delicate and slender as a
deer.[18]

While Brenda's writing paints a romantic picture of their

life in the mountains, it is John who recalled the difficulties of making a living:

> Sometimes there was a portrait to be painted, a drawing to be made: we repaired hymn-books for local chapels, gathered foxglove leaves for digitalis drug manufacturers, sold sheep-dog pups from time to time, and helped local farmers at busy times like shearing and hay-harvest. Nevertheless at times we were hard put to pay the grocer's bill.[19]

For a while the couple managed to survive on this insecure income, holding firmly onto their dreams of one day being able to make a living from their skills and art, but the reality of their situation pressed down upon them. One day, Mr Griffiths, the grocer, arrived on the doorstep with tears running down his face. 'I'm sorry, Mr Petts bach,' he said to John, 'I must ask you to pay your bill.' John was taken aback, and said to himself, 'John Petts, you must never cause a man to weep with embarrassment at your door because you cannot earn your living!'[20]

At the very least this experience turned their gaze back towards more worldly requirements. John Petts had always been interested in both engraving and typography and he borrowed the money to buy a small hand-press. They decided to call this the Caseg Press, after the river which drained the wild valley high above the village and also after their little pony mare (*caseg* in Welsh). The arrival of the press affirmed their conviction that they could work as artists. It heralded the start of a new creative era.

[1] John Petts, letter to the author, 24 April 1987.
[2] Ibid.

3 Brenda Chamberlain (ed.), *Alun Lewis and the Making of the Caseg Broadsheets*, (London: Enitharmon Press, 1970), p. 1. [Henceforth *ALCB*].

4 John Petts, letter to the author, Sept. 1983.

5 NLW MS 21502B, f. 2.

6 Ibid., f. 33.

7 John Petts in letter to the author, Sept. 1983.

8 John Petts in conversation with the author, 3 Sept. 1983.

9 Jean Ware, letter to the author, 16 July 1984.

10 John Petts in conversation with the author 3 Sept. 1983.

11 NLW MS 21504B, f. 23.

12 Ibid., f. 23.

13 Ibid., f. 25.

14 Ibid., f. 26.

15 Ibid., f. 27.

16 Ibid., f. 27.

17 Ibid., f. 28.

18 Ibid., f. 28.

19 John Petts, *Welsh Horizons*, p. 8.

20 John Petts in conversation with the author, 3 Sept. 1983.

Chapter 4
The Caseg Press 1939-44

Establishing the Caseg Press in 1938 gave Brenda and John a focus for their creative energy. Typography, graphics and engraving were particular interests of John and he taught Brenda to use the wood-engraving tools. She took to the technique right away and also enjoyed the hand colouring of the prints, but not being practical with any kind of machinery, she left the press work to John. As she became more proficient, Brenda preferred to carve her designs into the softer material of lino while John preferred the finer detail he could achieve by carving in wood. By 1939, John was engraving full-time, not only for the Caseg Press but for other presses and publishers. He had bought some of Eric Gill's Jubilee typeface and they began printing greetings cards with wood engravings of their designs. To publicise the venture, they printed a handbill which was widely distributed to shops, hotels and interested parties.

Most of the designs reflected their environment – the hills of Snowdonia, shepherds, sturdy women carrying hay – all strong figures engrossed in their lives on the land. From the distribution of their publicity and the work already executed, the work of the Caseg Press became known and commissions began to arrive. There were posters, handbills, illustrated brochures for hotels, letterheads and a whole variety of other work.

Initially they sold the prints for 6d but eventually had to increase the price as the hand colouring was time consuming and demand for their prints grew. Apart from advertising in literary magazines, they sent batches to bookshops to elicit orders and also sold directly from Tŷ'r Mynydd. Apart from local people, their clients included many well known figures, academics and writers including the architect of Portmeirion, Clough Williams-Ellis, Lloyd George, Sir Thomas and Lady Artemus Jones and Lady Elisabeth Babington Smith, and in 1939 the National Library of Wales began collecting their cards.

A great influence and encouragement at this time was Gwyn Jones who had begun *The Welsh Review*, in February 1939. He wrote to Brenda and John asking for articles and illustrations for the new magazine. Delighted, Brenda sent off some wood engravings and two were printed in the following issue, in March 1939. *The Poor Ones* (p. 83) is a study of four refugees with their cat, while *The Wild Riders* (p. 71) is a dramatic scurry of horses against a background of mountain peaks.[1] The latter was also used as a design for one of the Caseg greeting cards.

In the following month it was John's turn to be featured with a lino-cut, *The Sower,* and a wood engraving, *Carnedd Dafydd, Ysgolion Du*. The June number published John's essay, 'The Finding of Moses Griffith', and two wood engravings by Brenda. *Women of Afon Goch* is a rather heavy nude in the classical style, standing against a decorative floral background, while *The Bathers* illustrates two sturdy women washing.[2] Whereas these two works seem to echo her early academic training, *The Wild Riders* displays a new exuberance in line, composition and subject matter.

Merlod Mynydd (The Wild Riders), 1939, wood engraving, reproduced as a Caseg Press greetings card

Y Bugail ar y Trum (The Shepherd on the Ridge), 1940, hand-coloured wood engraving, reproduced as a Caseg Press greetings card

Both Brenda and John were delighted to see their work in print in the magazine. The money and the prestige were both welcome and requests for their work came from many quarters. Following an invitation from Margaret Leigh, a writer and sheep farmer in Ross-shire, they decided to go on a camping trip to Scotland. The idea was that the three of them would travel together and Brenda and John would provide engravings for her next book. As Gwyn Jones also offered to publish an illustrated diary of their journey in *The Welsh Review*, they decided it would be worthwhile both creatively and financially.

It was strange to be shutting up Tŷ'r Mynydd for so long. In the quiet of the Saturday evening I rode Polly over the mountain to Ffridd Corbri; she was hocks-deep in the new grass, and as I looked back through the larches she was ripping happily at the fresh bite. Here the furred bracken fronds were uncurling and lifting their arms – by the time we return they will have spread wide in greenness and drooped to a pattern of golden frets. In the morning I climbed the roof and covered the chimney-tops with slabs of red slate. It is strange to think that this year we will not be at Tanybwlch for the Hay or up at Buarth Braich for the Big Gathering.[3]

Brenda, John, and Gwyn, their dog, left Llanllechid on 5 June 1939 and travelled by train up to Inverness. Their meeting with Margaret Leigh did not work out as planned, because she abandoned the trip after the first day, but they continued on their journey and kept detailed notes, sketches and photographs to use on their return.

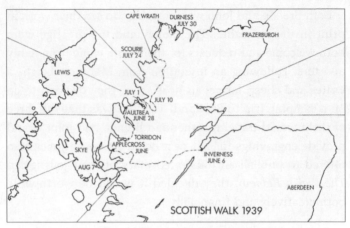

Map of Scotland showing the route of the walking trip,
June-August 1939

From Inverness, their journey was on foot and heading
west, pitching their tent in a suitable sheltered spot each
night. They went up Glen Cannich and over the pass to
Elchaig.

> Everywhere the bog-cotton is blooming in shining white
> tufts: when a breeze stirs, the ground dances alive with
> the sparkle of a myriad plumes. (Do some crofters still
> stuff their mattresses with this canna?)[4]

They made good progress that day and that night: 'We
cooked on a blazing fire of wood from the bogs: the roots
of the ancient Highland forest trees lie in the black peat
like bleached bones'.[5] By 8 June they had reached Strath
Ascaig where they stayed a week peat-carrying. On the
14th they headed north towards the hills of Applecross,
loading their possessions on Ladybird, a pack horse.

The towering mountains and the cascading rivers inspired Brenda and John to draw as well as to write, and they recorded many of the majestic peaks in their sketchbooks. At Torridon, in an area of land remote from the world in general, they stayed for a week, moving very slowly north and west. The mountains attracted them.

> The north face of Liathach lives in the mind like something seen in a vision. From the deeps of Coire na Caime, which is the Crooked Corrie, sheer cliffs rise up to spurs and pinnacles and jagged teeth. Its grandeur draws back the heart.
>
> Beinn Eighe lifts her white ribs above a tracery of pale screes, making ghostly shapes of birch trees on the grey-green of the slopes. Coire Mhic Fheachair is the soul of the mountain. A stupendous cliff of Torridon Sandstone rises about the deep loch-side in three bold buttresses capped with grey quartzite.[6]

Slowly they left the heart of the mountains, following the coastline round to Little Loch Broom. At the end of June Betsan joined them at Loch Maree and stayed with them till Achnahaird. John's wood engraving of *Betsan the Bather* was included in their article in *The Welsh Review*.

Although it was July, the weather had not been favourable, with rain and mists:

> For nearly three weeks we lived in sodden clothes. Our boots were a pulp, and our extra-thick stockings never dried out. It was a comfort to have one dry pair to wear in the sleeping bag at night, after the cold

dampness of the day. At times even the loaf was a spongy mass.[7]

But the cold and damp did not deter them and on they went and on 9 July, Brenda wrote:

> Ever since we came North I have been chafing to see the real coast, wild rocks with the surf breaking on them. At the sea-end of Loch Broom, the sky seems suddenly to lighten, the cliffs rise, and there is the smell of salt waves throwing white spray against the yellow-barnacled rocks. There is the *glut glut* of water smacked into dark hollowed caves, and the sandstone is rubbed smooth and round where water breaks ceaselessly upon it.[8]

At last they reached Ullapool where they had a chance to mend their boots and buy food. Then travelling northward once more they reached Scourie on 24 July. Their goal was Cape Wrath which was still fifty miles further north. They walked close to the coastline for a while following a rough cart-track that had been used by peat-carriers. One night they camped on a grassy ledge facing the Cape. It was in sight but still about ten miles away. The following morning, the rain came in with the dawn. Food was running low, they were hungry and wet and did not know how the land lay ahead. 'So the tent was made into a wet bundle to be hand-carried and we set off in the drizzle. Mist hung low and the Cape fog-horn boomed all day'.[9] In the late afternoon they pitched their tent to shelter while they ate a small meal and then travelled on. It was the first time they were really benighted.

It was about midnight. We were tired. Only the fog-horn booming ahead told us we were in the right direction. A dim white mist floated over the deep bog-holes. Nowhere to pitch a tent. The ground oozed water at every step. Suddenly we were on the brink of a deep gorge, vapour-filled; the roar of the water came up to us. There was nothing to do but camp above the ravine, on the wet bog. Tent pegs went into the ground with distressing ease. We prayed for a calm night. It was when we had crept into the sleeping bag after a frugal supper, that a great wind came out of the sou'west. After that the tent went mad. It cracked with reports like pistol shots, it sagged down into our faces, it bellied out, it shivered and groaned. We imagined ourselves tentless in the black night, our home blown into the sea... Tiredness made us callous, we dozed, only occasionally putting out a hand to feel that our gear was still there.[10]

The wind was still roaring the following day but the sky was clear with no sign of rain. Their food supplies were desperately low and after devouring the last scraps of bread, all that remained was a little oatmeal and two Oxo cubes. After walking for an hour they finally reached Cape Wrath.

On the cliff-edge, lighthouse and keepers' cottages dazzled the eyes on such a bright morning. Round the whole ran an immaculate white-washed wall. We wandered inside like hungry dogs. Food mattered more to us than the Cape that morning. We knocked at the Head Keeper's house. No one answered.

It was fourteen miles to Durness and food – the track

was rough and the gale buffeted us cruelly so we reeled like drunkards under our heavy packs. We lay on our sides resting once and ate the Oxo cubes reflectively.[11]

On 30 July they reached the Kyle of Durness where

The sea in its depths was purest blue, in the shallows vivid emerald, merging to mellow green where the water covered the sands of the traeth [beach]; through this cool harmony wound the red peat-water of the river like a stream of dark blood.

'Is not the sea the peacock of peacocks?
Even before the ugliest of buffaloes doth it spread out its tail;
Never doth it tire of its lace-fan of silver and silk.'[12]

After about 300 miles of walking, Brenda and John had reached their goal at the very north of Scotland but they did not stop travelling there but turned south-westward towards the Isle of Skye.

August 7: Finding ourselves in Easter Ross we had to come West again before turning home; now we are by Loch Scavaig under the Black Cuillin, with as much food as we could drag across the hills.[13]

They finally ended their journey there as the last entry in their journal shows:

There is so much to tell .... of climbing on the great ridge of the Cuillin, whose utter desolation grips the heart, –

of peak-encircled Loch Coruisk with the island of terns, of how Gwyn led us back through the black night over miles of cliff and crag, and of the loveliness of this green cwm where we are lying in the sun now, with mountain and sea and a rich froth of meadow sweet. Our boots have been finally broken by the harsh gabbro of Skye. We must go back, but it will not be to a place less lovely than here. When we next write it will be from the white house under Moel Faban.[14]

On their return to Llanllechid Brenda and John shaped their journal into the illustrated article for *The Welsh Review*.[15] This particular issue included a lot of Brenda and John's work. Apart from the Scottish journal, there was a lino-cut by John, *The Dance of Life* (on p. 153); a small wood engraving by Brenda, *Portrait* (on p. 143), and a poem and lino-cut by Brenda entitled *The Harvesters* (on p. 139). The image shows two sinuously lined women gathering armfuls of corn against a background of rugged mountains. There is an obvious enjoyment in the rhythm of line and texture which is echoed in Brenda's use of alliteration in the poem.

Young girls bind into sheaves the short-stalked corn,
    won with much labour from the mountain soil.
It has been beaten flat by wind and rain, but the
    straws are still yellow and the grain sweet.
When they rest under the shadow of a wall on the
    stubble-edge, they wind oat-straws about their
    fingers and laugh, calling them golden wedding-rings.
In the long afternoons they stook the corn and the air
    is full of the soft clashing of sheaves.

In the same issue of *The Welsh Review* there was a short story which particularly caught the attention of both Brenda and John. It was 'The Wanderers', a passionate tale about a family of gypsies by a writer, Alun Lewis, who was new to them.[16] The piece was fresh, poetic and very visual. John was particularly affected by it and said at the time, 'if ever there was a writer in Wales whose work I would love to illustrate, this is he'.[17] Although John had the urge to write to Alun Lewis, shyness stopped him and then a year later, at Christmas 1940, a letter arrived from Lewis saying, 'I've wanted to tell you, everytime [*sic*] I've seen any of your work ... *every* time so far, how exciting, how good with life it is'.[18]

Out of admiration for each other's work, a correspondence sprang up between the couple and Alun Lewis. Lewis came from Cwmaman near Aberdare, had been to university at Aberystwyth, where he received a first class honours degree in history, and had then continued his studies at Manchester University before becoming a teacher in Pengam, south Wales. In 1940 he had enlisted, joining the Royal Engineers as a 'tally clerk', and was sent to the Railway Training Centre at Longmoor in Hampshire. He had always enjoyed writing and since his schooldays had contributed his poems and prose for publication. Experience of army life had strengthened his resolve to write and determine him to want to educate 'the People'. Since the beginning of the war, the quality of his work had begun to gain recognition and he was now being taken seriously as a poet.

At the outbreak of the war, John Petts registered as a Conscientious Objector and was called to tribunal in Caernarfon where he was asked to support his views that 'killing fellow men is contrary to my moral sense of right and wrong'. The chairman of the tribunal happened to be Sir Thomas Artemus Jones, who was a patron of the Caseg Press, and his case was heard sympathetically. John volunteered to do agricultural work and was sent to a succession of farms leaving Brenda to take care of the Press.

Betsan had joined the Land Army and was working on a farm at Addlestead, near Headley in Surrey. She let John know that the farm was in urgent need of a cowman and he arranged a transfer to move down. At the end of January 1941, both Alun and John found themselves in the south of England and planned their first meeting although it was 13 April before they did manage to meet. Alun took a four-hour bus ride to visit John on the farm. Alun helped John finish his farm work then they gathered wood for a fire and sat talking over tea. John showed him photographs of Brenda and their home in Snowdonia and they exchanged their feelings about life, literature and art. The day after his visit, Alun wrote in a letter to Brenda:

> John told me too that you write poetry. I wish you would let me read some. I thought you must, but you'd said nothing – only in W.R. [*The Welsh Review*] The Threshers 'the soft clashing of the sheaves' and your letter about the mountain at Xmas made me think you write. Well, if you can send some, I'd love to read them.[19]

Brenda was pleased that he was interested in her writing and sent him a selection of recent poems. In the same letter, he had suggested that the three of them collaborate in a literary and artistic venture. He had seen an engraving by John called *Debris Searcher*, which he felt struck a similar note to his poem 'The Sentry'. He suggested that they produce a series of Broadsheets carrying a poem and engraving like the ones that pedlars used to sell around the farms in the seventeenth and eighteenth centuries. They could print these broadsheets on the Caseg Press, advertise them in the local paper and poetry magazines and sell them for a penny or tuppence a sheet. Brenda later recalled that

> He seemed obsessed with the idea of reaching 'the People'. John and I were caught by his enthusiasm though we thought Alun's belief that we could capture the eyes and ears and pockets of the multitudes was a fallacy.[20]

Even in Llanllechid, however, the war began to impinge on life. In April, a plane crashed on the hills near Tŷ'r Mynydd and Brenda, and John's younger brother Peter, who was staying with her, began sleeping in the garden in tents, because she felt safer outdoors as she felt it would be easier to escape if they saw the bombers coming close. By May, there were raids over Liverpool and refugees started arriving in Bangor. There was not much food in the shops but Brenda had plenty of vegetables from the garden and milk from the goat. John and Brenda corresponded several times a week and John sent parcels of books and money to pay the bills.

All in all, 1941 was hardly the time to begin a new artistic venture and apart from their enthusiasm, Alun, John and Brenda had little in common, as she later commented:

> Ours was an unlikely partnership. My husband and I were painfully engaged in earning the right to live in the

way that seemed best to us (obscure rebels, detached from the world) while Alun Lewis was moving in an opposite direction. He longed passionately to mingle more and more closely with humanity, to be involved with 'poverty and politics and economics'. There was a factor which overrode our differences. We were equally enthusiastic over carrying out his project. Though we wrangled over almost every detail of production – the appearance of a page, the translations, the size of lino-blocks, the pages, we never lost our interest in what we were trying to produce.[21]

However, despite their different ideologies, the correspondence between them continued with vigour and plans for the broadsheets were exchanged and discussed. Eventually they agreed that each sheet would have a theme such as 'War in Wales', 'War Epitaphs', 'The Welsh Peasant' and 'Love Poems'. The poems chosen had to be 'Welsh in character' and include work from both living and dead poets, and each sheet would feature engravings by John and Brenda. Choosing the poems was the next task. Alun was full of ideas and his suggestions included Glyn Jones, Dylan Thomas and David Jones.

I have chosen the poems that seem to have most tactile visual value ... They are all exciting images with a surrealist intensity in them that I feel would communicate a design for your knives.[22]

By the end of June 1941 they had finally agreed on the content of the first broadsheet and it was duly prepared for printing. It carried the wood engraving by John, *Debris*

Searcher, which had been Alun's original inspiration, and two poems by Alun – 'Raiders' Dawn' and 'Song of Innocence'. As the small Adana press at Tŷ'r Mynydd was really too limited to produce the quality they wanted, the block of the first broadsheet was sent to the printers, J.D. Lewis of Llandysul. Alun offered to pay the initial cost of the printing and 500 sheets were printed selling for 3d each. Brenda, as the only geographically stable member of the trio, was to coordinate the operation and deal with the correspondence and distribution of the broadsheets while Alun, for his part, contacted his literary contemporaries, Keidrych Rhys, Gwyn Jones and others, encouraging them to subscribe and to spread the word.

On 5 July 1941 Alun married Gweno Ellis of Aberystwyth in a very quiet ceremony in Gloucester. Time was at such a premium that the ring was bought only five minutes before the ceremony and for a bouquet Alun stole a spray of roses that were hanging over a wall on the way to the registry office. They had only their wedding day together before having to go their separate ways. As a wedding present, Brenda sent a hand-coloured copy of her lino print *Figures in a Landscape*. A double-page spread in *Picture Post* had inspired her to produce this image. The line is strong and confident, the figure still reminiscent of Gauguin's Tahitian women, and here the rugged landscape emphasises the hardship of rustic life. Frequently, Brenda took her inspiration from cuttings in newspapers and magazines – sometimes her attention would be caught by the acute angle of a head, the solid stance of a figure, a rich texture, a compelling shape. She hoarded these cuttings in files and notebooks until a later date when they would be retrieved, reworked and emerge transformed in her own work.

Alun and Gweno were delighted with Brenda's present and, in his next letter, Alun described what he saw in it:

The luminous tones in the dark colours of the valley running up from the river is as restful, and exciting at the same time, as a Beethoven Sonata: so are the colours moving from the clothes to the stones, the mauve theme & the yellow; & then the white aprons & the light on the cheeks & the skin & feet sets it all tingling with a reined life...

There are endless voyages for me in it, so I won't try to thank you in terms commensurate with my feelings.[23]

Brenda was pleased by his praise and enthusiasm. She had an innate need to have her work liked and accepted, and did not generally encourage criticism. But although she had not met Alun, he had won her trust with his earnest praise, and *his* critical remarks were acceptable to her. Sometimes they were harsh and sometimes complimentary, but always direct and honest and backed up with reason:

There is a simplicity in your poems that is very cool & soothing, like your mountain lakes, a kind of innocence, naivety that I do not find in your engravings where there is more criticism of life, more exploration of <u>human</u> flesh – & blood & emotion. That is, perhaps, why you write poetry, because it expresses a different, younger self ...

I wouldn't say any of this if I didn't think you were, although I've not met you, my friend, as John is, to whom I speak my thoughts, whatever they be.[24]

In the many versions of her poem 'Dead Ponies' in her notebooks, Brenda altered some words and lines according to Alun's suggestions but still clung to her version; keeping some lines awkward, stilted to the tongue, to emphasise the discomfort of the situation. An evocative poem, it was published in the *Dublin Magazine* later that summer and was included in two poetry anthologies in the 1940s, *Poetry in Wartime* and *New British Poets*.[25]

Although the first broadsheet had been ready to be printed about July, there had been setbacks and it was still with the printers at the beginning of October. As the war progressed, supplies of good paper began to be in short supply, inevitably there had been delays with deliveries, and the prices were continually rising. Alun was becoming anxious about the success of the venture but as he was committed to his Army training course at Morecambe, there was little he could do apart from write encouraging letters.

At the end of October 1941, Alun had his first leave in eight months and made plans to visit Tŷ'r Mynydd on his way south to meet Gweno. Brenda was particularly excited as she had wanted to meet Alun for a long time. Although her part at the centre of the organisation in Llanllechid was vital, she had been feeling left out of things recently, especially as John and Alun had been able to meet on several occasions. Alun was due to arrive in the afternoon of Friday, 31 October, and Brenda went into Bangor to meet his train. Alun had hoped she would bring her pony and cart to collect him as he could only stay overnight. Brenda had suggested the bus trip would be quicker and allow him more time at Tŷ'r Mynydd. Alun arrived on time and as the next bus to Llanllechid was not due for a while they sat and talked in an Italian coffee bar in the High Street.

He had a lot to say, but spoke in such soft running Southern Welsh tones that I could catch little of what he said, through the din of other people's conversation, the hissing of the coffee machine and the cars outside in the narrow street.[26]

Brenda was so anxious to make a good impression on Alun that at first she was very quiet.

I was also embarrassed as the hem of my skirt had begun to come undone at the back.[27]

But they had so much to talk about that Brenda soon forgot about her embarrassment and shyness.

They reached Llanllechid about teatime and after talking for hours, they walked by moonlight on the mountain, through Bwlch y Brwyn (the pass of the rushes) to the Caseg River – from which the press and the Broadsheets derived their name. Then they sat in the chimney corner by a roaring fire and talked till dawn. Alun had to leave a few hours later to catch the first bus and train to take him to Dyfi Junction where he was meeting Gweno. After a night with Gweno's parents in Aberystwyth, Alun went to Llandysul to see J.D. Lewis, the printers.

For some months Alun had been concerned about the delays in the printing of the first Broadsheet, so he had decided to go and investigate at the earliest opportunity. The printer 'seemed to have rather a guilty conscience and no real explanation for the delay except that he was waiting for a new machine to do the sheets with'.[28] Alun spent five hours there, sorting out the difficulties and choosing paper for the Broadsheets. By the time he left the printing room, the machine was turning out the five hundred copies of the first Broadsheet.

As the sheets came off the Press, it suddenly struck Alun that it was not a good idea to have his poems on the first Broadsheet. 'It may have seemed as if we're running the sheets to advertise me simply'.[29] As he did not want to give that impression, he wrote immediately to the printers asking them to hold on to the first Broadsheet for the moment, wait until the second one was ready and then dispatch the two together. He wrote to Brenda and John and asked them to prepare the second sheet as soon as they possibly could and send it on to Llandysul. Alun was rushing them because he wanted to distribute some of the Broadsheets personally while he was still in Wales on leave:

> I've asked Lewis to send 150 of each sheet to me, and 50 to Gwyn Jones; also to keep as many as he thinks the Swansea and Carmarthen booksellers will accept; and send the rest to you in the North Wales area. There'll be one prospectus and subscription form for each sheet. I think I can probably arrange to sell more than 150, after the first number. I'll send a specimen to Foyles, Richard Wilson, Llew. Wyn Griffith & Gwyn Jones and ask them how many they want. Then I'll tackle Cardiff – Smiths and Welsh Bookshop.[30]

Originally the sheets were going to be sold for 3d. each but it soon became obvious that this was not going to cover the cost and the price had to be raised to 4d. A prospectus was also prepared to publicise their venture and was distributed with each Broadsheet. Bookshops were asked to slip this manifesto into their books; and newspapers were sent samples and asked to write a review or feature about it. There were various versions of the prospectus and this was the final version as printed:

THE CASEG BROADSHEETS
are a new venture by Welsh artists, writers and printers which aim [*sic*] at publishing a series of 4d. broadsheets of new engravings by John Petts and Brenda Chamberlain and poems in English and Welsh (with the Bell translations into English) by Welsh poets over the last 1000 years. The Welsh Peasants, Wales at War, Welsh Love Songs for Penillion and Welsh Epitaphs by the medieval poets, as well as verse by such living writers as Dylan Thomas, R. Williams-Parry, Alun Lewis, Glyn Jones, Keidrych Rees [*sic*] and Lynette Roberts are planned for the first ten numbers.

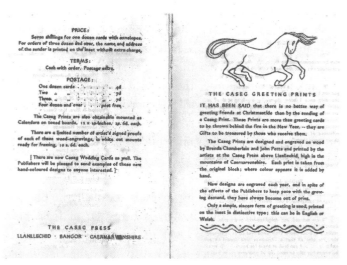

Subscription form for The Caseg Press Greeting Prints, c. 1939

If you desire to obtain the series by subscription, please send the attached form to –
The Caseg Press, Llanllechid, Caernarvonshire.

Within a month the first two broadsheets and the prospectus were released. The second broadsheet was of a sequence of traditional stanzas or Penillion in Welsh with English translation and accompanied by two wood-engravings, one by Brenda and one by John. They sent Alun the proof of Sheet no. 2 and he replied by return of post with a long list of his impressions. He was not happy about the English translation of the Penillion and suggested various amendments. Alun had an astute critical eye and was quick to articulate his feelings. About the illustrations he wrote:

> I like the engravings enormously – John's grain of wheat has an astonishing combination of vigour, lustre and delicacy. I would have liked some cover for the woman's skirt though, Brenda. The lower line is rather puzzling anatomically, as it were, making her look amputated. If you had a window bar thickly across her at the bottom I think it would improve the balance of the design and also effect a better union with the words.[31]

Brenda had come to the same conclusion as Alun about the typographical overload of the sheet. He felt

> It begins too near the top & ends too near the bottom. Don't you think one design is best? Or at least both designs on the same level of paper? And a certain amount of white space as relief to show the clarity and boldness of words and engravings.[32]

PENILLION

I

Gwynt ar fôr, a haul ar fynydd,
Cerrig llwydion yn lle coedydd,
A gwylanod yn lle dynion,
Och, Duw, pa fodd na thorrai 'nghalon!

II

Dod dy law ond wyd yn coelio,
Dan fy mron, a gwylia 'mrifo,
Ti gei glywed, os gwrandewi,
Swn y galon fach yn torri.

III

Nid oes rhyngof ag ef heno
Onid pridd ac arch ac amdo;
Mi fum lawer gwaith ymhellach,
Ond nid erioed â chalon drymach.

IV

Hiraeth mawr a hiraeth creulon,
Hiraeth sydd yn torri'm calon;
Pan f'wyf dryma'r nos yn cysgu,
Fe ddaw hiraeth ac a'm deffry.

Hiraeth, hiraeth, cilia, cilia,
Paid a phwyso'n rhy drwm arna',
Nesa dipyn at yr erchwyn,
Gad i mi gael cysgu gronyn.

Derfydd aur a derfydd arian,
Derfydd melfed, derfydd sidan,
Derfydd pob dilledyn helaeth,
Eto er hyn ni dderfydd hiraeth.

V

Blodau'r flwyddyn yw f'anwylyd,
Ebrill, Mai, Mehefin hefyd,
Llewyrch haul yn twnnu ar gysgod,
A gwenithen y genethod.

WOOD ENGRAVING. *Brenda Chamberlain.*

I

Wind on the sea and sun on the mountain,
Grey stones instead of woods
And seagulls instead of men—
Oh God! that my heart would break!

II

Put thy hand, if thou'lt not believe,
Under my breast, and see thou hurt me not;
Thou wilt hear, if thou hearkenest,
The sound of the little heart breaking.

III

There is nothing between him and me tonight
But earth and coffin and shroud;
I was many a time further from him,
But never with a heavier heart.

IV

A great longing, a cruel longing,
A longing is breaking my heart;
When I am asleep in the deepest night
Longing comes waking me.

Longing, longing, get thee gone,
Weigh not too heavy on me;
Get thee aside a little,
Let me sleep awhile.

Gold must end and silver must end,
Velvet must end, silk must end,
Ends all sumptuous raiment—
But longing never ends.

V

The flower of all the year is my beloved,
April, May, and June besides,
The brightness of the sun shining on shadow,
A grain of wheat among girls.

Traditional.
(Translated by H. IDRIS BELL)

WOOD ENGRAVING.   *John Petts.*

With acknowledgements to Mr. H. Idris Bell and the Publishers, Messrs. Hughes & Son, Wrexham, for permission to reprint the English translation from *Welsh Poems of the Twentieth Century.*

Published by the Caseg Press, Llanllechid Caernarvonshire and printed at the Gomerian Press, Llandyssul, S. Wales.

Caseg Broadsheet no. 2, November 1941

Tactfully he added,

> I admit it's the printer's job rather than yours, but I
> think we should be careful not to embarrass him with
> too much material for each sheet. Do you agree? Or
> hasn't he sent you sheet two yet?[33]

However, the second was duly printed in its original form
without any amendments and the two broadsheets were
distributed to subscribers and booksellers in Wales and
London. Interest was strong and in one of his letters, Alun
gave Brenda and John some feedback:

> I've had very high praise of sheet I from Robert Graves,
> Keidrych Rees [*sic*] & Lynette[,] & Phillip [*sic*] Unwin.
> The engraving was particularly lauded, John bach. You're
> in a rich vein. I'm afraid you know, that you two are
> going to be what you dread – a success.[34]

After the successful launching of the first two broadsheets
in November 1941, Alun, John and Brenda began making
plans for the rest of the series. Alun was now in
Woodbridge, Suffolk, serving as an officer with the South
Wales Borderers. It was an unhappy time for him, as
Brenda observed:

> He suffered from moods of black frustration, as was only
> to be expected from a writer forced into a life totally
> against his nature; and yet it must be remembered, he
> had chosen to become an officer. He had been
> withdrawn, was withdrawing himself, further and
> further from home.[35]

Alun did regret his decision to become an officer, finding it more depressing and shocking than he could ever have anticipated. It was

> somehow immoral and ludicrous. I have to make conversation in the Mess, assume anger or dignity to the men; I can't lounge about listening to the natural and earthy talk of the barrack room and pub any more. There is a whole world of caste and stiff tradition fencing me off. I don't like thinking about it.[36]

Later that November on the 14th, Brenda attended a special ceremony in Bangor in which her mother was installed as Mayor, a great honour. For eleven years Elsie Chamberlain had been the only woman member of the Bangor Borough Council and had also worked enthusiastically with many local groups and societies. She was thrilled to gain the position which she had always

Elsie Chamberlain as Mayor of Bangor, 1941

dreamt her father would reach and publicly thanked her husband 'without whose goodwill and co-operation she would not have been able to do the public work which had fallen to her lot.'[37] Brenda enjoyed the ceremony, and although pleased for her mother found it hard, as always, to understand her mother's obvious enjoyment of organising events and attending meetings and committees. In May that year Elsie Chamberlain had dealt with 1779 evacuees, providing them with advice, information and clothing. While her mother was a born organiser, Brenda was not, and she was finding it difficult enough to handle the paperwork for the production of the Caseg Broadsheets.

In December, Alun Lewis forwarded some subscriptions for the Broadsheets from two friends:

> I'm enclosing £1 being 10/- from Vernon Watkins the poet, in goodwill: he says don't send him any as he's joining the RAF, and won't carry nice things with him: but we could keep a set for him, couldn't we? And the other 10/- from my pal Dick Mills … who wants you to send copies of sheet one to several friends, with a prospectus in each, and written on them 'Merry Xmas from Dick Mills'. You see, he sailed for India last week in Khaki – and it's in the nature of a last request. Will you do it, Brenda?[38]

Brenda found it depressing to think that men were going off to war knowing that they might not return. The war was still a long way from Llanllechid and it was Alun's letters that really brought home to her the reality of the situation.

Plans for Broadsheets no. 3 and no. 4 progressed and

Brenda sent the proofs to Alun in February 1942. He replied on the 15th of that month:

About the 3rd & 4th sheets. I agree with you that you need a third poem for your Love Song sequence; if I still suggest that you end with an illustration, it is for 'editorial' policy, not poetic, that I say so.[39]

Despite the pressures of war upon him Alun remained optimistic and still adhered to his idealised view of the broadsheets.

Looked at broadly, the idea I have is that the sheets should work forward all the time, beyond individual love or failure or defeat, & should speak for a whole nation, all humanity in their small way. That is why I prefer the cosmic mood of 'these carried bitter tears to the sea' to 'A man has drowned my pride'. The latter is terribly true & real: but I want the great flow of earth and water & emotion of the second to be closing harmony, which opens a window onto the world, & does not nail trouble & anguish to its root. I also think the sheets need an engraving – that is the tradition we have set and I think the cause of their popularity.[40]

Aware that he could be posted overseas at any moment Alun tried to relinquish his involvement with the project: 'However, it is your work now; no use pretending it's mine; I never did approve of absentee directors.'[41] His protestations were just a gesture; he wanted so much to express his views and be involved but most of all he wanted to feel needed. His letter continued,

Please decide for yourself. But I say quite clearly that I regretted not finding one of those wonderful vignettes of woman's heads of yours ... I don't think the drawings of No 3 are half as effective as the bold engraving of No 1. I got little out of John's drawing – it was too small & obscured, as if a mist had come over the mountain. The eighteenth century sheets were clear to the point of caricature deliberately sacrificing sensitiveness for clarity & sturdiness – a sort of rollicking line. I don't want to go to that extreme but I do feel we're trying to reproduce something that cannot but weaken and lose itself in the process, when we try to reproduce your delicate and gradual drawings.

Do you think you could place a head and shoulders shawled woman or dreaming woman, on the sheet? If you omit No 1 of Lovesong and include No 3 say? I don't know. I'm only thinking.

This sounds carping; you know it isn't, Brenda, don't you? I'm proud of cooperating with you, and overjoyed at our friendship. Because of that, I must give my critical bent its fling, so's you can get to know and like or dislike me, if you choose...[42]

Alun's advice was sound, but sadly it was not acted upon and Broadsheet no. 3, the 'War and Wales' sheet, was overcrowded with words and illustrations with two half-tone drawings which really did lack definition. There were three excerpts from poems attributed to Taliesin, Peryf ap Cedifor and Gwalchmai, in Welsh and English. One drawing, *Study after Leonardo* was by Brenda and *The Slain* by John. Broadsheet no 4 was a crowded one too, featuring four modern poems: 'To a Welsh Woman' and 'The Circle of C' by

Study after Leonardo used on Caseg Broadsheet No. 3

Lynette Roberts, and 'From the Green Heart' and 'From Lovesong' by Brenda Chamberlain, accompanied by a wood engraving 'Snowdon ridge' by John Petts. Broadsheets no. 3 and no. 4 were published in March 1942.

In the same month, Brenda had news that three of her poems had been chosen for Tambimuttu's anthology, *Poetry in Wartime*. They were 'Dead Ponies', 'Christmas Eve by the Baltic' and 'Dead Climber'.[43] Alun wrote, expressing his pleasure that her work had been chosen and encouraged Brenda to send off her poems to other editors: 'You're not an easy poet to understand, Brenda; one must discover you gradually, moving from poem to poem as along a grass track leading to the long grass levels of the mountain tops where the air is & the heavens & so much, so little else'.[44] There grew an urgency in Brenda to write poetry and she read as much contemporary writing as she could with that same intensity.

89

Poetry became as precious as bread. I can remember buying a new magazine in Bangor (perhaps it was *Poetry London*) standing in the street to read it, as a starving person will tear the crust from a loaf. *Life and Letters*, *Poetry Quarterly*, and many other 'little' magazines, were printing new poems as they were written, with urgency; after all, tomorrow there might be no more paper, no more ink, no more world.[45]

Brenda had 'finished' about ten poems and in her notebooks there were the seeds for many more. She was working on a long cycle of poems which she called 'The Green Heart', and occasionally a short section of this would appear in print under another title. 'Christmas Eve by the Baltic', for example, is Part IV of 'The Green Heart'. These poems were based on the letters she had received from Karl von Laer, the German boy she had met in Bangor in 1932. Until the war broke out, their correspondence had been a 'constant, silent dialogue' which had inspired many of Brenda's poems.[46] But her writing was still young and naïve and often clumsy in construction. Alun again instructed her:

And may I in the friendship of poetry warn you of one thing? Words. I found myself using the same adjectives a lot over a period of say two years. 'Terrible' I used and 'lovely' – ordinary words which cannot be used often, for their poetic value lies in lifting their ordinariness – once or twice at most – into a high order of feeling. You use 'tormented' too often, sometimes in association with natural things which are naturally not tormented – e.g. 'tormented waves'. I suggest that your imagery & the words that express it are reaching the stage where they must change & grow and become something wider, deeper & more sinuous-reaching in their roots less 'oppressed by mountains'. Also that you will discard 'flat' words such as 'tinctured'. Rilke even in translation is a rich source of words for the same fundamental thoughts as you work in. It is only a kind of preparation, not a warning that I'm uttering, in so far as I can divine your future voyages.[47]

With all the recent interest in her poetry Brenda was beginning to take her writing seriously and poured more of her energy into that direction. Since the outbreak of war in 1939 she had felt unable to paint and had found it much more satisfying to express her feelings in words. As she had not been painting for a few years her confidence was weak and although she had enjoyed the success of the Caseg Broadsheets, she really felt that it was more John's success than her own, as engraving and printing were his particular skills. In fact, once the Caseg Broadsheets project came to an end, Brenda was never again to do any engraving or printmaking.

She was feeling the need to have her own work recognised and she began to think that writing might achieve this result. She desperately wanted to be a success and did not feel that her work was being taken seriously enough. It was about this time that differences began to arise between Brenda and John. Competition and professional jealousy entered their relationship as each of them vied for attention. To a close female friend, Brenda described John as holding her back in her creativity, seeing her 'as a weaver, a home-maker, a writer but not an artist

– that was his territory.' Wartime circumstances put an additional strain on their relationship and they began to drift further apart. Brenda took solace in her writing, words became all important and a pattern emerged in her creative behaviour; when happy, Brenda would paint, and when unhappy, she felt able to write. She found herself brooding over the fact that the war was steadily impinging upon her own life. Even in the wilds of Snowdonia the war encroached; and one dark night, bombs dropped around the village, killing a woman as she sat by the fire.

Images and strong feelings impressed themselves on Brenda Chamberlain and in subsequent years she would draw upon this store of memories as inspiration for both her painting and her writing. Throughout her life, death was a constantly recurring theme and her most vivid first-hand experiences were culled from these wartime years in the Welsh mountains. In comparison to the mass bomb victims in cities, and the mortality of those on active service, her experiences were minimal, but to Brenda they seemed provocative and awe-inspiring, and she drew upon these images over and over again. It was hard for Brenda to accept that in a land that had been so tranquil, war was now on her doorstep. Knowing the local area as she did from those long walks in the mountain, Brenda worked for the Red Cross searching for wrecked aeroplanes and their crews. Sometimes, the impact of the war came far too close for Brenda's liking.

One terrible spring evening when we were coming home with branches for the fire, myself and a young village boy, we came upon, in a hollow place between two hills, three Liverpool evacuee boys playing with a live mortar.

They were throwing it against a big rock, to make it explode. They would not listen to my protests; in fact having an audience, made them more eager to cause a sensation. Suddenly, with a fearful bang, the mortar exploded. The child and I threw ourselves to the ground, and covered heads with our arms. When the smoke had cleared, and fragments of rock and earth had ceased to fall, I went back into the hollow. One of the three boys was dragging himself along the ground screaming for his mother. One of his legs was perforated all over with holes the size of half crowns. The second boy had escaped injury, but the third was twitching in the death agony, his brains spilling out onto the grass. I told my young friend to stay with the boys, while I ran for help to the village postmaster. Afterwards, I heard that the unwounded boy had quietly run away to his foster-mother's, thrown his cap onto the peg inside the door and eaten his tea without a word, a sign of shock. It was a long time before I recovered from the horror of the happening. There was a military tribunal in Llanberis which I had to attend. Live ammunition continued to lie forgotten on the mountain. Accidents continued to happen, innocent days were over.[48]

In the meantime, more letters arrived from Alun Lewis stating his disappointment with the way the Broadsheets had turned out.

My feeling is that we haven't realised the ideal we envisaged at the start – typographically, artistically or poetically. The small engravings have failed to reproduce the detail & clarity of the larger originals: Leonardo's

Horsemen, for instance, was too archaic for the modern reality that WAR connotes. I think we need to be bolder, to use strong black and white contrasts <u>roughly</u>; and give the engraving a fullness it doesn't get when it's tucked into a corner. I prefer the Llandysul type to your italic type, I think, for that same black & white definition which I feel we should aim at.[49]

Both Brenda and John considered these comments seriously. He was right. Whereas the first two broadsheets had been strong and vital, the second two had lacked definition and power, and consequently, interest in the Broadsheets had dwindled. In numbers 5 and 6 they reverted to the original boldness. No. 5 featured part of a Dylan Thomas poem, 'In memory of Ann Jones', alongside a drawing by Brenda Chamberlain. Although this was certainly a more punchy presentation, Alun expressed his dissatisfaction.

I do still feel that the Ann Jones sheet doesn't balance in itself; the drawing on one side, the poem with a staircase formation, sort of hooked around it.[50]

Broadsheet no. 6 was 'Spring', a poem from the Cynfeirdd (the earliest Welsh poets) in Welsh and with an English translation by H. Idris Bell. A wood engraving *Flower of the Bone* by John Petts dominated the sheet giving it structure. Alun approved of this one and wrote to Brenda, 'I think John's Gwanwyn [Spring] sheet is wholly happy and satisfying'.[51] These latter two sheets were published in June 1942. Two more were planned and reached the proofs stage but were never published. Alun was sent to India just before Christmas in 1942 and although his letters continued to flow, the impetus to continue producing the Broadsheets had been lost.

The activities of the Caseg Press had affected Brenda's life quite dramatically. Since she was situated at Llanllechid, Brenda had become the main focus of the interest generated by the work of the press and the Broadsheets. John's farm work had taken him away from

Self portrait, 1942, wood engraving

home a lot and her almost reclusive life at Tŷ'r Mynydd became transformed by her introduction to a new circle of friends and acquaintances, people who had expressed interest in and admiration for the Caseg Broadsheets. One of these was Lord Elgin's daughter, Lady Elisabeth Babington Smith, who exchanged friendly letters with Brenda and subsequently invited her to stay in Scotland.

By the end of 1942, John was running a small farm, Tyddyn Cynal close by, near Conwy, and he occasionally managed to return to Tŷ'r Mynydd at weekends, but their relationship was now becoming quite strained and although the farm was close by, Brenda also found it difficult to visit him there:

> If I came over just for a day what would it be like? You've no idea how horribly awkward I feel coming there now, because I know every word or look I give is being criticised.[52]

In May 1943, in response to another invitation from Lady Babington Smith, Brenda went to Scotland. While there, she met Friedl Bleier, a tall charismatic Jew who had fled Austria with his mother. Brenda became infatuated with him and wrote about him in great detail to John extolling his love of climbing, his knowledge of poetry, his dark handsome face and flashing eyes. Inevitably, John questioned her intentions but Brenda was adamant in her response:

> It is marvellous that you have such understanding, John. But I think it is far too ordinary an interpretation of my relationship with Friedl, to say that I have fallen in love

with him. I haven't; we don't fall in love with lightning, or fire, or a mountain torrent, & he is all these things.[53]

On one such weekend he returned to discover Brenda just back from one of her visits to Dunfermline and Edinburgh. He was taken aback to discover that she was not alone. 'I entered the house to find a very handsome young Jew, tall and dark, sitting by the table in my particular armchair, wearing my best sweater'. Apparently he seemed surprised to see John. After they had a meal, Brenda said to John, 'Let's walk on the mountain; I've got to talk to you.' 'Then,' John explained, as they walked along the green track, 'she dropped a bomb on my heart and soul. All was over between us.' She said, 'This is the love of my life – I feel a woman at last.' She was returning to Edinburgh to begin a new life. John asked, 'Surely you'll <u>want</u>, you'll need to keep Tŷ'r Mynydd as a home?' 'You can have it.' he added. But Brenda refused, as she was adamant that she was starting a new life elsewhere.[54]

So Brenda left for Scotland; leaving John no address. The blow was hard. After Christmas 1943, John gave up his commitment to the Conwy farm and returned to Tŷ'r Mynydd to wait for his call-up papers. Although he had not changed his views about war, he had decided to volunteer for active service with the non-fighting section, the Royal Army Medical Corps (RAMC). Then the second blow struck: he received a letter from a solicitor in Bangor, addressed to him at the farm, informing him that Brenda was returning to Tŷ'r Mynydd, that 'she regarded it as her property' and that John 'must not take up residence there and had no right to return'.[55] John was amazed by this and replied in the strongest terms, stating that he knew of no law in Britain which could keep a man out of his own home and that anyway, he was in fact living there. 'I was sick at heart', he later recalled, 'that Brenda would find it in herself to go to such extreme lengths to, in fact, try to steal the place from me (we were in fact joint owners of the property).[56] When John did receive his call-up papers, and before joining the army, he left Tŷ'r Mynydd, taking his basic possessions – easel, painting materials and tools, canvases and frames – to store with his friend, John St. Bodfan Gruffydd in Edern. He explained,

> Quixotically, I wrote to Brenda, saying that since she wanted the house so much that she had tried to steal it, I would give it to her. She never replied but returned to live there, making it her base, enjoying the fact that now people came up the hill to see her alone.[57]

Having joined the RAMC, in the spring of 1944 John volunteered for parachute training and eventually became a member of the Parachute Field Ambulance on the blood transfusion team.[58] It was a dangerous occupation. His duties took him to many parts of the world and the survival rate in the Parachute Regiment was low. He was still unsettled by the way his relationship with Brenda had ended. It felt very unsatisfactory. He had shared so many happy times with Brenda and now felt the need to contact her and settle their differences in case he, like many of his companions, did not survive the war. He wrote to Brenda and yet again she did not reply, which saddened him a great deal.

Brenda must have been distraught too, for her sojourn in Scotland had been brief. Although she had been warned by Friedl's mother that he was a philanderer who took advantage of women, she returned to Edinburgh clearly thinking that she was going to be living with him, but he didn't turn up and she had no choice but to return to Tŷ'r Mynydd. Friedl Bleier had passed in and out of her life very quickly, leaving no trace except sadness for Brenda. She and John were now divorced and he was away at war. In March 1944 news came that Alun Lewis had died in Burma of wounds received in what was said to be a revolver accident.

> Domestic rupture and then death – it was the end of the Broadsheets. I retained no copies of the sheets, or if I did, they lay around the house, and their backs were used by children for their drawings, and then thrown away. The Broadsheets were lost, but good memories remained.[59]

Brenda had grown up very quickly in these war years. When she first arrived in Llanllechid, she was full of youth, joy and optimism. The years Brenda and John spent together, a time of growth and development for them both, were brought to an end by Brenda, who, having decided that she and John no longer shared the same view of the world, had followed a romantic dream to Scotland. Thwarted by its failure to blossom, Brenda returned to Llanllechid. And at thirty-two she found herself alone.

[1] *The Welsh Review*, 1.2 (March 1939), 71, 83.
[2] *The Welsh Review*, 1.5 (June 1939), 131, 143, 247, 267.
[3] Published as Brenda Chamberlain & R. John Petts, 'From Other Hills (Letters from the Western highlands, with Wood-engravings by the Writers)', *The Welsh Review*, 2.4 (Nov.

1939), pp. 197-205 (p. 197, 5 June). Eleven wood engravings were included.

[4] 'From Other Hills', p. 197 (7 June).

[5] Ibid., p. 197 (7 June).

[6] Ibid., pp. 198-99 (21 June).

[7] Ibid., p. 201 (8 July).

[8] Ibid., p. 201 (9 July).

[9] Ibid., p. 203 (29 July).

[10] Ibid., pp. 203-204 (29 July).

[11] Ibid., p. 204 (29 July).

[12] Ibid., p. 204 (29 July).

[13] Ibid., p. 204 (7 Aug.).

[14] Ibid., p. 205 [7 July?/Aug].

[15] See note 1 above, and illustration, p. 63.

[16] *The Welsh Review* 2.4 (Nov. 1939), 128-39.

[17] John Petts, *Welsh Horizons*, p. 11.

[18] Ibid., p. 11.

[19] Letter from Alun Lewis to Brenda Chamberlain, 14 April 1941, NLW MS 20798C, f.6.

[20] Brenda Chamberlain, *ALCB*, p. 2.

[21] NLW MS 18969E, 'How the Caseg broadsheets began', ff. 2-3.

[22] NLW MS 20798 C, f.9.

[23] Letter from Alun Lewis to Brenda Chamberlain, [July 1941], NLW MS 20798C, ff. 18-19.

[24] Letter, 2 June 1941, from Alun Lewis to Brenda Chamberlain, NLW MS 20798C, ff. 10^v-11.

[25] Published as 'There is death enough in Europe' in *The Dublin Magazine* 16.3 (July-Sept. 1941), 9-10; as 'Dead Ponies' in M. J. Tambimuttu (ed.), *Poetry in Wartime. An Anthology* (London: Faber & Faber, 1942), p. 27; in Kenneth Rexroth (ed.), *The New British Poets* (Norfolk, Conn.: New Directions, 1949), p. 23; also in Brenda Chamberlain, *The Green Heart* (London: Oxford University Press, 1958), p. 31. [Henceforth

GH].

[26] NLW MS 18969E, f. 4.

[27] Ibid., f. 4.

[28] Letter from Alun Lewis, 4 Nov. [1941], NLW MS 20798C, f. 22.

[29] Ibid., f. 22.

[30] Ibid., f. 23.

[31] Dated 'Nov. 18?' [1941], ibid., f. 27^v.

[32] Ibid., f. 27^v.

[33] Ibid. f. 27^v.

[34] Ibid., f. 28.

[35] *ALCB*, p. 26.

[36] Letter from Alun Lewis, 5 Jan. 1942, NLW MS 20798C, f. 32.

[37] *The North Wales Chronicle*, 14 Nov. 1941, p. 4.

[38] Letter from Alun Lewis, 9 [Dec. 1941], NLW MS 20798C, f. 31^v.

[39] Letter from Alun Lewis, 15 Feb. 1942, NLW MS 20789C, f. 36^v.

[40] Ibid., f. 36^v.

[41] Ibid., f. 36^v.

[42] Ibid., ff. 36-37.

[43] *Poetry in Wartime*, pp. 27-31.

[44] Ibid., f. 38^v.

[45] *AW*, p. 48.

[46] *GH*, p. 35.

[47] NLW MS 20798C, f. 39.

[48] *AW*, pp. 49-50.

[49] Letter from Alun Lewis, Sun., 9 [?Aug. 1942], NLW MS 20798C, f. 41^v.

[50] Letter from Alun Lewis, Sat., 26 [?Sept. 1942], NLW MS 20798C, f. 42^v.

[51] Ibid., f. 42^v.

[52] NLW MS 23207F, f. 143, letter dated 11 May 1943.

[53] NLW MS 23207F, f. 172, dated 'Tues. June? [*sic*] 1943'.

[54] Letter from John Petts to the author, 30 Sept. 1983.

[55] Ibid.

[56] Ibid.

[57] John Petts in conversation with the author, 3 Sept. 1983.

[58] Petts joined the 224 Parachute Field Ambulance with the 6th Airborne Division. The unit consisted of conscripts and volunteers including conscientious objectors who had not wished to bear arms.

[59] NLW MS 18969E, f. 4.

Chapter 5

Across Deep Water 1944-47

Brenda was alone in Tŷ'r Mynydd. Feelings of melancholia swept over her, and saddened by her recent unfulfilled experiences, she withdrew into her shell. She took solace in words and her notebooks were filled with a disordered array of phrases, half-written poems and fragments of prose. To allow plenty of room for revision, she wrote her original version on the right-hand pages and left the left-hand sides blank for alterations and corrections. Writing was certainly no easy process for Brenda; it was a battle she took on when she was unhappy and allowed her to earn herself a few pounds as her work was still enjoying popularity in the small magazines. Despite her recent experiences, she wrote nothing in her notebooks about her parting with John or her trip to Scotland to meet Friedl, and found it difficult to share her thoughts with friends. Instead, her sadness and bitterness began to emerge through characters in her writings. In her poem 'Blodeuwedd' Brenda identified with the guilt Blodeuwedd felt when she was punished for taking a lover, Gronw:

When Gronw came to her he thawed
Winter's long frost and on her melting thigh
Planted the Spring:
Her body fructified
But after joy returns
White rain, wind driving of the wombed
Blind rain of loneliness
November sorrows and the cold nights
Broken by rats eating of stored delights.

Love's mirror lies thin splintered in the
    abandoned room.
Damp rots the marriage bed and the air reeks
With fog and sodden leaves
Choking the gutters and the eaves
O Soul, could we foresee our ends?[1]

In her notebooks Brenda explained how the cry of an owl
led her to write the poem:

When I was a child, lying in bed one morning in our
house below the wood, an owl battered itself against the
bedroom window. Memory is fixed in the channels of
childhood: of brown soft body and flat faced falling
suddenly at the glass; of my father's horror.

'An owl in daylight. O misfortune. Someone of ours is
to die.' My uncle was killed soon after, and from that
time on, the owl has sent ice through my blood. I think
it chills its own heart with its cry.[2]

Now, years later as Brenda was out walking her dogs, she
recalled that memory:

A white owl circles me and cries once more from her feather-wall of snow. Owl, why of such ill omen? Of such import of evil? I think of Blodeuwedd in the *Mabinogion*.

So they took the blossoms of the oak and the blossoms of the broom, and the blossoms of the meadowsweet, and produced from them a maiden, the fairest and most graceful that man ever saw. And they baptized her, and gave her the name of Blodeuwedd.[3]

When he had transformed her into an owl after she had sinned, Gwydion said:

I will not slay thee, but I will do unto thee worse than that. For I will turn thee into a bird ... Thou shalt never show thy face in the light of day henceforth; and that through fear of all the other birds.[4]

Night after night, up at the farm when field work is finished and the others have gone visiting, I work at my poem 'Blodeuwedd'.

Many miles we have run
Many bitter lakes swum
Fleeing our ghosts and discarded loves
Thinking to build new lives.[5]

It was the lament of both Brenda and Blodeuwedd.

The image of the bird, of death and references to the *Mabinogion* recur in another poem that Brenda was working on in this spring of 1944. 'Poem for Five Airmen' was prefaced by another quotation from Lady Charlotte Guest's translation of the *Mabinogion*, this time from the tale of Lludd and Llefelys: 'The second plague was a shriek which came every May-eve over every hearth...'[6] In the poem Brenda likened the second plague to the disturbance of war:

> Now horror feeds upon our sobered hearts.
> Air's treachery, land's harshness, water's malice.
> Most, fire's dragon tongue
> All, in this twisted wreckage
> Prove power to break our peace.[7]

The bird was a phoenix which consumed the burnt bodies of the five airmen as their plane crashed into the valley of Cwm Pen Llafur. The airmen

> Became the fires wherein they blazed and shook
> Their bone-fine bodies off; withstood the shock
> Of all their lost
> Identity; and lastly know
> That in the flames
> Their spirits grew.

Just as Blodeuwedd was transformed into the form of an owl, here the airmen were transformed into

> Birdmen at last
> Feather-ruddered
> Wind-tipped of living quill.[8]

Despite the theme of rebirth, the poem expresses little hope, and the reality of disaster in war leaves a bitter taste. While sections of the poem flow smoothly, Brenda's excessive use of hyphenated words (there are twenty-nine examples in this poem alone), such as 'feather-ruddered', 'tongue-dumb', 'thought-prick', sound contrived and awkward. Brenda sometimes became too bogged down in the texture of words. She applied them as boldly as the paint from her brush but instead of blending and harmonising like the paint they sat together in obvious discomfort. She describes her way of working:

> I was in the habit of carrying scraps of paper about with me, on which to put down word-gems, the secret life of poetry.
>
> Becoming obsessed with the making of a poem, I would work at the words, always cutting away; trying to make a little express much; condensing, clarifying, and finally forging. Page after page of the notebook would become covered with countless variations of the one poem that might be taken up and laid aside of a period of weeks, months or even years.
>
> The making of a poem is for me an almost endless process; even when at last it sounds to be complete, it seems best to put it away for further ripening and more dispassionate assessment at a later time.[9]

Amongst all of these 'countless variations of the one poem' in her notebooks, it is difficult to see any real development and it seemed to indicate a lack of confidence and uncertainty. Brenda was rarely satisfied with her poems and found it extremely difficult to declare a poem finished. Even when a poem had been accepted for publication Brenda could not leave it alone. She would change a line and often the title before a poem was published in another magazine or anthology. It was not uncommon for a poem to have as many as four different titles in print. However, there were the rare occasions when Brenda wrote quickly and left the poem alone in its original form. It was in this manner that she wrote her third poem of that spring in 1944. Called 'For Alun', it was written to commemorate the death of Alun Lewis who died in Burma on 5 March. For Brenda 'the bulk of his letters and his short story THE ORANGE GROVE are the most completely rewarding things he wrote. There is something contrived about the poems, a shade too much "poetry".'[10] To echo this preference, Brenda based her poem around a line taken from Alun's last letter to her, dated 7 February 1944: 'I'll come walking the hills with you in flesh or ghost, surely I will.'[11]

FOR ALUN
Now his sweet singing spirit leaves the orange grove:
The blood-hibiscus and dust-wheeling suns
Burn through tranced leaves about earth-resting body
Of Alun, son of the grey valleys,
By whose hearths' ash we weep him
In his own land.
Slowly returning on our tidal tears,
The homing spirit smiles through mountain rain.
Throws war's dirt from him
In the barren lake;
Becomes complete.
The dreaming poet,
Lover and soldier
On rock begins promised pilgrimage.
For he said, surely he would come again
In flesh or ghost beside me on the hill.[12]

For three cold months Brenda remained more or less in seclusion, sublimating her feelings of sadness in her writing. But as the weather brightened, so did her spirits. Her 'Poem for Five Airmen' was published in *The Welsh Review* in March, 'For Alun' found a place in *Wales* in June and three of her early poems were included in the anthology *Modern Welsh Poetry* edited by Keidrych Rhys.[13] As Brenda shook off her introspection she felt the need to have people around her again. She wrote to her friends, inviting them all to visit Tŷ'r Mynydd, but only those living close by could respond as war-time restrictions were still in force and long distance travel was difficult. She encouraged the local children and neighbours to call in and see her, wrote more letters to her friends, went out walking much more and very soon found that she was regaining her old energy and vigour.

But despite Brenda's change in spirits, Elsie Chamberlain was still worried about her daughter. To her, Brenda seemed 'such a quiet little mouse', a 'bohemian' with a broken marriage and now living alone in an old stone cottage without electricity and with no running water. Her mother sent people to visit her and tried to introduce Brenda into Bangor society but Brenda was not at all interested. The prospect of mixing socially with her mother's fellow committee members was not an attractive one. Brenda could not cope with bureaucracy of any kind and had no desire to meet people who actually enjoyed it.

Occasionally, however, Elsie Chamberlain did put Brenda in touch with some people she liked. It was due to her that Brenda re-met Esmé Firbank (later Kirby) and her husband Thomas, who lived near Capel Curig. Esmé remembered seeing Brenda and John before the war at a friend's house in the Ogwen valley. Brenda had sat quietly watching while her husband held everyone's attention with his stories. Having heard that Brenda was now alone, Esmé had felt sorry for her, assuming that it had been John who had left Brenda, and she invited Brenda to visit them on their farm. Brenda took up the invitation, trekking over the rugged twelve miles with her dogs to the hill farm set high on the side of the valley, Dyffryn Mymbyr, across from Moel Siabod and high above the twin lakes, Llynnau Mymbyr. It was to be the first of many visits spread over many years and the beginning of a lifelong friendship for Brenda.

View of Llynnau Mymbyr

Esmé was small and lithe like Brenda, but much more down-to-earth and practical. Brenda was the dreamer, the writer, the artist; Esmé was the sheep farmer, the homemaker, the organiser. Although they were very different in temperament and outlook, they were both spirited, determined women who shared a love of mountain walking. Brenda began to visit regularly. She would stay for a day or two, turning up at busy times in the farm calendar to 'help' with the sheep gathering and dipping and with the harvest. Despite being an independent person who was quite capable of looking after herself, Brenda was very dependent on her friends. She felt the need to belong and wanted to feel needed. It was important to her to believe that she was essential to the success of these farm events. Sometimes it was almost as if shearing could not go on if she was not there. Brenda saw herself as a sturdy practical worker on the land, but it seems that the farmers held a different view and because she was so tiny and not considered strong or capable she was given the lighter jobs to do. Esmé found her totally and utterly hopeless as far as farm work was concerned. 'Brenda probably thought she was doing great things but really she was ineffective. If she shut a gate, she would be on the wrong side of it.'[14] But Esmé accepted her help on the farm and Brenda enjoyed every minute of being part of a working life there.

In the 1940s the farm, Dyffryn Mymbyr, had become well known throughout the country with the publication of Thomas Firbank's book *I Bought a Mountain*.[15] His vivid account of the early years running the 2,400 acre sheep farm at Dyffryn Mymbyr with his wife became a major international bestseller. Inspired by Thomas's account of life at there, Brenda wrote her own abridged version of farming life. Under the title *Mountains of Rock* Brenda wrote a series of eight short accounts; 'Late Spring', 'Foxhunt', 'Fire', 'Shearing', 'Electric Storm', 'Hayharvest', 'Midwinter' and 'Blizzard'.[16] She set the stories in an indeterminate landscape, and although she named landmarks such as Y Tŵr Du, Bwlch y Ddwy Glyder, Cwm-y-Ffynnon, which exist in the area around Dyffryn Mymbyr, she described events which did not take place there at all. The 'Foxhunt', for example, is more likely to have taken place around Llanllechid although Brenda sets it in the Glyders. She tended to superimpose a little of one landscape upon another, and often she changed the names of her characters, sometimes using only an initial to create a sense of mystery. To Brenda, events were there to be dramatised, names to be romanticised and the truth to be embellished.

Occasionally though, she did keep to the facts, as in 'Hayharvest' which, according to Esmé, gives an accurate account of haymaking at Dyffryn:

> E. works in the haymeadows like one possessed, when the men have gone to dinner she works on steadily, a small figure in the long meadow, seated on the machine behind Bell who is slow and timid because of the soft areas of marsh under much of the hay, where shoe flounders helplessly and the weight of the machine holds her down. The mechanical forks as they strike out and toss the hay are like monstrous iron claws of a robot fowl scratching in the dust. Where the ground is too soft for the horse, we turn the heavy swathes by hand. Much of the hay is taken to the barns on a sledge.[17]

But then, almost as if writing the facts was too straightforward, Brenda added:

> K. E. still lies upstairs, propped with pillows so that she may see down into the fields. When it rains, she says, it will never be dry on our lands again, but she holds her peace when the sun comes from behind a cloud, drying grasses and withered harvest flowers.[18]

After the fact, we have the fiction. K.E. was not known to Esmé and she suggested it was probably a vignette about someone unconnected with Dyffryn Mymbyr, which Brenda invented here just to add a little mystery, or it is quite possible she simply reversed Esmé's own initials.

This same 'Hayharvest' account reappears with slight variations in a later collection of Brenda's writings. In *Tiderace* published in 1962, the scene takes place on Bardsey Island off the north Wales coast and the worker is now called Jacob.[19]

These adapted versions of her stories became real for her, and when the names of place, person and time are so subtly altered it becomes very hard to determine which of the many variations of a story is true. Her notebooks, although many are dated, were not used consecutively and often she would pick up an early notebook ten years later and add another version to the original. Typescripts of her writings were seldom dated and in most cases there is no obvious chronological order in which to place the various versions. As most of her writings were autobiographical, by sweeping sand over her footprints and leaving ambiguous trails, Brenda created herself as the most enigmatic character of all.

In her autobiographical essay in the volume *Artists in Wales*, Brenda wrote: 'I worked for a year on the sheep farm of a friend, whose farm is on the slopes of the Glyders'.[20] Although neither the friend nor the farm were named, it was obvious to Esmé that it was the farm at Dyffryn Mymbyr, as there is no other farm in that area with which she was connected.[21] Brenda's 'year' is a little doubtful though, as the longest length of time she spent at Dyffryn Mymbyr was a month when Esmé had a poisoned leg. Perhaps if all the visits were added together it would equal a year, and perhaps it felt like a year to Brenda if she had experienced something of each season there. She was becoming more and more involved in herself, seeing the world from her point of view.

Back in Llanllechid she was now leading a much busier social life. Some of the local children used to go up to Tŷ'r Mynydd to do their homework since their own homes were crowded and noisy, and some of the more eccentric village characters would drop in for tea and a chat. Llanllechid was a predominantly Welsh-speaking, staunchly chapel-going village, and for the most part Brenda felt hostile to the villagers. They in turn found the gaunt-faced little woman, who rode her pony down to the village post office, very strange indeed.

Visitors were arriving from further afield now. Peter Petts came to visit Brenda when he was on leave. Now a handsome young man of nineteen, he would arrive either alone or with his friends, Peter Kahn and Jean van der Bijl. In their eyes Brenda was an unusual and fascinating creature: a writer, an artist and an animated talker. She revelled in the attention of this entourage of young men while, down in the village, the tongues wagged.

Despite the attention of these young men, the memory of her German friend, Karl von Laer, still haunted Brenda. As the news reported bombings on Germany she worried for his safety and once again she pulled out the letters he had sent her before the war began:

During the enforced silence, while our countries were at war, I suddenly realised that there was still a means of communication, that it might in fact be possible for me

114

to get closer to Franz (Karl) during the separation. I began to study his letters, all of which I had kept. It was an easy task to turn some of them into poetry, they were already poems in prose. As the project grew, it became far more complex: the first poems were in his voice, and were simple in form and feeling. Later poems showed dual personality, his and mine. *Some had philosophical argument.* There was no hint of passion in any of them, only an idealised romantic love. *How could there be anything more? We were very young in those days.*[22]

In his last letter to Brenda before the war, dated 12 January 1937 Karl told Brenda:

... no I don't still study the law. I passed my examinations two years ago, was then for one year a soldier in the army and now I am a forester and a farmer and learn to manage a big estate.[23]

He was going to marry his fiancée, Bummi, in the autumn of 1938 and he would need these new skills when they moved to his family home, a little castle called Schlotheim in Thuringen. He invited Brenda to visit them there. But since that letter, the war had interrupted their correspondence and she had no idea where Karl was or even if he was still alive. Now, as well as continuing to work on the cycle of poems which she called 'The Green Heart', a new theme began to emerge in her writing. In 'Young Fisher Brought to Land' the tale of the drowned fishermen is unfolded and in 'Women on the strand' Brenda writes of a gathering on the shore praying for the fisherman to return home:

But the sea's a woman, desiring them
Has she not bones enough yet
That she must beggar our hearths?[24]

They are two of a series of poems with sea connections, full of foreboding and the recurring image of death by drowning. Although swept to sea by her pen, physically Brenda was still firmly based in the slate quarrying area of Llanllechid. Her only means of transport was Polly, her pony, and she had no inclination to travel far. The extent of her boundaries stretched south to Capel Curig to see Esmé and Thomas and north to Bangor to visit her mother.

Although Brenda did not follow her mother's enthusiasm for bettering living conditions for the poor or fighting for higher wages, she had a kind heart and was always ready to help any person or animal in need. As her school friend, Jean Ware, said, 'The under dog, the spurned one, the ones battered by life, animals, little boys – she would share her last seagull's egg with.'[25] When the war finally came to an end in 1945 groups of young Dutch children were evacuated to north Wales. They had been found homeless and starving, reduced to eating tulip bulbs and were near to death. Lady Artemus Jones from Bangor had spearheaded the project to bring them to Wales so they could be fed and looked after for a short while until Holland recovered after the devastation of war. Brenda immediately offered to take one of the children under her wing and a young boy called Louis Eveleens came to stay with her in Llanllechid.

Brenda enjoyed having his company but at times found it difficult to communicate with the young Dutch boy.

When Lady Artemus Jones became aware of this, she suggested that Brenda invite Raymond Garlick, a student friend of hers from Bangor, and his Dutch friend, Louis Soeterboek, to visit her. The young boy would then be able to speak to someone in his own language. Louis Soeterboek was twenty-nine and a brilliant linguist and poet, while Raymond Garlick was a shy young man who was studying English at the University in Bangor. Exempt from war service because he was disabled, Garlick had joined a small group of undergraduates who were taught by an even smaller group of professors. Although Brenda's intention had been to attract the Dutch student to Tŷ'r Mynydd to talk to the boy in his own language, it was Raymond Garlick alone who responded.

He made his first visit in the winter of 1945 and to the young nineteen-year-old student, Brenda seemed a remarkable person. He was a very reserved man whose sheltered upbringing had not prepared him for meeting such a colourful character. Her long gaunt face and her distinctive way of dressing distinguished her from anyone else he had ever met. She had a strong impact on him and he was flattered that Brenda wanted to paint his portrait. That first visit led to further invitations and Raymond Garlick would frequently go up to Llanllechid for tea in the afternoons. He began to meet some of Brenda's other friends and often Esmé Firbank, Peter Petts, Peter Kahn or Jean van der Bijl would be there when he called. The company was always lively and animated and he would later remember Brenda more for the quality of her conversation than for her art or writing.

Whatever she talked about she made absorbing, vivid, memorable. Analysing this many years after, I realised that underlying it there was a process of ruthless selection, quixotic imagination, deliberate hyperbole; but the effect was exhilarating, salutary and hugely extended one's awareness of life.[26]

In December 1945, Brenda wrote to Raymond Garlick to postpone one of his visits, a sitting for his portrait. She had just had news that the young Dutch boy was returning to Holland that week so she had decided to have a few days' break and go up to Newcastle to visit Jean. They would both be returning to Tŷ'r Mynydd for Christmas where they would be joined by Peter Petts. On her return Garlick resumed his visits, but his portrait was never completed.

Bardsey from the mainland

118

Soon after Christmas that year, one of Brenda's friends, Henry Mitchell (Michalski), suggested that she should go for a short trip to Bardsey Island off the Llŷn peninsula in north Wales. Brenda responded eagerly to the suggestion and began to plan a visit. She managed to weave a mystery around the companion who made the suggestion and he appeared under different names – Friedrich, Kurt and H. in the various accounts of her trip.[27] Brenda and Henry set off early in May to drive to the village of Aberdaron, at the tip of the peninsula, where they were to await their boat. The prospect of visiting the remote island of Bardsey filled Brenda with great excitement:

Six miles across the Sound from the white village lies the sea-crag to which three pilgrimages equal to one to Rome. At the ruined abbey of Saint Mary I will pray for the souls of my friends. The treasures of Britain are to be found in the fertile earth of the fields and bays of the southwest or in the seal-cave to the east; for Merlin buried or planted here in some secret place certain mystical properties. If they can be found, you shall learn from them.[28]

It is a notoriously rough crossing to the island but on this, her first visit, the sea was almost dead calm, like 'the inner side of an oyster shell, or silk shaken out in shallow folds.'[29] The boat arrived and

The sea took us, and it became immaterial whether we made landfall or not. We began to live in the present moment and, Miracle! time did stand still on the waters between here and there.[30]

Brenda became absorbed by the sea and entranced by the prospect of the dark hump backed rock which held so many mysteries.

> It was so calm that we seemed not to be moving; it was the island that moved slowly round to meet us out of the blue ocean. On her eastward side her five hundred foot mountain stood sheer behind salty vapours that gave her austerity, an aloofness.[31]

After years in the mountains these new images were welcomed, absorbed, recorded in her notebooks and eventually used in *Tide-race*.

> We passed close under black and lichen-encrusted cliffs; nearer, nearer, close, close, until the fangs of wet rock were snapping at us; but in this proximity there was safety, for we were in slack water, in a sullen backwash. Rock rose in galleries and on every shelf stood solemn congregations of sea-birds. We slowly crept past the ramparts of this world of birds.
>
> And still there was no sign of any place where a man might build himself a shelter.
>
> At last, the high land fell away and we were in the anchorage.[32]

In the shelter of the harbour they had their first view of the inhabited side of the island; the flat west sheltering beneath the curved arm of the mountain. A cart track ran south to the lighthouse and wound north to the abbey connecting all the dwellings along its way.

Although the visitors had asked the postmaster to book

View of Bardsey Island

them a place to stay overnight they now discovered that nothing had been arranged for them. As they had brought no food or blankets or tents with them, their most immediate task was to seek shelter with one of the islanders. But the islanders seemed very wary of the strangers and were reluctant to offer their hospitality. Brenda relates that she and her friend walked north along the track and stopped at the first farm to ask for lodging.

From the open doorway came a smell of freshly baked bread and cakes.

'No.' said the woman. 'I cannot take you in. My house is full of children.'

'No.' said the stout blonde woman barring the door of the second house. 'There is no room here.'

She was openly hostile.

The third house was empty, dark, and locked.

The fourth house lay away from the path at the bottom of a steep field. A thread of smoke was rising from its chimneys. Out in the meadow, a foxy-looking dog barked at us, and a tall man came out, but quickly went inside again. I knocked at the door. A Scots voice called:

'Come in.'[33]

A man Brenda called Stewart Hopkinson gave them tea and invited them to stay. His wife was on the mainland; he was lonely and welcomed their company. They were relieved to have found a place to sleep and eat and once they had had a cup of tea and a short chat with Hopkinson, they were keen to explore the island before it grew dark. They walked towards the abbey ruins.

From the north, one could see the whole island; a handful of farms, a lighthouse, a ruined monastery, an earth made fertile with the bones of men.[34]

There were so many new shapes and colours and atmospheres for Brenda to absorb, and she was drawn to the sea where the waves washed into the dark sea caves.

The waves were green, greenly came they, waves came ever-green out of Ireland, to fall upon the cliffs of Wales and glut her caverns with salt and broken things.[35]

122

Everything about the island entranced Brenda; she rushed around peering through the windows of the empty houses, clambered down the rocks and into the caves, watched the rabbits scampering through the fields, discovered the withy beds which each farm used to make lobster creels. Down on the rocky shore she saw a seal cow basking and imagined that it called to her:

Seal, *Tide-race*, p. 37

Come to me, come to me. Her arms extended, folded again to her creamy underside. So great was the human mermaid attraction that I could have leapt to my death by drowning.

A woman on land and a silkie in the sea.[36]

They returned to the house and as darkness fell, the air became full with the cry of the shearwaters as they came in to land, crying 'like banshees from their winding passages among the rocks'.[30]

Brenda found everything so different from Tŷ'r Mynydd, even the light at night:

Bardsey lighthouse

Before getting into bed, I crouched at the window. There were no sash cords, so the frames were held open by pieces of stick. Across the slope of the mountain the lighthouse beam flashed like a scythe with stronger radiance than moonlight. Illuminating night: such innocence was in the cool winds and mooncast shadow. There was no nightmare, no dream. The house being in the middle of fields, took the full flesh of the beams, the uninquisitive arcs passing over with a scythe's movements or like ground-lightning.

How different it was from those nights in Galloway, in the dark house above the Firth of Solway. That bedroom's leaf-heavy, tree-haunted gloom, where on entering, my heart felt the midnight shiver of massed foliage breathing and growing.

And the sea makes clean our hearts.[38]

And the sea was to trap them on the island for another day, for overnight the wind had grown too strong for the boat to cross the Sound. Brenda was delighted:

> O joy, another day with the seals.
> I thought, how cosy it must be in winter,
> securely cut off from the world outside.[39]

Her travelling companion, however, felt differently. The island had not lived up to his expectations. He was disappointed by the delay and was ready to return to the mainland. During that extra day, Brenda walked from end to end of the island and explored the precipitous east slope with the guidance of Stewart. There were many nesting birds on every ledge and everywhere chicks were chipping through their shells. The air was loud with the screaming of gulls. Brenda clambered along the ledges.

> Feeling like a pigmy, I climbed up and down among the crags. The sea was emerald, frothed with white. In lee of the land, submerged rocks of the reef showed as soft purple stains under the water.[40]

All too soon it grew dark so they returned to Stewart's house where they sat talking by lamplight and Brenda wrote about the day in her journal. She was so overloaded with new images and experiences that she had no time to revise her writing. It remained fresh, vivid and evocative of her first impressions of the island.

On the following morning icy rain poured down but it was calm enough for the boat to sail. The island men loaded the boats with crabs, lobsters, rabbits, gulls' eggs and an old blackened stove. Brenda and her friend squeezed aboard:

> The rain was chilling. In long grey shrouds the resting-place of the holy fathers fell away. Already it was the past: time had not after all stood still. The seal cave dropped astern; the yellow-stained rocks, the ledges lined with sober birds, vanished. The sheltering cliffs slid backwards. The tide rip of the Sound was under us and around us. How deep and savage was the sea, how cramped our craft. We were sprayed with salt and switchbacked over those waves that spouted so viciously.
>
> For as long as they could see it, my eyes did not leave the rain-shrouded mountain. On her slopes I had left anew self, and had vowed to return.[41]

Brenda had fallen under the spell of Bardsey Island, Island of the Bards; or as the Welsh call it, Ynys Enlli, Island in the Current. Brenda was determined to return, she felt that she had no choice:

> From that day the island is in me. Before going there, my mood was placid and blank; now a physical pain of yearning never leaves me: to be there again. The island has entered my consciousness – ever to leave it? Only personal issues, being intangible, shifting, are blurred.[42]

The personal issues she alluded to concerned a man. She had asked herself '...could I dare plunge into the hermit-life, into the fisherman-farmer's?' And her answer had been: 'Alone; most certainly not. With a man, perhaps'.[43] The man to whom she was closest was the Frenchman, Jean van der Bijl, who had been visiting Tŷ'r Mynydd over the last year. Would he be interested in living on the isolated island with her? Brenda was uncertain but determined to suggest it to him. In her heart, she knew she could not live on Bardsey Island alone. Now in her mid-thirties, she had developed a strong sense of the way she wanted to live her life; she was determined to make her living as an artist and writer and was prepared to reject comfort and security to fulfil that aim. As long as there was enough money to allow her to eat and buy writing and painting materials she was content; having clothes or possessions did not concern her and she was just as happy to sleep on a hard bench as in comfortable bed. Her needs were few, far fewer than those of most people, but one thing that she definitely wanted was a man to share her life with. As she was dependent on her friends she drew her energy from her exchanges, whether in person or via her prolific letters. And, besides, she had already had her warning from Cadwaladr, one of the islanders:

Unless the man and the woman pull together in this life, there's bound to be trouble; and it's no use for a woman to try living here on her own, because she's a liability to everyone.[44]

It was with great trepidation that she told Jean about the wonders of the island. So much depended on his response. She was prepared to take the risk and live with him on Bardsey, but was he interested in such a venture? Having sown the seed, Brenda allowed Jean to think about it. Her mind was awash with questions, ideas, doubts and thoughts and she poured this energy into her writing.

Excitedly she recorded her experiences in her notebook, wrote to friends and exchanged letters with the man from the island whom in *Tide-race* she calls Stewart Hopkinson. He encouraged her to settle on Bardsey. In July Brenda made a second visit, this time for two weeks. Having decided to be more self-sufficient, Brenda had arranged to stay in one of the empty houses and took a sleeping bag and plenty of provisions.

As the boat arrived at Aberdaron, Stewart leapt ashore to greet Brenda.

'How are you?' I asked, happy with relief that the boat had come.

'Bearing up,' he answered, with an embarrassed grin adding, 'My wife's back; and our furniture arrived last week, but the house is still untidy.'[45]

It took hours for the islandmen to empty the boat of its lobsters and crabs and reload with coal, provisions and meal-sacks. It was seven o'clock before they left and eight thirty by the time they reached the island anchorage. Once more Brenda felt the pull of the island:

It is so familiar, this world that is just outside life. My ancestors never moved so strongly in my blood as now. I belong to the sea in a way that strengthens me. It is familiar yet stronger than dream.[46]

As she and Stewart walked down the island track his words shattered the peace.

Alice said she would leave me again for good if you set

foot here again,' he said. 'She can't bear the place and she's jealous of you because you seem to like it.'[47]

Stewart and Alice had planned to settle on the island, to become partners with the 'Levens' family who were moving to Bardsey later in the year, but Alice had taken a dislike to the island from the start and Brenda's obvious appreciation of the place acted as an irritant. When they reached the gate of Garthwen, Stewart stopped and said nothing. Brenda walked on up the lane to Tŷ Bach, the grey stone house which faced south. The house had been lying empty for some time and was coated with dust, cobwebs, trapped butterflies and moths:

> I wandered from room to room upstairs. It began to grow dark. The bedroom was foul with decay; there was a hole in the ceiling; dry-rot in the floor under the window; a smell of cobwebs and decay.
> … The lamp was lit in the lighthouse as the sun went into the western sea. I spread my sleeping bag on the floor and formed my spare clothing into a pillow. Strips of mouldy paper lay about; the walls were pocked with a damp rash.[48]

She tried to settle down to sleep but felt uncomfortable about the Hopkinsons. She got up and went down to Garthwen to talk to the couple. There was still a light on in the house and Stewart and his wife were sitting in front of an empty grate in a small room. Brenda tried to talk to Alice but she was not very friendly and Brenda quickly left. When Stewart followed to apologise to her, Alice locked him out. There seemed to be little that Brenda could do, so she returned to her dusty house and tried to sleep. Sleep did not come and her mind was filled with confused thoughts. 'I've dreamed for weeks of this day; and being free of everyone I knew before ... to be able to sit quite alone and think without interruption.'[49]

About an hour later there was a loud knocking at the front door. It was Hopkinson:

'Alice sent me to bring you to sleep at Garthwen.'
'What! Alice sent you?'
'We couldn't rest .... Anyway, you can't stay here in this dirt. Get dressed and come to the house. She's getting a room ready for you.'[50]

Plas Bach or Garthwen in *Tide-race*

Reluctantly, Brenda dressed and followed him down to Garthwen. A tired and unhappy Alice appeared and they silently sat and ate supper before going to bed. It was now about 2 o'clock in the morning and Brenda was feeling very tired. 'Sleep would not come. In their bedroom across the passage, the husband and wife kept up a monotonous conversation until the sky greyed into morning'.[51] Brenda was relieved when morning came so she could escape from the unhappy couple. By bush telegraph news soon circulated that Stewart's wife was threatening to leave him again. Brenda's presence was looked on with a certain amount of unease. One islander declared to his wife, 'That woman's here again, all by herself in the next house'.[52]

A woman living alone was considered not only to be strange but to be a burden; she would inevitably lean on her neighbours. Life on an island was perhaps not as smooth and idyllic as Brenda had imagined it to be. 'Terror. Violence. Greed. I was not passing over to a dream life, an escapist's paradise, but to one that whitened the hair and bowed the back, that would raise sea-monsters of hatred and despair'.[53] Although uncomfortable at the time, in retrospect Brenda revelled in the experience and wrote a lively account in her notebook. Her writing is often at its best when exploring the tensions in human relationships; and while we learn little of the background of the characters, she allows us to relive their troubles, torments and desires.

As well as enjoying the emotional excitement on the island, Brenda found time to paint. All through the war years her canvases had remained blank and it was with relief and pleasure that she resumed her painting and drawing activities. The weather was hot and Brenda worked on the cliffs, painting the smooth shapes and varied colours of the rocks.

Rocks, *Tide-race*, p. 45

A rock shore; cliffs of mussel-blue shell. Wine-red, icy
pink, pure white, yellow and green. The surf creamed at
the foot of the coloured walls. Colours evoked images,
images evoked words. Wall of jasper, tower of quartzite.
How can a common seacliff be a wall of jasper? I would,
knowing this salt channel and these bastions, make a
new hymn to the virgin; say she was a wall of jasper with
eyes clear as the running tide.[54]

This trip had certainly been an eventful one for Brenda. As
well as upsetting the Hopkinsons, Brenda also found she
had unknowingly disturbed 'the balance of power then
ruling island politics'.[55] As she explained in a letter to
Raymond Garlick: 'Of course I have chummed up with the
most disresputable family here, trust me. They are awfully

kind and have a wonderful little boy also, Guto, a real gypsy with merry eyes'.[56] As in many close-knit communities, the inhabitants were split into two distinct camps. On Bardsey,

> Almost without realising it, I found I had taken sides for the Bull-necks and their one or two friends such as Dai Penmon, the young lobsterman, and against the Rest who were only names to me in those first few days ...
>
> So I became a rebel without knowing what the war was about; and become a cause of great annoyance to the people on 'the other side'.
>
> Cadwaladr played on my weakness and sense of insecurity, on my ignorance of the true state of affairs between him and his neighbours, and on the embaressment now existing between me and Hopkinson.[57]

Already Brenda was being drawn into the lives of the islanders. They had accepted her and she had accepted them. Here on Bardsey Island she had discovered a haven where she wanted to make her home. She knew it would not be an easy life and she still had doubts about moving there alone. Jean had expressed an interest but he had not yet seen the island for himself. He was staying at Tŷ'r Mynydd for the whole of August and became infected with Brenda's enthusiasm when she returned home after her second visit.

Brenda sent two excerpts from her journals to the editor of *Life and Letters Today* who accepted them for publication, and they later appeared in the September and October issues.[58] As September arrived Brenda was drawn back to the island whose Welsh name, Ynys Enlli, she often

Cadwaladr, *Tide-race*, p. 69

used. She stayed only a week this time and concentrated on her writing and painting. She took delight in recording the everyday events of the islanders in word and line. The island children became her models. It was a novelty for them to have a stranger on the island and they enjoyed her attention. Now that she had gained her desire to draw and paint, Brenda wanted to do as much as she possibly could in her week on the island.

The next few months proved to be very busy ones. Brenda wanted to write more about her visits to Bardsey and develop her recent drawings into paintings. She had to fit these activities around her visits to see her father in Bangor. He was unwell and Brenda was visiting him every day, as her mother was in Germany seeing for herself how bad things were after the war. Elsie apparently gave an impressive public meeting in Bangor on her return, but Brenda neither attended nor commented on it in her journal. Although her mother's trip abroad had not interested her, the reminder of troubled Germany brought Karl von Laer to her thoughts once more. She wrote to him at his ancestral home, the castle of Schlotheim in East Prussia, with little hope of a letter reaching him. She was both surprised and delighted when some weeks later, in the middle of October, she received a reply. In his letter Karl explained how, with the Russian invasion, his family had been driven out of Schlotheim. His sister had died and one of his brothers was still missing in Russia. He wrote:

My mother stayed in Streckentin, in Pommerain until this Spring. It was terrible there; the Poles plundered and laid the village waste: the hall of our house has been turned into a stable for calves and the fields have not been cultivated. My mother and Fräulein K went to live in the house of the wheelwright: later, they were turned out into the British zone. In Schlotheim two of my aunts, Vera and Kilian, are still living, and they forwarded your letter. My grandmother and the old aunts were arrested last winter by the Russians, but were freed after three days because they were too old for the journey to Siberia. A few weeks later, my grandmother died. The aunts are now living in one room in the town.[59]

By good luck, I came wounded from the eastern front in February 1945 and was taken prisoner by the Americans. At first I was in an infirmary, and then with Bummi I got through the Western zone. We worked for a year on a little farm in Hessen, and came on this summer to Westphalia to rejoin my parents, my younger brother Hans, and my brother Johannes and his family.[60]

Although it was a very depressing story, Brenda was greatly relieved to hear that Karl was still alive. She had often worried for his safety and had yearned for news of him, this man whom she regarded as 'My soul's soul, my double'.[61] The year 1946 was proving to be an important one for Brenda; she had renewed contact with her German friend and had discovered the island of Bardsey.

The first restored my spiritual life-line, the well of poetry was refreshed; the second led me to the Atlantic waves which I had desired all my life, the sea which had been in the blood of my Irish and Manx forebears. From the restored link with my German friend, I began to see that there is a pattern in life, strong links we form are never really broken. The second wonder was, that after two days of running wild on Enlli, it was the only place for me to live; it became home after that brief contact.[62]

The third wonder was still tentative; Jean had agreed to visit the island and consider living there.

In the meantime, Brenda lost no time in sending a copy of her 'Green Heart' cycle of poems to Karl von Laer. He wrote back very quickly and was obviously delighted by them:

I read with emotion that the song cycle is directly inspired by my letters and therefore the lines are easily as much mine as yours. But is it not also that I can understand so well your verses and you can understand so well my letters because similar thoughts and feelings are in us, and I do not wonder that you can describe so truly the Baltic shore...[63]

He offered some words for Brenda to use as a preface to the poems. In a form edited by Brenda with the names changed, Karl becomes Klaus and Brenda, Elizabeth Greatorex; it reveals the development of their bond:

I first met Elizabeth in the Welsh mountains in a hot summer in the 1930s. It seemed to me that they were like brother and sister, she and the mountains: that the hills stood in affliction with wrapped heads when she was absent: when she was not there, rain ran down the barren shoulders like tears. The mountains were desolate for me when she was not there, to weave a magic veil round their heads with her store of sad and mirthful legends, when her light foot was not going before me over the wild summits ...

Out of this unity with Nature in which the ruling of God is visible, the natural melody of her poetry found its source. For me, her poems gave expression to our youthful thoughts and emotions. Similar thoughts, similar emotions, made us apprehend more clearly the powerful beauty of the world.

The same natural forces rule the Baltic shore as rule the native shore of the poet. Solitude and far horizon of sea and sky: against them the human heart suffers great loneliness.

The images employed by my friend to clothe words written by me in halting English, form a distillation of poetry out of prose. More, they speak of the closeness of our friendship. In our student days a similarity of temperament drew us together. Despite all the horrors that have swept our world since then, we both retain our faith in the ultimate coming of the Angel.[64]

Now that they were in contact again, Brenda was able to share her enthusiasms for Bardsey with Karl. After the gap of almost six years their letters began to flow back and forth with their customary ease.

Events in Brenda's life continued to move quickly. Tŷ'r Mynydd seemed to be constantly crowded with visitors of all nationalities. As a pair of French friends took their leave and Jean left for Newcastle to collect the rest of his belongings, there were plans made for Jean's Indian friends to visit. The staid villagers of Llanllechid were now used to strange processions of visitors trooping up the street to the house on the mountain. With the Indians, Choudra and Moti, Brenda, Jean and Peter Petts had a very lively Christmas. As she told Raymond Garlick,

> ...Peter had bought [*sic*] a fez home and you should have been here to see him and Moti going down the village on Christmas Eve afternoon. Moti was wearing the fez (a Hindu in a Fez!!) and Peter some other monstrosity. *C'était énorme.*[65]

Once the main celebrations were over and the Indian visitors had gone, Brenda, Jean and Peter went walking across the slopes of Carnedd Dafydd

> ... to the snow cornice hanging over towards Ffynnon Lloer. We descended in almost darkness down the very steep slopes of Pen yr Oleu Wen to the Ogwen Bridge. Jean forgot his stick some distance from the bottom and toiled up the slopes again in the dark. Quite mad but he found it 'Thanks to his grandmother. She had taught him at an early age to pray for anything lost, to St. Anthony of Padua.' He is most serious about this and prays like mad to St. Anthony of Padua as he combs the rocks and crannies.[66]

In the lull of early January, Brenda and Jean went over to visit Esmé, whom Brenda had not seen since the previous spring, so there was a lot of news to exchange. Brenda was in a very excitable mood: ever since Jean had agreed to visit Bardsey, she had been impatiently waiting for the weather to improve to allow a crossing. That visit was now just a few days away and Brenda was tormented by the excitement of showing her island to Jean and the fear that he might not like it.

> For nearly three months now we have talked of going, have lived in dreams of the island though neither of us has spoken much of his thoughts. Are we not both at a disadvantage? I, because my reverie is of the known rock overlaid by the weaving of imagination; and he? Since no one can understand the dreams of another when his own are of such tenuous structure, I cannot speak for him. This alone is certain: he has never been on the island, and so sees it through my eyes ... He feels the pull but cannot see the magnet. How can we speak of settling down there together when one of us has not yet visited the place?[67]

Brenda maintained this tension in her account of their attempts to reach the island. In line with her policy to change the names of people and places, in her narrative she refers to Jean as Paul and she remains nameless as the first person narrator.

It was early in January 1947, the wind was icy and the land laced with frost. Aberdaron looked bleak.

> How different an air our port of embarkation wears in wintertime, with no one but ourselves moving in the street. The two hotels and the boarding house are shut, and hanging askew on the door of the small café is a black card with white letters spelling SHUT framed in ice and many-pointed stars of frost.
>
> Only the sea is abroad; along the desolate beach run hungry waves that would like to devour the houses and

140

the hotel; the grave-yard and the church at the top of the strand.[68]

Although the sea looked too rough for crossing, Brenda was still hopeful a boat might venture across the Sound to collect them. She had waited so long for this visit that she would not easily accept defeat and be stranded on the mainland without making every possible effort to cross. Brenda and Jean walked up the hill out of Aberdaron to St. Mary's Well on Uwchmynydd where Bardsey Island can be most clearly seen. Once a traditional resting place for pilgrims on their way to the island, the well was the spot at which Cadwaladr had instructed Brenda to light a fire to signal for a boat:

'Signal by fire from above the well, as near as possible to the bottom of the gorse patch. We will answer from the field near the mountain. As soon as you can see our smoke put out your fire, and we will quench ours, so that we shall both understand that it is a signal for a boat and not someone making a gorse fire for pleasure or clearance of the land ... If we think the sea is too rough or any crisis on the farm should stop us from coming; we will relight our fire a minute or two afterwards. In this way you will not have to wait indefinitely'.[69]

They lit their first fire and sat in its warmth staring at the island.

The sun stood in the west; our slope was strongly lit; the island was in a haze. I tried to concentrate on the field at the mountain foot, for I knew that the answering signal would be lit there. Whenever I looked away to rest my eyes, orange stains blotted the sky.[70]

It was an hour before they saw any smoke rise from the island.

Overjoyed, we leaped up and stamped out our fire until our boots grew hot.

They had lit only one beacon on the island. Good; it meant they were coming for us; and that in about an hour they would be in the Sound. We huddled against the piercing cold in the rock bay; after a time I thought I heard the throb of an engine far away, but it came no nearer. There was no sign of any craft.

Another, much bigger beacon burned up in the farm field over there. At last it looked as though they were coming for us. To show that we were still at the well, and to warm ourselves, we made a fire at which we crouched eagerly.

The sun was sinking; the earth became colder and colder. The red and misshapen sun fell from the sky.

We sat over the flames, squatting now by this, now by that bed of glowing ash, while the ground became ever more intensely frozen. At last we lost heart and grew weary of watching the grey emptiness of the Sound.

Suddenly, another beacon went up from the island. Once more we put out our fires and waited for the second signal from Cadwaladr. In a few minutes it came. Further along the island there was a red glow, then smoke poured towards the west. So they could not come for us; there must be engine trouble or a cow was calving, or it was too late on the tide. Dispirited and hungry, we trudged back to the village through the dusk.[71]

Early the next morning they were out on the beach again but there was no sign of a boat.

In the village they said that no one would set out in such weather from the island, with the wind blowing so strongly from the north west.

Only Cadwaladr might do it. 'He's the only man who might,' said one. 'He's willing to take a risk.'[72]

They had lunch in the village before once more walking up to the well where they lit a fire. Within five minutes they spotted the smoke of a fire on the island. Brenda withheld her excitement.

Yesterday, I had wasted too much emotion; today, I was determined to show no interest until the boat was actually in view. So I lay down, washed of all feeling.

Paul had walked over the brow to the headland. After an hour he came back shouting loudly.

'The boat! The boat!'

He was trembling violently, and his arm shook as he pointed towards the Sound. It was only then I realised how much the journey meant to him, and it left me dumb with surprise.[73]

Very, very slowly the dark speck of the boat grew larger as it moved closer to the shore. The sea proved too choppy for them to get aboard at the beach and Cadwaladr called for them to go to Porth Felen over the other side of the mountain. They had to climb a steep hillside and find their way into the gully where the boat was waiting in slightly calmer water. Eventually they managed to scramble into the bobbing boat and then Cadwaladr steered the craft into the rough sea. The journey seemed long:

We tracked through water lanes, this way, that way. The sea was what Cadwaladr calls neither good nor bad. Swells ran under the boat, and we would find ourselves flung sideways as a wave piled itself against our frail craft. The water was at its roughest along the back of the island mountain where wind and tide combined against us. We had to sit in the stern so that the bows should be free to ride lightly on the hurrying waves; even with the engine at full speed we remained stationary opposite a

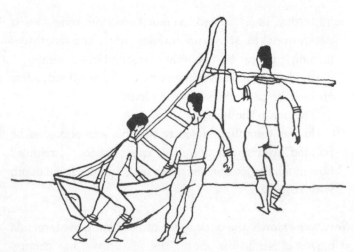

Men with the island boat, *Tide-race*, p. 109

144

deep gully for a long time. The propeller threshed the water, but we scarcely moved.

At last, we ran out of the strongest pull of the current at Pen Clogwyn, and knew that we should soon make landfall.[74]

Exhausted and hungry Brenda and Jean made their way with Cadwaladr to the north end of the island where they were staying with his family. It was particularly cold and windy that night. Jean slept on a clothes-chest in the kitchen while Brenda shared an icy cold room with the elder daughter, Myfanwy. It was hardly the best time for Jean to see Bardsey. They had arrived in the severest of the island's weather; there was frost, ice and fog and a wild storm had blown up overnight. In the morning Brenda and Jean walked along the west coast 'beside a roaring surf of glass and cream. The waves were empty of seals; gulls were sitting about on the land above the sea, waiting impatiently for the storm to blow itself out'.[75] Brenda desperately wanted to know what Jean felt about the island, but it was still too soon to ask what he thought of living there. She was watchful of Jean's every nuance, every look, and every mood. Days went by. They explored the windswept island, helped Cadwaladr with his work, played cards with the children – and still Brenda did not know what Jean might have decided.

One afternoon when they were walking at the south end Brenda could hold back no longer.

At last I dared to ask him whether he would care to farm and fish here. Had he shown any hesitation, I should have known that everything was over.

He said, 'Of course, of course. I think it is wonderful'.[76]

Brenda could hardly believe the words she had heard and it took some hours for them to sink in. That evening in the house, with frozen snow on the window and a howling gale outside, contentment began to grow in her. But that feeling did not last long. From the elation of that moment, she plunged into doubt and worry.

There were dark thoughts, rooted in nightmare and the untrusting mind. I asked myself whether happiness could come to me here; whether it was wise in relation to my work, to my future life, to cut myself off from the outside world. I had done it once before with disastrous results. Now I proposed to do it in an even more uncompromising way.[77]

Brenda's moods fluctuated, constantly pulled like the tides – now up, now steady, now down. She needed constant assurance that all was well, that her work was good, that her friends wanted to visit and write to her. Now, more than ever Brenda felt the need for reassurance. She was about to take a risk and would it work?

I wondered whether Paul was as prepared as he thought for this revolutionary change which for him would be far more novel than for me. Could we pull together like strong rowers or would we fall apart as so many others had done before us?[78]

1 'Blodeuwedd', first published in *Poetry London*, 2.10 (March 1944) pp. 33-34; quoted here from 'Blodeuwedd', *Wales* 6.24 (Dec. 1946) 19-21.

2 NLW MS 21501E, f. 7.

3 This paragraph quoted from Lady Charlotte Guest's translation of the *Mabinogion*, probably from the Everyman edition.

4 Quoted from Guest's translation.

5 NLW MS 21501E, f. 7.

6 Ibid., f. 7.

7 Ibid., f. 7.

8 'Poem for Five Airmen', *The Welsh Review*, 3.1 (March 1944), 18-20.

9 *Tide-race* (London: Hodder & Stoughton, 1962), p. 82. [Henceforth *TR*].

10 *ALCB*, p. 14.

11 *ALCB*, p. 39.

12 'For Alun', *Wales* 3.4 (June 1944), 7; also printed in *Poetry Chicago* 1946.xi (Sept. 1945), 303.

13 See note 11 above; 'Song – Talysarn', 'To Dafydd Coed mourning his mountain-broken dog', and 'You, who in April laughed', appeared in Keidrych Rhys (ed.), *Modern Welsh Poetry* (London: Faber & Faber, 1944), pp. 18-19.

14 Esmé Kirby in conversation with the author, 14 March 1985.

15 London: Harrap, 1940. At her death in 1999 Esmé Kirby bequeathed the farm to the National Trust, which now lets the house as a holiday cottage.

16 'Mountain of Rock', *The Welsh Review* 4.3 (Sept. 1945), 190-7.

17 'Mountain of Rock', p. 196.

18 Ibid., p. 196.

19 *TR*, p. 157.

20 *AW*, p. 50.

21 Esmé Kirby in conversation with the author, 14 March 1985.

22 NLW MS 22493C, f. 216. The words italicised were drawn through with a line in her notebook.

[23] NLW MS 22493C, f. 216.

[24] *GH*, p. 26.

[25] Jean Ware, letter to the author, 16 July 1984.

[26] Raymond Garlick, in Meic Stephens (ed.), *Artists in Wales 2*, (Llandysul: Gomer, 1973), pp. 83-97, (p. 87). See also Raymond Garlick, 'Some Painters', *Planet* 108 (Dec. 1994-Jan. 1995), 67-73.

[27] He is called Friedrich in *Tide-race*, Kurt in 'Silkie and Tide-Race', published in *The Welsh Review* 7 (Autumn 1948), 176-83, and 'H.' in 'From a Journal: Silkie and Tide-Race', *Life and Letters Today* 50.110 (Oct. 1946), 3-14.

[28] *TR*, p. 16.

[29] *TR*, p. 17.

[30] *TR*, p. 17.

[31] *TR*, p. 19.

[32] *TR*, pp. 20-1.

[33] *TR*, p. 22.

[34] *TR*, p. 25.

[35] *TR*, p. 35.

[36] *TR*, p. 31.

[37] *TR*, p. 30.

[38] *TR*, pp. 29-30.

[39] *TR*, p. 40.

[40] *TR*, p. 32.

[41] *TR*, pp. 43-44.

[42] 'From a Journal: Silkie and Tide Race', *Life and Letters Today* 50.109 (Sept. 1946), 138-43.

[43] *TR*, p. 16.

[44] *TR*, pp. 83-4.

[45] *TR*, p. 47.

[46] 'Ynys Enlli', *The Welsh Review*, 6 (Summer 1947), 82-85 (p. 82).

[47] *TR*, p. 48.

[48] *TR*, p. 49.

[49] *TR*, p. 50.

[50] *TR*, p. 52.

[51] *TR*, p. 54.

[52] *TR*, p. 56.

[53] *TR*, p. 56.

[54] *TR*, p. 25.

[55] *TR*, p. 58.

[56] Letter from Brenda Chamberlain to Raymond Garlick, July 1946, National Library of Wales, Raymond Garlick MSS 2.

[57] *TR*, p. 58.

[58] 'From a Journal: Silkie and Tide race', *Life and Letters Today*, 50. 109 (Sept. 1946), 138-43; 'From a Journal: Silkie and Tide race', *Life and Letters Today*, 51. 110 (Oct.1946), 3-14.

[59] Typescript draft of letter dated 5 October 1946, with revisions by Brenda Chamberlain, NLW MS 22493C, f. 218.

[60] NLW MS 22493C, f. 229.

[61] 'The Green Heart', III, vi, *GH*, p. 42.

[62] *AW*, p. 51.

[63] NLW MS 22493C, f. 234.

[64] Ibid., pp. 6-8.

[65] Letter from Brenda Chamberlain to Raymond Garlick, Dec. 1946, Raymond Garlick MSS 2.

[66] Letter from Brenda Chamberlain to Raymond Garlick, 29 Dec. 1946, Raymond Garlick MSS 2.

[67] *TR*, p. 110.

[68] *TR*, p. 111.

[69] *TR*, pp. 112-13.

[70] *TR*, p. 113.

[71] *TR*, pp. 113-15.

[72] *TR*, p. 115.

[73] *TR*, p. 115.

[74] *TR*, pp. 116-17.

[75] *TR*, p. 117.

[76] *TR*, p. 132.

[77] *TR*, p. 134.

[78] *TR*, p. 134.

Chapter 6
The Prolific Years 1947-52

Tŷ'r Mynydd was turned upside down. The proposed move to Bardsey spurred Brenda into action. Living on an island would present very different problems and demands than life in a north Wales village and every forgotten item meant a long boat trip to the nearest shop. Although Brenda's needs were simple and she had never consciously collected ornaments and material goods, there was still a lot to pack. Apart from her painting and writing equipment there were household goods, clothes, books, furniture and the two dogs, the cat, and Polly, her pony. On 17 March 1947 she was relieved to hear that her divorce from John Petts had finally come through. Although he had filed for divorce in 1944, the papers had gone astray during the war and it had taken several years to settle everything. It was timely and gave her closure on her life at Llanllechid.

Brenda vacillated between excitement and trepidation about the move to Bardsey with Jean. Fortunately the large amounts of energy required to make all the necessary preparations for the trip prevented too many doubts from creeping into her mind. There was the problem of Tŷ'r

Mynydd too. She did not relish leaving it totally deserted and so contacted Raymond Garlick who had been trying to find somewhere to live in Llanllechid for some time. Brenda invited him to rent the half of Tŷ'r Mynydd that had formerly been used for the Caseg Press. Garlick was delighted with the offer. The rent was to be £13 a year, which he paid in advance on moving there in May 1947.

On 19 May Brenda and Jean loaded all their belongings and the cat and dogs into a lorry. Goodbyes were said to Polly, the pony, who was to be collected on a later trip, and they set off to drive to Aberdaron. On this first crossing there was only room to take the small animals, bedding, food and the bare necessities. Furniture and other belongings were stored in a shed on the mainland, to be transported on future crossings. Twm (called Cadwaladr in *Tide-race*) arrived with his boat about midday, and after helping unload the boxes of lobsters and collecting the groceries and mail, they set off for Bardsey.[1] On their first crossing to establish a new home, they were blessed with a calm sea and they quickly reached the island.

Brenda and Jean were eventually going to live in Carreg Fawr ('Pencraig' in *Tide-race*) but until the 'Levens' family moved from there to Plas Bach ('Garthwen') they were to stay in Tŷ Bach ('Tŷ Bychan'), which Brenda had occupied on an earlier visit to the island. It was at the north of the island near Nant ('Pant') and had been empty for some years. Although the house was badly in need of repair, Brenda and Jean decided that they could manage there until Carreg Fawr became vacant.

That first evening, after supper with their neighbours, Brenda and Jean walked along the shore.

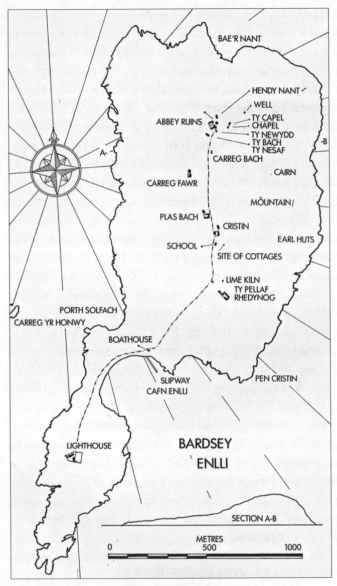

Map of Bardsey Island

Lathers broke on the beach, where we were alone with the evening fishers, screaming terns that, scimitar-winged, quartered the bay.

The planet Jupiter was burning in the east. All the other shiners in the heaven were pale, pallidly setting over the summer sea.

Today, we became islanders.[2]

And what did that mean? This was no tropical island where one could live off the rich fruits of the land and lie all day in the sun, as Brenda knew:

People dream up a lot of romantic moonshine about islands, talking of complete freedom; actually it is a life of strict behaviour, self-discipline, self-reliance, and duty to one's neighbours; a highly formalised code of behaviour that evolves elastically to fit new situations as they arise.[3]

On Bardsey Brenda found herself on a windswept, often fog-enshrouded island of 144 acres, frequently cut off from the mainland by high winds and rough seas with several sturdy houses, a chapel, a ruined abbey, and a lighthouse, but no telephone or electricity. The eastern half of the island is mountainous, dropping sheer to the sea, while its western flank is flat, populated and divided by earth dykes into small fields where rabbits and shearwaters have their burrows, sheep and cattle graze, and crops are grown. Few trees survive the salt winds and only scrubby hawthorns, gorse, fuchsias and the marshy clusters of the withy beds are able to grow. Through the seasons the island is tinted with the purple of heather and foxgloves, the golden hue of gorse and yellow flag iris, the rust of the autumn bracken and a scattered sprinkling of daisies and violets. Being an island, Bardsey has its own particular habitat and microclimate which attracts rare forms of marine life, insects, vegetation and birds. Consequently it has long been a favourite haunt of specialists in these fields. Bardsey is particularly well known for its wide variety of resident and visiting birds. The revolving beams of the lighthouse often attract migrating species of birds to land though sadly many are killed each year as they collide with the lighthouse tower.

Brenda Chamberlain was especially interested in the island's past, which is steeped in religion and mystery. The earliest record of habitation can be seen in the remains of ancient hut settlements on the hillside and apart from a reputed visit by the legendary Myrddin (the Welsh Merlin, who is said to have kept the Thirteen Treasures of Britain in a glass house there), the next known community dates from the fifth century. Then, Einion Frenin of Llŷn, king and saint, founded a religious house on the island in 420 AD. About a hundred years later another saint, Cadfan, visited Bardsey and established a monastic order there, becoming the first abbot. While he built an abbey at the north of the island, his cousin established a church at Aberdaron on the mainland.

Dyfrig (Dubricius) was the next reported visitor of importance. He had been bishop of Llandaf in south Wales until, as Brenda recounts, 'he suddenly threw up the honours of the church; the rock-hump in the Sound was calling him. And there he joined the community of saints, and lived with sea-fowl until he died in the year of our Lord, 612'.[4] On his death, Bardsey acquired sanctified status as a place of pilgrimage. The island reputedly became known as the 'Rome of Britain' and it was so highly regarded that three pilgrimages to Bardsey were considered equal to one pilgrimage to Rome. Over the centuries many pilgrims had risked their lives in crossing the treacherous waters to reach the holy island. Some went to pray, and many went to die and join the twenty thousand saints reputed to be buried there.

In the nineteenth and twentieth centuries excavations took place on the island, and indeed a great number of bones were uncovered in the area around the ruined abbey, although no detailed record has been made. Brenda recounted an incident which happened during her stay on the island. When digging in his garden which was close to the abbey, Cadwaladr 'came upon many skeletons; skulls and thigh bones, teeth all brown like pre-Columbian pottery; shards that crumbled at the touch of a spade and fingers even as the air flowed over them ...'[5] When Brenda heard of this she rushed there to share the excitement and discovery.

> By evening, we had grown disgusted with ourselves for having handled the skeletons, for it was clear, the warning on the saints' cross in the churchyard:
>
> 'Respect the remains of 20,000 saints buried nearby: in hoc loco requiescant in pace.'
>
> 'Safe in this island where each saint wished to be buried near the sound of the ever-changing tides.'
>
> Feverishly, we washed and washed our hands, to deny having touched the bones.[6]

After the dissolution of the monasteries, when the island's religious community dispersed, its history took a surprising turn. The Duke of Northumberland is said to have given

Bardsey to Sion Wyn ap Huw of Bodfel in Llŷn in recognition of his services as a standard bearer to the Duke in the battle of Norwich in 1549. For a time a band of pirates took refuge on the island, making it their headquarters under the auspices of its owner, who is said to have benefited from the buccaneers' spoils.

Until the late nineteenth century little of the island's history is recorded, but the community is known to have settled into a lifestyle of fishing and farming. Then, in the 1870s, a dramatic change occurred when the owner, Sir Spencer Bulkeley Wynn, the third Lord Newborough, undertook a major rebuilding programme. Stone was plundered from the abbey leaving only the thirteenth-century tower standing. Ten large solid farmhouses were built mainly in pairs, with a shared yard sheltering behind high buttresses and castellated walls. The rebuilding was completed within ten years and there followed a new influx of population. By the turn of the century there were 124 inhabitants.

In re-colonising the island Newborough felt that Bardsey was really a separate kingdom to the rest of Britain and decided that it should be ruled by its own king. One of the islanders, Mr John Williams, was chosen and duly crowned on the shore by Lord Newborough's cousin. His crown was of decorated tin and he was given a 'treasure', a silver snuff box, and an 'army' to guard this treasure in the guise of a wooden effigy of a soldier. As king he was asked to rule honestly, justly and soberly. The custom continued until 1926 when the last king, Love Pritchard, left the island. He and a group of the elder folk decided that they had become too old to manage the island boat in rough seas and moved to the security of the mainland.

As soon as she settled there, Brenda seized upon all the details of the island's past to enrich her work, particularly her writing. She especially liked the idea of the island having a king and in her own way attempted to keep his memory alive. In her fictionalised account of her very first visit to Bardsey Brenda includes a description of him sitting on the beach as her boat pulled into the anchorage.

The King, Tide-race, p. 21

Seated four-square on the middle of the beach was an ancient man with a neptune beard and flowing hair. He had a light metal crown chased with a design of seahorses and shells, worn slightly side-ways on his head, and in his crablike fingers he held a plug of twist from which he was cutting thin wafers of tobacco. By his side lay an empty rum bottle. He was gross with majesty, and must have been a good trencherman and an heroic drinker. He reeked of fish and salt and tarry ropes.[7]

To Brenda he was as alive as any of the other residents even though the last king had left the island some years earlier. He frequently appears in her later accounts of life on the island, another example of Brenda blending fact with fiction. He, like many of the islanders, was to have his character transformed and exaggerated by her pen.

The initial enthusiasm of the new settlers of the 1870s soon declined and by 1934 the population had dwindled to forty. There was a small influx of new blood in the late 1930s, together with wireless sets and oil engines. But the newcomers did not stay long either, and when the war came, many families moved back to the mainland. The rapid decline of population ended the need for a resident minister and schoolteacher, so in 1945 the school closed and the Methodist minister moved back to the mainland. By 1947 there were only twelve islanders left. On such a small island no detail about one's daily life could be hidden, and Brenda soon discovered that she could not escape this constant scrutiny:

> Life on a small island I had found out at once and had been horrified at the discovery is almost entirely public so far as one's outside movements are concerned. There was almost no privacy; wherever one went, one was watched, usually through a telescope.[8]

After she had fallen asleep outdoors one day an islander triumphantly confronted Brenda with details of where, when and in what position she had slept. Living in a tiny island community there was little real news or scandal; it was natural for the inhabitants to magnify whatever happened. After life in the open country around Llanllechid, Brenda found the island very small.

But she did not have too much time to dwell on this disadvantage. Gathering *broc* (driftwood) and hunting for food were immediate daily priorities and deciding how to make a living was of paramount importance. She and Jean were poor; their only income was the small fees paid at irregular intervals to Brenda for the publication of her poems. There was no land attached to their temporary home so they could keep no animals, and it was not worth planting the garden as they would be moving house in the autumn. Much of their food had to be hunted – rabbits, fish and seagulls' eggs – so it was necessary to learn new skills simply in order to eat.

The novelty of our life was compensation for much hardship.

The Tomos Bullnecks were at first, but only for a short time, our stay and stand-by. Owain helped us to master the practicalities of our new way of life; teaching me how to make bread; showing Paul [i.e. Jean] how to skin a rock-fish by nailing it to a piece of wood and tearing off the skin with a pair of pincers to reveal the greenish flesh of the succulent fish. Cadwaladr was proud to instruct me in the art of making crab-paste; pounding the cooked meat while still hot with butter, salt and a little vinegar.[9]

Being befriended by Cadwaladr had its initial advantages but it was not long before Jean and Brenda realised that it also had its disadvantages. After about six months Cadwaladr tired of them and they realised how cut off they had become from the other families on the island:

> we began to make tentative approaches to the other islanders; and found to our surprise that they were mild, long-suffering men and women who had been amusedly and cynically waiting for us to see the light with regard to Cadwaladr, and to turn to them. We were simply following the pattern that had already been formed by many before us; the stranger was courted and encouraged to settle on the island by Cadwaladr. Then, once he was lulled and confident and installed, Cadwaladr would begin the vendetta, until the newcomer was either driven off, or into the arms of the other islanders. Since those early days, I have seen the pattern repeated many times.[10]

Because so many newcomers had tried and failed to make a living on Bardsey, the islanders were weary of efforts to settle amongst them. For the most part they were first-language Welsh speakers too, and found it difficult to express themselves in English and to accept anyone from 'foreign' shores. Although Brenda was born in Wales she spoke only English fluently, and unlike her mother who had learned Welsh, she had only a few phrases which she could understand and use. Jean similarly had no Welsh, although he was bilingual in French and English. But despite the initial apprehension of the islanders, they were slowly accepted as part of the island community. They were charismatic figures and proved their commitment to life on Bardsey. From her several visits to the island, Brenda was already a familiar face and the islanders found it a novelty to have a writer and artist amongst them. Jean's good looks were attractive to women, while his quick appreciation of boat-handling and lobster-fishing won him due admiration of the men. They both helped with the communal island chores such as sheep gathering, and the ritual loading and unloading of the island boat.

> The island boat, above all else, was the mainstay of life on Bardsey.
> 'The boat is going over.' That phrase had an electrifying importance for us, always; for it meant mail and food and news from the outer world. The men would shave and wash and change their clothes in a frenzy of impatience while the women made out shopping lists, carefully checking up on the sacks and tins of emergency stores.[11]

It was customary for only the men to go ashore but the women were always there help load the boat with precious potatoes, rabbits, lobsters, hay, wheat or whatever they had to sell on the mainland. As the women helped push the boat out to sea, they would shout last-minute items as the engine chugged into action. Almost immediately, the boat would move out of sight behind the mountain. Waiting for the boat to return was always an intense time, and when the sun was setting the women would climb up to the lookout hut on the mountain and stare out to sea, watching for the first sign, the first bobbing speck that could be identified as their boat. When

Island Boat, 1960s ink on paper

at last it was spotted they would slowly walk down to the Cafn to await its arrival:

A dark mass became detached from the rocky entrance to the anchorage, to float out onto the water. Here they come ... Are all safe; are they all there, our men? One, two, three, four, five, all are safe.

... Lighting a hurricane lamp, we slithered across the naked rocks to the beach.

Silently, carrying the sacks and boxes of provisions, we passed one another on the slippery seaweed. It smelt like long-rotten cabbages. Then began the procession to the boathouse.[12]

Next came the ritual of the mail, which was sorted and handed out in the boathouse after the boat was unloaded. To have handed out the letters any earlier might have meant a reduction in the labour force! All but the essentials were left in the boathouse till the morning when they could be sorted out in daylight.

One of these early trips to the mainland was especially important to Brenda for it gave her an opportunity to go ashore to collect Polly, her pony. Both the pony and its little cart proved very useful for transporting goods from the Cafn to their house on the north of the island. In their first few months on Bardsey Brenda and Jean threw themselves wholeheartedly into island life, and Jean became more adept at fishing and handling a boat as it was apparent that fishing would be the most profitable way of making a living. They decided to invest in a seven-foot-six dinghy, a four horse-power engine to propel her, and six lobster creels. Thus equipped, they hoped to fish for lobster, crayfish and crab. Whereas the islanders were adept at finding the right places to drop their lobster pots, Brenda and Jean were

> ... hit or miss tyros; at first, it was rare for a lobster to be found at the bottom of our traps. The currents in their amazing complexity baffled and sometimes frightened us, and it was with a sinking heart that I took the boat almost on to the cliff-foot, so that Paul could lean outboard to hook up the lobster line.[13]

Initially Brenda went out in the boat with Jean, but she soon tired of it.

> For our pains, the return was pitifully small; and I suddenly had enough potting to last me a lifetime, and realising that Paul was already showing signs of becoming a good seaman which meant that he would soon be capable of going alone round his pots as only an expert does in his young days, retired to the land thankfully, and became the housewife again.[14]

Although strongly drawn to the sea, Brenda always felt happier on dry land. She worried about Jean's safety as he began to go out to sea in all weathers. 'How I had grown to hate his long rubber thigh-boots because, wearing them, he would have no chance of survival in the sea, if by ill-luck he was swept overboard'.[15] Before living on the island, Brenda had written poems about drowning and now, faced with its reality she became even more horrified and enthralled by the image, as in 'Island Fisherman':

The island fisherman has come to terms with death;
His crabbed fingers are coldly afire with phosphorus
From the night-sea he fishes for bright-armoured
    herring.

Lifting his lobster pots at sunrise,
He is not surprised when drowned sailors
Wearing ropes of pearls round green throats
Nod their heads at him from underwater forests.[16]

This echoes her fears expressed five years earlier in 'Five Poems' where the face of man is:

Struggling and writhing at the bottom of the water.
He looked up at the reeling mountain
And at the dark cloud reeling over it.

They cared nothing for his impotence.
He is mortal and must die.
But they were immortal,
They will live, crumbling to rebirth, for ever.

Therefore he fled from the presence of water and the
    mountain.[17]

This realisation of the fragility of human life compared to the power and longevity of the mountains and water, particularly the sea, haunted Brenda. In 'Five Poems II' she explains further:

It is the fear I have of returning
To broken stairways of rock,

To the crumbling rottenness of stone;
Thou water-treacherous
Ysgolion Duon.

Let my sleep be death-at-night.
Let it not be to dream of flowers, and sprayed water
Thrown out in fine drops by a wind moving in the
    mosses.

May not my mind forget the cleft;
Wet gulf in the rottenness of stone,
Where meshes of sprayed water move, that slaked my
    hairs'
thirst to the roots.[18]

Living on the island with the sea all around her, there was no escape from water and although Brenda had no fear of the sea, she was obsessed with its power and action. She was intrigued by the way it took old glass, stones, shipwrecked boats or drowned bodies and wore them down, smoothed them out and encrusted surfaces. The image of the drowned body particularly fascinated her.

The sea is full of faces, and it is a sea of faces, the incredulous fixed faces of the doomed. This is the death by drowning: not for me; for him, for you: but not for me. The faces go down, and the arms; the disbelieving eyes begin to understand. One woman in a cotton skirt hooped in bell shape of wire, floats in to the shore, still breathing, one breather to remember a drunken voyage; one inherited memory to fill a woman's sight when she sits in the summer rain.[19]

Brenda's character was one of extremes, her moods ebbed and flowed between joy and melancholy, and her writings echoed these fluctuations. However, Jean proved to be a supportive companion, able to make her laugh and coax her out of her sadder moods.

She set aside one of the rooms as a studio and while Jean was out fishing she settled down to write and paint. Her furniture gradually arrived, brought over a piece at a time by Cadwaladr. This prolonged process took until the autumn to complete and Brenda was surprised that everything arrived safely despite rough seas and the poor state of Cadwaladr's boat. Brenda felt very happy; she loved the island and she was enjoying living with Jean. Things seemed to be going very smoothly. But in early September,

> ...the inevitable happened: there was a disastrous gale, in which among much general damage, our six pots broke from their ropes and were never seen by us again. Gritting our teeth, we planned to have more pots for the next season.[20]

Although their daily needs for money were few, they had used up most of their capital on the boat and the pots and could receive no income from the fishing. Brenda had been too busy with 'living' to sit down and write, so there was no money due from publications either. She decided that she would have to sell Tŷ'r Mynydd. She felt that part of her life was over and Bardsey was where she wanted to be. Impulsively she contacted the estate agents, fixed a price and put it on the market. She had no thoughts for Raymond Garlick who had paid a year's rent in advance to live there.

The first he knew of it was the arrival of a prospective buyer to view the cottage. He was puzzled and thought it must be a mistake, but when he complained to the estate agents, he was assured that Tŷ'r Mynydd was indeed up for sale. Brenda's selfish action shocked him. Their correspondence lost its tone of camaraderie and became reduced to the minimum of formal exchanges of information.

Tŷ'r Mynydd had certainly been a source of some of Brenda's problems. It was only four years since the difficulties arose between her and John Petts, when she had assumed ownership and had her solicitors request his departure. Frequently, Brenda looked no further than her own immediate needs. She was not conscious that her actions were selfish and could hurt other people. Her needs came first. As it happened, no buyers took an interest in Tŷ'r Mynydd and apart from a few enquiries, Garlick was left in peace to live there until he chose to leave. This did not, of course, solve the immediate money problem but Brenda just had to shrug her shoulders and tighten her belt.

Despite poverty, the first winter was full of novelty for us. Paul made a draught board from a piece of paper on which he drew squares, and we used coins as counters, so that in the evenings we could play an alternative game to the eternal Whist or Patience. Sometimes we read aloud to one another in front of the driftwood fire; or on rare occasions, visited our neighbours.[21]

As the 'Levens' family had delayed their departure, it was necessary for Brenda and Jean to stay in Tŷ Bach all winter. It was a cold house; there was already a hole in the roof and when the winds howled across the island they constantly feared even more damage. It took a lot of wood to keep the fire burning once the icy winds started blowing and that meant a good many visits to the shore to collect driftwood. As the shipping route from Ireland to Liverpool passed by the island there was plenty of flotsam washed ashore. All sorts of useful items were captured in the rocky coves: buckets, tyres, crates, great chunks of candle wax which could be melted down to make candles and seasoned planks for shelves and cupboards. There was always a healthy competition in the hunt for driftwood after there had been a storm or a high tide and some of the islanders would rise especially early to be first on the shore. But collecting *broc* had its honourable side too, and anything laid above the high tide line was considered claimed and left untouched for its owner.

Living on such a small isolated island, it was inevitable for frustrations to build up through boredom, friction or just being trapped indoors by stormy weather. As Brenda observed, 'Life on Bardsey is controlled by the moods of the sea; its tides, its gifts, its deprivations'.[22] The weather and more especially the sea enforced a pattern and rhythm of behaviour much more strongly than the clock or calendar. As Brenda recognised these rhythms, she became curious about how the individual families on the island ordered their days. She soon discovered that each farm adhered very rigidly to its own timetable. A typical day would begin early, searching for *broc* before breakfast. Then there was the milking, making and mending lobster pots, afternoon milking and then the evening would be spent by the fire. Brenda found that mealtimes were fixed but varied greatly from family to family. Her neighbours to the south fitted in five meals to Brenda's two or three. There was actually a lot to fit into each day merely to ensure one's survival and Brenda was annoyed by anyone suggesting that living on the island was all fun and no work.

She was fascinated by the way the islanders lived and interacted, and was intrigued how the rules of the island, although never articulated, were always adhered to without question. Although women were not restricted from going on the weekly shopping expedition ashore, it became customary for them to stay on the island. Similarly it was only the men who would visit the lighthouse keepers at the south of the island and not the women. They did not venture there except in strict emergency, in illness or to report that a boat was overdue. Although the other women seemed content to accept these ways, Brenda found such restrictions difficult; as an individual she wanted freedom of movement, yet at the same time she did not want to upset the other islanders. Unlike most women on Bardsey, Brenda's interests extended beyond the boundaries of the island rock and although it was considered strange, Brenda did leave the island quite often – to visit her mother in Bangor, friends on the mainland, or to spend time on the Trinity House Vessel when it made its regular supplies trip to the lighthouse.

In her short story 'The Return', Brenda vividly drew out the prejudices of the people from the mainland towards a single woman striking out for freedom. In the piece she drew upon some of the difficulties she herself had experienced. The story centred around Bridget Ritsin, a young woman living on an island with an older married man, Alec Morrison, who was dying of a chest complaint. When she crossed the perilous Sound to collect provisions she suffered the sharp-tongued criticism of the gossiping villagers who castigated her both for her adultery and her audacity to manoeuvre a boat across to the island alone. They felt justified to taunt a woman who dared to break away from the accepted behaviour of women that had been well-established for centuries.

Brenda captured the mocking tone in the postmaster's voice when he asked about Captain Morrison:

'It isn't as if the Captain took reasonable care of himself', said the postmaster.

'No', she answered. She was on guard against anything he might say.

'A man needs to be careful with a lung like that', said the postmaster.

'Yes', she said. She waited for the sentences to be laid like baited traps. They watched one another for the next move. The man lifted a two-ounce weight from the counter and dropped it with fastidious fingers into the brass scale. As the tray fell, the woman sighed. A chink in her armour. He breathed importantly and spread his hands on the counter. From pressure on the palms, dark veins stood up under the skin on the backs of his hands. He leaned his face to the level of her eyes. Watching him, her mouth fell slightly open.

'The Captain's lady is very nice indeed; Mrs Morrison is a charming lady. Have you met his wife, Mrs Ritsin?'

'No', she answered; 'she has not been to the Island since I came.' She could not prevent a smile flashing across her eyes at her own stupidity. Why must she have said just that, a ready-made sentence that could be handed on without distortion. She has not been to the

Island since I came. Should she add: no doubt she will be over here soon; then I shall have the pleasure of meeting her? The words would not come. The postmaster lodged the sentence carefully in his brain to be retailed to the village.

… why, she asked herself, why did she let herself fall into their cheap traps? The sentence would be repeated almost without a word being altered, but the emphasis, O my God, the stressing of the 'I', to imply a malicious woman's triumph. But all this doesn't really matter, she told herself, at least it won't once I'm back there.[23]

In *Tide-race* Brenda includes the same story, but it is interesting to note that in the opening, she changes the emphasis from criticism of the woman's adultery to the villager's distrust of a woman's ability to handle a boat.

'It isn't as if you need to live out there, in such a god-forsaken place', said the postmaster.

'No', I answered, on guard against anything he might say.

'It isn't as if you had been born to the life', said the postmaster.

'No', I said, waiting for his sentences to be laid down like baited traps … He leaned his face to the level of my eyes.

'You'll soon get tired of it', he rapped out. 'Have you thought what it will be like in the winter? Can you bake bread? What if you break a leg, and the sea is too rough for a doctor to get across?'

O, my God. But this doesn't really matter, I told myself. At least, it would not, once I was back on the island.[24]

But the villagers had little confidence in her ability to make a safe return to the island. 'My dear madam, no woman has ever before navigated these waters alone. Why, even on a calm day, the Porth Meudwy fishers will not willingly cross the Sound'. One woman spoke out particularly strongly: 'It isn't right for a woman to ape a man, doing a man's work'.[25]

Despite the criticism and hostility shown towards the woman, however, she sets out for the island, and in both variations of the tale she has a long, eerie crossing. Thick fog forces her to anchor offshore for the night, her mind alive with the taunting words and with vivid dreams. It is a sad, intense tale, later dramatised as a half-hour television programme.[26]

As their first winter passed and the brighter, warmer days of spring appeared, Brenda began to paint in earnest. The light of the island was vibrant and bright, and Brenda found herself choosing crisp, clear, bold colours. Her portraits of the island children and of Jean excited her. A gap of five or six years had elapsed since Brenda had been fully involved in her painting and now her work showed a new confidence and strength of line. *Island Man*, an oil painting of Jean, typifies this. No longer feeling restricted by her academic training, Brenda boldly outlined the head and shoulders in rough red brushstrokes. It has a very different quality to her portrait, *Mountain Cottager* (1938), where she moulded the soft roundness of the figure with small, careful delicacy. Here, in *Island Man*, there is

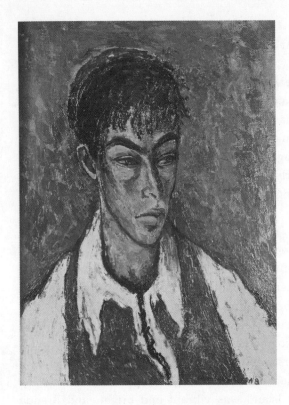

Island Man
(The
Bardsey
Boy), 1948,
oil on
canvas

exuberance in her brushwork and a forceful strength in the confident outline. In another portrait, *Boy with a Blue Head* (1948), she again used the technique of outlining the head with another strong colour. Here, a broad black line separates the turquoise of the face from the turquoise of the flat background.

As Brenda's attention settled on her painting it seemed inevitable that her writing would suffer, and in fact she wrote very little at this time. This meant that there was no income from publications and they had to rely solely on the sale of fish, lobsters and rabbits. They still had the rent from Tŷ'r Mynydd and the arrival of a cheque from Raymond Garlick for six months' rent allowed a few luxuries and some painting materials for Brenda. She was still determined to earn money by selling her paintings, but needed to paint more to have enough for an exhibition. It had often been difficult for Brenda to find time for her creative activities but now that their life was settling into its own pattern and rhythm, she found it possible to work.

I managed by sheer stubbornness, to continue my real life, which was of the imagination.

This was at all times less than easy, but I gradually adjusted myself to constant and violent changes of occupation: after hauling a boat or herding cows, to turn with minimum strain to painting or writing.[27]

Brenda on a boat loading cattle, 1 August 1950

She was relieved of one of her chores for a short time in May when her old school friend, Jean Ware, and her four-year-old son came to visit. As Brenda was absorbed by her painting and wanted to spend as many daylight hours as possible at her work, she asked Jean if she would look after the cooking. She was surprised by Brenda's kitchen; the oven was a nest of bricks and the refrigerator two biscuit tins covered by a wet towel which floated in two basins of cold water. The water supply caused even more alarm: 'The well was covered in green slime and there were ducks on it'.[28] Although Jean had taken a rucksack of cakes, biscuits, fruit and cheese, she wished she had brought more. Brenda and Jean van der Bijl had become used to their diet of seagull's eggs and rabbits and Brenda's rubbery bread, but Jean Ware and her son were continually hungry. But she had happy moments too, and her son particularly enjoyed his stay. Brenda amused him by drawing a mural in chalk on one of the whitewashed walls of the house and Jean van der Bijl would often take him on rabbit trapping expeditions.

When the visitors left, Brenda reluctantly resumed her cooking duties and reduced her painting time once more. There was further disruption in August, when the time came to move house. The 'Levens' family were moving at last, leaving Carreg Fawr empty for Brenda and Jean. Their temporary home was by now in poor repair, as Brenda noted: 'Just in time! The week after we vacated the old house, the last remaining good bedroom became uninhabitable when in a severe gale the big skylight blew out of the roof to shatter in fragments on the cobbles below'.[29] Along with the sturdier house, they rented a couple of fields in front and a withy bed where willow was grown to make lobster creels. Access to the fields meant that they could now consider keeping cattle and it was not long before they bought a Welsh Black cow which was about to calve. Brenda named the mother Sophia, and the calf Marie. A black bull-calf was added to their stock not long after. Brenda adored his long eye-lashes, christened him Jos, and took on the task of hand-rearing him.

Carreg Fawr, 1960s, ink on paper

Brenda and Jean were pleased with their new home which had eight rooms and stood within a small walled garden about four fields' distance from the sea. It faced west and its back looked on to the mountain. Brenda wrote:

> Now that I live here, in a four-square granite house that no winds can shake, I feel differently. It is good to have a little distance between the house and the sea; even so, on winter nights the roaring of the surf is monstrous. It booms as if under the foundations. There is no escape from the raving wind and water.[30]

It was both practical and homely:

There are no dark corners in the rooms. At breakfast-time, the living-room is bright with sun shining over the mountain, and supper-time on a summer evening, in the little study facing west across the Irish Sea to the horns of the Wicklows, it is a time of molten gold and flame-coloured sea, and of a peace so intense as to be a benediction.[31]

As they settled into Carreg Fawr, Brenda felt able to concentrate on her art once more. Preferring to work in the morning light she arranged her daily routine around her painting activities. She worked in a downstairs room, facing the mountain, pinning her paper or canvas directly on the wall, preferring to use no easel.

Interior, *Carreg Fawr*, *Tide-race*, p. 184

Painting and writing are obsessional activities, and as long as they function with reasonable smoothness, they give colour and energy to the rest of living. While one is looking for driftwood on the beach, the mind can run on, planning the next move on a canvas or the first line of a new poem.[32]

Whereas her writing of poetry was tentative, Brenda's painting was confident and self-assured and she began to produce some striking paintings. The other islanders were her models and she depicted them as dark, static, monumental figures. In *Fisherman's Return* (1949) Brenda featured two men sitting in a boat towing a dinghy behind them. Her viewpoint is from a low angle in the prow of the boat. The men are dark haired, dark eyed, solemn and still, their limbs set in a bold, relaxed splendour, poised like cats ready to leap into action. The shapes of the spaces between the figures were as important to Brenda as the figures themselves, who seem detached from the catch of fish at their feet, cluttering the boat. There is a minimal use of shading in the flat painted area of grey, rust and deep blue. In *The Fishing Net*, painted at the same time, Brenda used a softer, curving line while retaining the same style of monumental figures. Here, two fishermen carry their net while a mother and child sit alongside their boat. The barefooted fishermen, with their trousers rolled up to the knees of their sturdy legs, stare directly out of the picture.

Brenda showed no interest in developing any detail in the background of her paintings until *Fisherman Resting*. Here Jean was her model for the fisherman whose angular figure reclines on the colourfully adorned settle. To add to the decorative nature of the painting Brenda included the plate of fish and the wine bottles on the foreground table and the owl perched on the settle.

Often she painted directly onto the walls. As well as being an attempt to throw off the convention of easel painting and to decorate the house, it was often because she had run out of paper or canvas. She drew freely in charcoal or red ochre and often painted finished murals. According to her friends, there were life-sized horses, a big-eyed monkey, a woman with a head-dress, a girl at a table, a jar of flowers and the towers of a cathedral. Inevitably, over the decades many of these have been whitewashed over but there are still a few to be seen on the walls of Carreg Fawr.

It was around this time that Brenda's paintings were seen by Charles and Peter Gimpel from Gimpel Fils Gallery in London. Periodically, they travelled to various parts of Britain looking for new artists to exhibit in their London gallery. Brenda's bold figurative work caught their attention and they offered her a one-woman exhibition in March 1950. It was a major breakthrough for her. She was thrilled, and worked feverishly to produce enough work to show. The gallery exhibited nine watercolours and eleven oil paintings which all depicted her life on Bardsey. Although few sold, she found the experience exhilarating and encouraging.

At the same time, interest grew in her writing too. Although she had submitted little new work for a while, she heard that five of her poems had been included in the anthology *New British Poets*, while others appeared in the periodicals *New Directions*, *Poetry Quarterly*, and *Botteghe Oscure*.[33] She was especially pleased by the Italian publication. It meant that her work was now in print in

Europe and she was closer to attaining the international reputation that she desired.

After the London opening of her show, Brenda rushed back to the island armed with paints and canvases. In the flood of work that followed, there was a series of paintings of fish on plates. She tirelessly painted them in watercolour, in gouache, in oils, on their own, in pairs, with fruit, in their various hues of red, blue, blue, brown silver grey but

Pollock on a plate, 1950, oil on canvas,

almost always sitting on the same blue and white patterned plate. While she was in this feverish mood to paint, Brenda became more dependent on Jean to look after the animals and run the household. They had slowly gathered fifty-six sheep and a herd of eight cattle, so there was always plenty to be done. Jean also had the lobster pots to check and bait and the regular shopping trips to the mainland so it put a lot of pressure onto him. But despite her preoccupation with painting, Brenda would not miss any of the island 'events' such as the harvest, sheep-shearing and transporting of sheep to the mainland. These were the times which drew the islanders close as they worked with a common aim. Brenda would be there both to participate in the activity and to record new material in her notebooks.

Although Brenda enjoyed the farming aspect of Bardsey, she was never attracted to draw it. Indeed, of all the animals on the island, it was only the horses, cats and fish that she regularly drew and painted. While her literary work described in some detail the wildlife and the island environment, it would be very difficult to tell from her art that she was actually living on the island. She seldom painted the landscape or buildings; it was her imagination which provided her subject matter rather than her immediate surroundings. Her neighbours remained a source of fascination, and although they appear in identifiable portraits she did not place them in a recognisable location.

There was only a tiny shingle beach on Bardsey, yet in her painting *Children on the Seashore* (1950) Brenda portrayed the children on a vast empty shore. The perspective was exaggerated by lines drawn on the background leading to a vanishing point in the sea. At the water's edge, a silhouetted figure rolls a large hoop along the shore. She became obsessed with the composition of this particular picture, filling her notebooks with drawings and written descriptions:

... These young children are of dark Iberian stock. Through the action of the winds, their black hair stands stiffly, as if some kind of seaweed covered their heads. Their faces

182

Children on the Seashore, 1950, oil on canvas

have already the closed unexpectant look of their elders, for they know none of the small intimate delights and surprises of childhood that are commonplace in more civilised and mother-protected regions of the earth.

... They walk then, on this day after the night of extremely high water, down on to the clean sand; five children, three boys and two girls. It is a calm day. On the newly exposed beach no wind walks, but the air is full of the distant menace of surf breaking on the long shore. The children play among the herring-net screens.[34]

She made several small versions of this painting, and then finally, she began work on a large, carefully prepared canvas. Her journal records:

I wrote a piece of prose about the painting I was about to put on canvas, echoing the original drawing made on newsprint, but now I had greater freedom as the words could be placed exactly where I wished to give dramatic effect or tone. The canvas was left for six months, and then painted. I used only black, and the white of the canvas; and for half tones, black removed partially with a rag.[35]

Brenda's long dissertation about this painting reveals more about her process of creative thinking than any piece of her published prose. She was interested in the inward journey of analysis, and exploration of shape, image and colour. In this particular painting Brenda also proved to herself that she was able to combine her writing with her art. For a long time she had believed that at some point she was going to have to make a decision to be either a painter or a writer but now she had been able to resolve that conflict. She felt that here the painting was not superimposed on the words but blended with them and the spaces between the paragraphs. 'This painting gave a sense of real satisfaction, because I could not imagine the painting without the words'.[36]

Brenda emerged drained from this period of intense concentration. Quite unexpectedly, she received a letter from Karl von Laer. After almost a year's gap in their communication, he sent news of his formal engagement to Hildegard. Brenda was puzzled. She could not imagine what had happened to his first wife, Bummi. They had seemed very happy and Brenda wondered if she had died or they had divorced. She felt unsettled by this mystery.

During this time Brenda had gone to London to replenish her painting materials and to visit the Gimpel Fils Gallery.

The Gimpel family liked her work and offered to act as her agent. Since Brenda found it difficult to promote her own art and disliked the paperwork and organisation required to mount an exhibition, she was delighted to accept. More importantly, it left her more time to paint and enjoy life on Bardsey. Brenda found she was quickly developing a friendship with Charles Gimpel and his wife, Kaye, and this artist-agent relationship was to mature into a strong and important anchor for her. The gallery had become her focal point for art other than her own, and she developed a new interest in the international art world.

After her break in London, Brenda returned to a wild, blustery Wales. Aberdaron was awash with sea-spray and the wind was rising at a terrific pace. The island men were worried about waiting any longer for her and were about to cast away when she arrived on the shore. Breathlessly she ran onto the beach, shouting out to the men. At the last possible moment, Jean heard her and rowed the dinghy swiftly ashore to collect her. Brenda was unprepared for the rough weather and although enveloped in Jean's duffle coat, she was soon soaked through by sea spray.

Such a sea was running that I was taken far away beyond the mere fear of drowning; that we should be overwhelmed and sunk at any moment seemed too obvious. Strangely, inky phrases began to press upon one another in my numbed mind.

'Whole seas went over her decks.'
Literary tags came to mind.
'Green seas poured over her hatches, tearing out the strongly battened-down covers.'[37]

185

Even in the midst of the storm Brenda's mind was focused on its artistic possibilities and from such experiences her poems emerged. At last they swung around the headland into the Cafn. The anchorage was uncannily calm. It was a relief to be on dry land once more. 'The island was a core of silence at the heart of thundering surf that surrounded it on every side'.[38]

In the rush to scramble aboard the boat Brenda had left all her supplies and luggage on the shore. There was no worry about its safety for it would be stored away by one of the villagers but the main problem was the lack of food. The storm had taken everyone by surprise and no one had stocked up with emergency food supplies. For weeks the foul weather continued. The island was battered by wind and rain and it became impossible to walk upright against the wild gales. Food supplies began to run out. Under cover of darkness bartering took place: margarine was exchanged for candles; tobacco for tea and sugar. Every night they all prayed for a lull in the storm, but there was no end to its fury. After four weeks' isolation, Christmas arrived, but passed by frugally, for they had no celebratory food, gifts or Christmas cards. It was a gloomy occasion.

There was always the fear of illness on an isolated island with no doctor, but on the whole the islanders were a sturdy bunch and managed with their own medication. However, while they were still cut off by the storm, a thistle seed was blown into Brenda's eye and neither she nor anyone else on the island was able to extract it. The bandaged eye watered for days but still she continued to paint. With the skies heavy with storm clouds and the windows encrusted with sea spray, the daylight was very poor. Despite these conditions, Brenda struggled on with her painting to keep her spirits up.

By the New Year the radio batteries had completely expired leaving no connection with the outside world. Eventually, after five weeks, news came from the lighthouse that a passing lifeboat was preparing to venture near the island to deliver provisions for the islanders. It was a successful mission despite the wild seas.

> Our reaction to the food was strange and unexpected. Besides the common staples of life, my mother had sent a basket of exotic delicatessen foodstuffs. These, we spread out over the table, to gloat over. After careful examination, and a close reading of labels, they were put away in the cupboard. We had gone for so long on an austere diet, that we were unprepared for richer fare. It was some days before we had the desire to open the gift-food.[39]

Christmas was eventually celebrated in the middle of January, 'when the gorse bushes were already ablaze with gold; putting out our greetings cards at about the time when we should have been taking them down'.[40]

When at last the storm abated and the boat was once more able to cross to the mainland, life returned to normal on the island. With the first boat came a parcel of thirty copies of the *New Yorker* from Kaye Gimpel. This was a rare treat, and on a whim Brenda sent some poems to the magazine. Much to her delight, five were accepted and she received a cheque for £64, a large sum at the time.

It proved to be a productive year and Brenda painted around forty canvases, which was by far her greatest output to date. One of the larger compositions, *Children on a Hopscotch Pavement* had echoes of the earlier *Children on the Seashore*. It had a similar formal arrangement of children with their elongated heads, the shell, the ball, the bird, set against the lined background of a hopscotch pavement. Brenda was particularly pleased with her next painting, *Girl with a Siamese Cat*, a sensitive portrait of one of the islanders with Brenda's cat, Filitz. She entered the painting in the competition for Fine Art at the Royal National Eisteddfod at Llanrwst, where it won first prize.

On 19 July 1951, Brenda's father died and was cremated two days later in Landican Cemetery, Birkenhead. As there were no telephones on Bardsey and letters only reached the island when the boat came across, unfortunately Brenda did not hear the news in time to attend the funeral. The irregular post affected her again just a week later when she failed to receive the news that she

Children on a hopscotch pavement, 1951, oil on canvas

Study for Girl with a Siamese Cat, c. 1951, ink on paper

had won the Gold Medal in Fine Art at the National Eisteddfod in time to attend the ceremony on Monday, 6 August and did not manage to arrive at the Eisteddfod until Wednesday, 8 August.

She attended with her London agent and posed for photographs with her Siamese cat, who had appeared in the winning painting. She had expected an informal presentation in the Art Pavilion and was surprised to be invited onto the stage in the Main Pavilion where she was presented with the medal by Mr C.O. Jones, the vice-chairman of the Arts and Crafts Committee. Although there was no monetary prize attached to this honour, Brenda received 50 guineas (£52.10s, or £52.50 today), her high asking price for her painting, as the Arts Council bought it for its permanent Welsh Collection. They also bought paintings by the Highly Commended artists: Kyffin Williams, John Elwyn, Hywel Harries and George Little.

Having received the unexpected income from the poems and the purchase of the painting, Brenda and Jean decided to take a break from the island. After arranging for neighbours to take care of their animals, they set off at the beginning of October 1951. Despite the repeated invitations of Karl von Laer for them to visit him and his family in Germany, Brenda and Jean chose to go to France. Karl's letters were such an inspiration to Brenda, particularly to her poetry, that although she wanted to see Karl again, she feared that they would not live up to each other's expectations after twenty years apart, and preferring not to risk losing this friendship, she did not take up the invitation. They went instead to the south of France, travelling by train to Ménerbes where they planned to stay for about two months. Having arrived on 9 October, Brenda recorded her first impressions:

Ménerbes, narrow streets, tall houses, a white dust. The rough village street with exotic flowers, trees, La

Carmejane [*sic*] high up, near the church; the bell of the Hôtel de Ville hangs in a surrealist iron openwork cage.[41]

They stayed in 'La Carmajane' in the village and spent their days walking into the hills and exploring the local sights:

Vineyards and more vineyards, hills and more hills, limestone quarries cut into like cheese, white escarpments tree-covered. Les cigales lizards coming out of cracks in the sunny wall. Hawks, ravens, flowers. Olive trees. The fig tree in the courtyard, dropping its ripe pulped fruits onto the earth. Great tomatoes lying in the soil, melons. La chasse somewhere over the valley. The far echoes of dog-barking. Every inch of landscape is sculptured by man towards one end, the cultivation of the grape.[42]

Although Brenda obviously enjoyed the French countryside, she was constantly comparing it to Wales:

For two days it has rained, gently but persistently; this morning the clouds began to roll up from the lowlands, until, by the evening, the landscape is as sad as a Welsh Valley, La Montagne du Luberon like the foothills around Bethesda quarry, becoming soft blue with moisture.[43]

Brenda was always hungry for new subjects for her work, and she avidly recorded the architecture, people and landscape in word and image in her notebook. On the way to Roussillon they walked

... up the hill towards the red earth. The fieldworkers were in bright blue against the red, pink, magenta, yellow ochre, burnt ochre earth. We climbed through a wood and came to a wide, deep ravine full of tender green fir trees, of the tenderest yellow-green against the red soil.[44]

Brenda was already mentally planning her next paintings as she found herself swamped by these vivid stimuli, colours and images which she did not experience in Wales. When they reached the end of their holiday, she felt a certain reluctance to return to Bardsey. It was well into November and by the time they got back the island was cold, windy and grey.

I came back to my prison on the sea rock, everything put from me but the ambition to succeed as an artist. It is only in voluntary imprisonment that I can bring out the painful fruits of experience. Having spent most of my days too close to Nature, I have discovered that Nature is not enough. Living cheek by jowl with her deepens nobody's mind. The island has only succeeded in giving me love for mankind, for crowded streets, quaysides, foreign towns, exotic fruits, sophisticated gatherings, architecture.

Down with the nature lover.

My fellow islanders are empty of everything but the lust for gold.[45]

It was the first time that Brenda had found it difficult to return and settle on the island. The house seemed cold and grey, and the responsibility of tending all their animals weighed heavily upon her. As well as the dogs, cats, hens, geese and the pony there were eighty-six sheep and the extra work of wintering eight bullocks for Esmé Kirby. Brenda wanted to paint but found it difficult to combine both chores and painting in the short hours of daylight. However, once she began, the vibrant colours of Ménerbes brightened her mood and filled her paintings with rich reds, blues, greens and ochres.

Brenda with *The Wildmen*

She contacted Gimpel Fils with the news of her new French series of work and was offered an exhibition at the gallery in April of the following year. Because there was so little time to complete the series, Brenda became totally absorbed by her work, painting furiously. Her subject matter for this series was much more exotic than the Bardsey works; aubergines were substituted for apples, elegant furnishings replaced basic tables and chairs, rich

193

reds and ochres appeared instead of dull blues and greys. She gave all in this series French titles; *Les Figues Sauvages*, *La Maison des Italiens* and *Jeune Fille aux Aubergines* (see plate 7). This last work was a well-composed study of Dora Maar, Picasso's mistress, who lived in Ménerbes. Brenda portrays her as a young woman in white, seated on a high-backed rust and brown curvaceous chair. Beside her stands another carved chair and a plain table with a plate of aubergines on green leaves. The background is a delicately floral-patterned blue wall covering.

In *Red Coffee Pot* (1952) (see plate 8) pattern dominates. Although there is a realistic arrangement of fruit, bread-basket, bottles, bowls and coffee pot on a table, the painting is almost abstract. There are obvious references to Cézanne in the arrangement of fruit and the distorted angles of perspective. The tablecloth has a lively zigzag pattern and the back wall is traced with curves and swirls suggestive of wrought-iron. The colours are bold and the canvas (35 x 40 in., 89 x 101.5 cm) quite large for Brenda.

The trip to France had opened Brenda's work to foreign influences, and she was keener than ever to reach an international audience. To further this aim she exhibited with the Women's International Art Club. Although she chose to live in a Welsh-speaking area Brenda did not wish to be narrowly defined as a Welsh artist. She described herself as 'of Celtic blood', which she saw as placing her in an international context.

Her exhibition of French-influenced paintings opened in Gimpel Fils Gallery in April. By now her work was selling slowly but steadily, and apart from paintings owned privately in Britain, France and America, examples had been bought by the National Museum of Wales, Arts

Council of Great Britain, Contemporary Art Society of Wales and the National Library of Wales.

Although there were many other artists working in Wales in the 1950s, Brenda tended not to interact with them. This was partly because of geographical separation, lack of patronage and more particularly the lack of good spaces to exhibit. Most artists remained quite isolated and it was hard to find recognition. Some artists, particularly in the more populated areas, founded exhibiting groups such as the South Wales Group, the 56 Group and the Rhondda Group, to give each other mutual support and better opportunities to exhibit their work, but she remained outside such associations.

Living on Bardsey, Brenda was not only cut off from her fellow artists in Wales but quite frequently from the mainland itself. Sending paintings for exhibition was always a nerve-wracking experience. To compensate for rough weather and delayed crossings, Brenda would always allow at least three weeks to transport her work to the gallery. The canvases had to be well packed, then wrapped in tarpaulin and loaded onto the boat. The weather conditions were vital and if it was rainy or there was a rough sea, they risked damage during the crossing. Brenda would often travel ashore with them to reassure herself of their safe arrival. Once on dry land, their journey was relatively straightforward – by road to Bangor and then by train to London.

In June, Brenda was shocked to hear the news that Peter Petts had died in a mountaineering accident, descending the face of the second peak of Les Diablerets in Switzerland. He had slipped and fallen more than a thousand feet to his death. He was twenty-seven. It was sad news for Brenda and Jean who had both been very fond of him. Brenda turned to her painting to absorb the grief she felt. The result was a portrait of Jean, called *Man with a John Dory*. Again it featured the distinctive elongated head, the statuesque pose and the interest in decorative pattern in the fishing-net backcloth, the man's chequered jumper and the scales and fins of the huge fish. The colours were subdued greys, browns and blues with a splash of red in Jean's woollen cap.

During the summer she produced another outstanding painting, *The Cristin Children*, an intricate composition of four island children with four of the island's cats. It was a stylised arrangement of interlocking blocks of colour where on the diamond tiled floor two pairs of cats swirl and fight, their bodies entwined in the style of Escher. Seated on a sofa, chair and cushion the children stare blankly, their stocky bodies frozen in poses, their sad faces adult rather than childlike. Soft pinks, greys, and blues subtly blend together.

Brenda was pleased with these recent paintings. She seemed to have settled into a pattern of working, and was inspired by the stimulus of working towards regular London exhibitions. Her writing had not progressed so well and although she had continued to revise her work about life on Bardsey, she had written very little for publication. She did enjoy writing and receiving letters though, and she kept in regular contact with her friends. Her correspondence with Karl von Laer continued and Karl sent news of the birth of twins into the family. In almost every letter, Karl extended an invitation for Brenda and Jean to visit, and at last Brenda agreed they should spend Christmas there. Karl was delighted, though Brenda and Jean were apprehensive.

1. In her accounts of events on the island, Brenda frequently used alternative names for places and people. As her use of these names is not constant, it can easily cause confusion. To clarify the situation, the real names, where known, are used in the text with fictitious names in brackets. Where there is uncertainty about the identification, the fictitious name appears in single quotation marks alone.

2. *TR*, p. 138.

3. NLW MS 21501E, f. 66.

4. *TR*, p. 119.

5. *TR*, p. 181.

6. *TR*, p. 181.

7. *TR*, p. 21.

8. *TR*, pp. 145-46.

9. *TR*, p. 138.

10. *TR*, p. 141.

11. *TR*, p. 193.

12. *TR*, p. 196.

13. *TR*, pp. 139-40.

14. *TR*, p. 140.

15. *TR*, p. 140.

16. 'Island Fisherman', published in *Botteghe Oscure* 4 (1949), 367; *The New Yorker*, XXVII.xxi (7 July 1951), 22; *GH*, p. 27; *TR*, pp. 120-21; John Stuart Williams & Meic Stephens (eds), *The Lilting House* (London: Dent & Llandybïe: Christopher Davies, 1969), p. 71.

17. 'Five Poems', *The Dublin Magazine* 16.3 (July-Sept.1941), 8-10, (poem II, p.8).

18. Ibid.

19. *TR*, p. 62.

20. *TR*, p. 141.

21. *TR*, p. 141.

22. 'The Islanders: Eight famous people define their joys of island living', *House & Garden*, April 1959, p. 71. See below, Chapter 8, p. 253.

[23] 'The Return', *Life and Letters Today* 54 (1947), 215-16; *The Penguin Book of Welsh Short Stories*, p. 151.

[24] *TR*, p. 161.

[25] *TR*, p. 162.

[26] 'The Return', in the BBC2 television series *Sea Tales*, transmitted 12 May 1977.

[27] *TR*, p. 182.

[28] Jean Ware, letter to the author, 16 July 1984.

[29] *TR*, p. 184.

[30] Brenda Chamberlain, 'Brenda Chamberlain's Bardsey', *House and Gardens* (April 1959), p. 71.

[31] Ibid., p. 71.

[32] Ibid., p. 71.

[33] 'Dead Ponies', 'Lament', 'Song (Bone-aged)', 'You who in April laughed', 'Song (Heron is harsh with despair)', in Kenneth Rexroth (ed.), *New British Poets. An Anthology* (Norfolk, Conn.: New Directions, 1949), p. 23; 'Christmas Eve', *New Directions in Prose and Poetry* (1949), 323-26; 'New Year's Eve', *Poetry Quarterly* II, ii (Summer 1949), 79; 'The Green Heart' part I,i, *Poetry Quarterly* (Autumn 1949), 147; 'Island Fisherman', *Botteghe Oscure* iv (1949), 367.

[34] *TR*, pp. 180-81.

[35] Notebook dated Dec. 1953, private collection.

[36] 'The Relationship of Art and Literature', NLW MS 21501E, f. 57.

[37] *TR*, p. 214.

[38] *TR*, p. 215.

[39] *TR*, p. 219.

[40] *TR*, p. 219.

[41] NLW MS 21508B, f. 93, (9 Oct. 1951).

[42] Ibid., ff. 92-93 (text reversed).

[43] Ibid., f. 89 (text reversed).

[44] Ibid., f. 88 (text reversed).

[45] Ibid., f. 20.

Chapter 7

The German Waves and the Green Heart 1952-58

On 21 December 1952 Brenda and Jean left Bardsey Island for Germany. The journey proved long and tiring: first a crossing by boat to Aberdaron, then bus to Bangor, train to London and on by another train to Harwich where they caught a ferry to the Hook of Holland. They arrived in the early morning and caught a train to Löhne in north-west Germany, where Karl had arranged to meet them:

> The nearer we came to Löhne, the more blanched and derelict was the landscape. We stepped down into icy mud and slush on the station platform. We had several pieces of luggage; suitcases and small grips, and skis. Porters stood about; grey-clothed men, in peaked caps over grey faces. They refused to notice us or our belongings.[1]

There was no sign of Karl, and Brenda was worried in case he was there and she had not recognised him. Both she and Jean were anxious and, tired and after a long wait at the station, they decided to take a taxi to the Schäferhof, the small house in the woods where Karl and his family lived.

Instead of their long awaited meeting with Karl, the first person that Brenda saw was his wife Hildegard or Hilde:

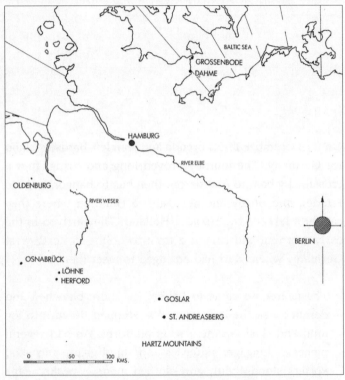

Map of Germany showing locations named in the text

A massive woman great with child, in a full-skirted blue dress, clogs, and ribbed woollen stockings, a red and white kerchief over her dark hair, came out of the house door. Her head was beautiful, with a fine hooked nose and dark eyes; but her body was gross and untidy. She had the haunches of a brood mare. This I realized, must be Klaus's [Karl's] second wife, of whom I knew nothing, except that she had been his wife for three years. Antoine [Jean] was overcome by the vastness of the woman crossing the yard. He said aloud. 'My God'.[2]

Hildegard greeted them warmly and invited them inside. She could not understand why Karl had missed them as he had left in good time to meet their train. While settling into her room upstairs, Brenda heard someone arrive. Karl ran up the stairs to meet her.

Hilde, ink on paper

I do not remember what we said to one another in our excitement, but I was aware of Antoine watching us from the hall below. Klaus was dressed in a green overcoat;

on his head was a grey felt hat edged with green braid, and worn pulled down over one eye. He wore spectacles. The hair at his temples was almost white. His laugh was the same, his eyes were the same, so blue they gave him almost the look of a blind man, the blue of an icefall. What I was unprepared for, was his warmth, his exuberant delight that I had come on a visit at last.[3]

Meeting Karl again entranced Brenda. She became infatuated by everything about him: his words, his family, his past. She desperately wanted to feel close to him, to have time alone with him to talk about their exchange of letters and her poetry, to catch up on the last twenty years of separation. Before setting out on the journey Brenda had decided to keep a journal of all the events as they happened. In these writings, later published in novel form as *The Water-Castle*, Brenda retained the chronological account of events and most of the real place names, but changed the names of her characters as she had done in *Tide-race*. So Karl became 'Franz', and in later versions 'Klaus'; his first wife, Bummi, became 'Brita'; his second wife, Hildegard, known as Hilde, and sometimes referred to by Brenda as 'Matthilde', became 'Helga'; Brenda was 'Elizabeth Greatorex' and Jean was 'Antoine'.

On her second day at the Schäferhof Brenda had time to explore.

As far as one can see, the land is flat and melancholy, with low hills forming the horizon. Farm dwellings stand apart from each other over the plain, like dolls' houses put down at random. They have steep-pitched roofs, small windows and enormous doorways, and are variously painted; white, green and chocolate-coloured.[4]

She was not so enamoured of the interior of the Schäferhof.

> The house is sordid: a miserable mongrel called Yula messes wherever she pleases, in the living-room or in the hall, and a ginger and white cat is always in the room where we eat. A sickly smell of babies fills the air.[5]
>
> The hall stinks of pig food and brussels sprouts. There is a smell from the stable as well, but most overpowering of all, is the stench from the lavatory.[6]

Although Karl had trained in law, he had gone on to study forestry and now ran a farm on which he grew Brussels sprouts. To her surprise Brenda discovered that Karl and Hilde were first cousins and had married only a few months after they had met. Hilde had been visiting her relations on the eve of her departure to South Africa, where she was going to practice as a veterinary surgeon. Karl had impulsively proposed to her and though she had already bought her ticket she decided to stay and marry him. That was three years ago, and she had since given birth to twins and was now six months' pregnant. Brenda did not know how to respond to Hilde with whom she felt awkward. Even though she was polite and charming, Brenda did not feel that she could get close to her:

> I came to Germany prepared to like her. Now, by a conversation we have just had together, my heart is estranged from her; I am on my guard. She was preparing to rest in her room after lunch: with what I

took to be gentle kindness, she called me in for a little conversation. She immediately began to criticise Klaus, naming a list of petty annoyances mostly to do with the horse and cart.

She smiled, and dismissed me, leaving these small poison drops to infect my ears.[7]

Brenda could not believe what she had heard.

Infinite care will be necessary to carry me through the coming weeks. The need for tact became obvious at once, when Klaus first ran up the stairs to greet me on my arrival, when he gave me the pot of cyclamen.

Helga said to me yesterday:

'You have known Klaus for twenty years. I have only known him for three.'[8]

Brenda was not a naturally tactful person and she enjoyed the dramatic tension of the situation. Even now the writer in her was active, feeding off the new people and circumstances.

What made it additionally exciting was the discovery of so many images that were familiar. Brenda first experienced this on Christmas Eve when she, Jean, Karl and Hilde went to a service in the village church.

The building was lit simply by the candles on the two tall Christmas trees by the altar … it was a familiar experience of my soul, like all else happening so suddenly, threatening to overcome my usual calm. These candled fir trees were synonymous with those translated from Klaus's description, to form an image in one of my first poems.[9]

This appears in *The Green Heart* sequence of poems:

> At the birthday feast
> Of Christ Son of Mary
> We see the young priest
> By the altar where
> Two candled fir trees
> That a salt wind stirs
> Arch over Him. He cries
> Softly to the mangered Child
> Who is comforted.[10]

As Brenda states in *The Water-Castle*:

> Having made the poem out of his experience, I now so
> late shared his experience and found the poem true. I
> felt myself to be going backwards in time.[11]

Brenda felt uncomfortably aware that although she was
enjoying herself, Jean was probably not: 'I could imagine
how Antoine, as a Roman Catholic, must have been
repelled by the stark Lutheran service.'[12] After only two
days in Germany she realised that she was treading on
delicate ground. She was surprised at how close she felt to
Karl:

> ... we were so attuned that we instinctively avoid
> speaking or even looking at one another when Helga or
> Antoine are in the same room. How is it possible that we
> should have remained the same to one another after so
> many years?[13]

Although she was aware that her obvious feelings for Karl bothered both Jean and Hilde, Brenda did not hide how she felt. Throughout her writings she intimated that Hilde did not appreciate Karl and that Jean had become moody and did not understand her feelings towards her German friend. A rift began to grow between her and Jean which was emphasised by the sleeping arrangements: Jean had to leave the Schäferhof every night to sleep on a neighbouring farm. Brenda wrote that this was because there was only a single bed in her room, while Karl later explained that as the couple were not married, it would go against convention for them to sleep under the same roof.

Karl, ink on paper from a 1950s notebook

On Boxing Day they all went to a hare-shoot at Oberbehme (the Water Castle), the moated mansion which was owned by Karl's cousin, Cef Krüger and his wife, Ulla. It had been Karl's home for a few years, and his parents still lived there. In his letters, Karl had told Brenda a great deal about Oberbehme and she was excited to see the place which had inspired some of her poetry.

So this was the reality behind the dream, the reality behind the poem of the ice-covered moat round the sleeping castle. It is exactly as it was in my imagination.[14]

After receiving a descriptive letter from Karl some ten years earlier, Brenda had written in *The Green Heart*:

Snow covers the mountain and the silent forest.
The frost has built an ice bridge
Over the lake round our house
Where the wild duck swam in warm weather
The wild duck that roused us each morning
Have flown away to the river.[15]

One feature had puzzled Brenda.

My mental picture had been a curious one though, for all it had been crystal-clear, showing the pale-coloured façade from the end of the wall to the bridge over the moat, on the left side. There had been nothing of the other half of the façade. The focus of the image had been the dark windows at the furthest end of the wall above the stagnant water.[16]

Later in the day she discovered from Karl that the two windows at the end of the façade were the rooms in which he and Bummi had lived. Brenda found this fact very significant.

> This was my proof, the reason why, in my mental image, I had seen only half the façade. The bridge, the frozen waters, the windows had been there. They were all I needed. The link between Klaus and myself had been so strong that I had been almost unconsciously living in him and through him these many years.[17]

Brenda began to see great significance in every experience with Karl. She described him as 'My soul's soul, my double' and as her 'other self'.[18] Every moment spent in his company became precious. When Karl spent time with his family and friends at Oberbehme, Brenda felt slighted, wishing to be at the centre of his attention.

> To see Klaus again after the few hours of separation filled me with a singular sensation, disappointment that he had shown no interest in me during the day, and a sudden happiness, a sense of homecoming, as I walked to where he stood talking to Johannes.[19]

Despite her obsession with Karl, Brenda spent time talking to other members of the family who had come to the hareshoot. She felt drawn to Ulla, whom she quickly discovered was fond of painting. She was taken to meet Ulla's children, Bylle and Krischan, who were having a painting lesson in the house. Brenda recorded in her journal how Ulla beckoned to her daughter, who ran forward,

There are three wooden bridges spanning the moat, from the Castle into the fields. A stone bridge leads to the main arched gateway leading into a cobbled yard round which the castle is built

The Water-Castle, 1950s, ink on paper

'and taking my hand with feverish fingers, curtsied so violently that her long black pigtails flew about her inquisitive ears. A fine sweat dewed her brow and upper lip which, coupled with hectically-flushed cheeks, gave her an overwrought intensity. Her eyes were black, large, and wide-open. Her young brother had a more reserved nature, but the same intentness of gaze as his sister and father'.[20]

Brenda also met Ulla's mother, Oma Strengel, and several other members of the family and their friends. Through them she began to learn more about Karl's past. All the family had been forced to flee from their sumptuous homes in East Prussia by the Russian advance. The journey west had been arduous, and memories were still vivid, as Ulla told Brenda:

'These carpets', she went on, pointing to the wall and the floor, 'they formed the walls of our house on the journey. We were six months on the roads, and many of us died, particularly the young children and the very old people.'[21]

Brenda was very surprised to learn that at the end of the trek from the east ninety-five people had been housed in Oberbehme. They consisted of family, friends and servants. Even then in 1952, there were still twenty-eight people living there. Although they had lost much of their wealth, they still clung to remnants of the past by surrounding themselves with elegant furnishings and holding lavish events such as the hare-shoot, where servants ran back and forth tending the finely-dressed sportsmen.

Of the future, they speak but seldom; when they do, it is with dread of the Russians, and of what they may do next. They have no future such as they were born to expect. Klaus for example, was a doctor of law; he took a degree in forestry too, in order to be fitted for the life of a landowner. He was the lord of Schlotheim. He talks at times of past pleasures: carp pools, rose gardens, horses, foreign holidays, tutors, nurses.[22]

Of all the places with which Karl had been associated, Schlotheim, his lost ancestral home in East Prussia, appealed most to Brenda. From his descriptions of the estate in letters, Brenda had plucked phrases for her poems, and she was excited when Karl showed her an album of photographs of it.

What a contrast there is between this ugly Westphalian farm and the baroque schloss with its elegant proportions, its statues, its rose garden, its peacocks![23]

The Schloss felt very special to Brenda and from that vital link of letters between her and Karl before the war she had dreamt of being there. Now, she found it abhorrent to hear Hilde talking about returning as mistress of Schlotheim. In Brenda's eyes, Bummi had been an ideal and happy match for Karl and Brenda had never felt any resentment at her presence there even though she had never met her in person. Faced with Hilde, Brenda was adamant:

It has become quite clear in my mind; since Brita [Bummi] cannot return there, then it is for me to go. Schlotheim is part of my myth-inheritance. It would be as familiar to me as the Obenburg [Oberbehme] is familiar; I could walk out onto the terrace from the cool interior and know the individual shape and colour of each flower hanging between lacquered leaves.[24]

Jean must have found Brenda's fantasies difficult to cope with, but Brenda did not express any understanding for his feelings in her journal. She appeared to take him for granted, to be annoyed when he became moody and jealous and to point out areas where they did not agree. Although Brenda declared, 'There is nothing left between us: our natures are too opposed for us ever to be close to one another again', she also confessed her need for him.[25] Over the years she had grown to rely on upon his companionship and support, and she definitely did not want to live alone on Bardsey. Brenda wanted too many things at once.

She was still puzzled by the mystery surrounding Karl's first wife, Bummi. It was Ulla who eventually explained to Brenda what happened:

'She was a diabetic, and very ill before the baby came; but she wanted so much to have one. They had been married ten years and had no children. It was a great joy to her, preparing things for the baby. She and Klaus were happy: it was a good marriage. They only lacked a child. Because she was diabetic, she had to take injections. The child was born alive; it was a boy. The doctor had given orders that Brita should not be given an injection after the birth. She was left alone for a few minutes; she gave herself an injection. She died; and the baby died two days later. It was terrible for Klaus, they had been so happy. He felt that if only the baby had lived, it would have been part of Brita, something to remember her by.'[26]

Brenda was relieved to know at last what had happened even though it was so tragic. She now understood why Karl had suddenly stopped writing to her. However, she was still puzzled why Karl had married Hilde as they did not seem at all compatible. Brenda found it very hard to believe that any woman could be unhappy with such 'a wonderful man'.

While they were in Germany Brenda and Jean wanted to spend some time skiing and planned to go to Sankt Andreasberg in the Hartz mountains for three weeks. Hilde was too pregnant to go, but Karl hoped to join them for the last fortnight. They left on 3 January, travelling to Goslar by train. From there they took a bus up the narrow valley to the mountains.

We were in a black and white world; black tree trunks, black river, white earth, white-capped boulders. We

Bille, ink on paper from a 1950s notebook

crossed sensational bridges over mountain torrents. From the moment when we had left Goslar for this silent country of solitary escarpments and endless forest, we had been in the enchanted world of Goethe.[27]

On arrival at Sankt Andreasberg they discovered that they had not been booked into a hotel although they had organised it with the Reisebureau in Herford before they left. The same mistake had happened to six other holiday makers and they were all sent to sit in a hotel lounge until the problem was sorted out.

Antoine took an instant dislike to the waiter in the hotel. We were both tired and cold and deflated, and extremely hungry. I ordered a black coffee; Antoine had a beer. The coffee gave me a certain measure of courage: the beer on an empty stomach made Antoine surly and arrogant. The waiter's large ears, and his servility, infuriated him.[28]

Brenda's pared-down prose style was aptly suited to capturing the essence of such small moments of drama which would normally pass by unnoticed and unrecorded.

After a couple of hours, officials from the Reisebureau arrived and allocated everyone to accommodation. Brenda and Jean were sent to the house of 'Frau Schmidt' who was not at all pleased to see them. Noone had told her they were coming and she had no room. Stubborn and weary, Brenda and Jean refused to leave and 'Frau Schmidt' eventually gave way and let them in. They soon discovered how full the house was. The guest room was taken and 'Frau Schmidt' had already given up her bedroom for a guest. All she could offer them was the small room where she had been sleeping, while she would have to sleep on the living-room sofa for the night. Tomorrow the guest room would be free and they would have more space. This settled, they went straight to bed and slept soundly.

Thoughts of Karl's forthcoming visit filled Brenda's head from the first day at Sankt Andreasburg. She was impatient. She wanted Karl to be there and as the days went by she felt a distance growing between herself and Jean.

I carry the weight of my thoughts up and down the dead-white shadowless slopes. I wonder how much Antoine knows. He probably guesses that I was prepared to leave him as long ago as last autumn.[29]

Yet with pleasure she admired his skill on skis: 'he swoops past me effortlessly, with the easy movements of a mountaineer. He becomes identified with a roebuck glimpsed as it leaps across a clearing'.[30] Although Brenda had done a little skiing each winter in Snowdonia, the snow conditions were rarely ideal for the sport and she had not become very proficient. She had to work hard to keep up with Jean, yet both took delight in seeing the trees, mountains and snow – all experiences not at hand on their island home.

Brenda and Jean arrived back at their pension after a long day's skiing, to find a message from Karl saying he had arrived and had gone for a walk. When Karl returned, Brenda heard him go into the next room where Jean was sitting. She writes in *The Water-Castle*: 'I did not join them immediately, for I had been surprised by such a flood of pure joy; so vibrant a sensation had run through me at the sound of his voice, that I could not trust myself to meet him'.[31] Brenda composed herself and entered the room: 'Everything is changed because Klaus is with us. The village has become magical, the lights of the Bahnhof burn more brilliantly.'[32] Karl was in high spirits too and suggested they all go dancing. Brenda was soon swept up in his enthusiasm but Jean was less pleased by Karl's arrival. Brenda noticed him become tense and start chain-smoking, and she saw his hands were shaking violently. As she began to glow with happiness, Jean's spirits sank lower. When Brenda danced with him she was irritated by his rigidity: 'His body, so used to exercise and usually so fluid in his movements, was now that of an automaton.'[33] For the rest of the evening Brenda danced with Karl, leaving Jean alone to smoke in another room.

Despite the protestations in her writings of her concern for the situation, her behaviour made it apparent that she selfishly enjoyed the tension and the drama. She felt flattered to have the attention of two attractive men, although her main concern was to impress Karl and live up to his expectations of her.

> If, after keeping a friendship alive for twenty years, we should fail to sustain it when we are together, it would be a calamity. During this week, our sensitiveness to one another will be strained to the utmost … We expect a great deal of one another, perhaps too much.[34]

Karl made many drawings in the mountains and on one occasion, when Brenda went over to sketch beside him, her mind flashed back twenty years to the times when they sat together sketching in the hills of Snowdonia. While they sat there, Brenda was ever conscious of Jean's watchful gaze. Her continual attempts to exclude Jean from the intimate conversations she wanted with Karl, caused still more tension. The situation came to a head on the day Karl was leaving. Brenda's distress at his departure and Jean's anger at her selfish behaviour resulted in a bitter quarrel. Brenda felt that Jean misunderstood her feelings for Karl. He repeatedly asked, 'Why did you not tell me before about yourself and that man?'[35] Brenda felt exasperated: 'It is useless to protest the truth, that up to now there has been nothing to tell.'[36]

Karl left and Brenda found the last few days of the holiday extremely difficult: 'Nothing can ever transcend the joy of last week; the despair of the present.' On 24 January, she and Jean left the mountains and returned to Löhne. Karl met them at the station, but he was in low spirits and hardly spoke. When questioned, he told them that Hilde and the children had gone to Oberbehme for a few days. The weather worsened and they were forced to stay indoors for most of the time. Brenda felt uncomfortable as she wondered if she had been the cause of Hilde's sudden departure. She even suggested to Karl that she and Jean should leave straight away but Karl insisted that they stay until at least the following weekend.

Goslar in the snow, 1950s, ink on paper

As the days passed and Hilde did not return, Brenda found the situation increasingly tense. Having decided to ask Karl directly, she told Jean that she was going upstairs to talk with him. When it transpired that his quarrel with Hilde had been unconnected with Brenda, she was very relieved. Then they talked about their separate relationships and she told Karl of her unhappiness, Jean's jealousy and their many arguments. Karl spoke to her firmly, insisting that she must not be pulled in two ways:

> Stay close to Antoine whom you know to be a good man. Let me go with you in your poetry, this most difficult way, but don't forget the other way with your husband. I like him, and I think he is your counterpoint, and you would be unhappy without him.[37]

Brenda was not so easily convinced: 'It will be difficult because we are so different.' But Karl was adamant: 'Often, it is difficult to live with a man whose soul is different ... Let us be good friends, and we shall be closer together than lovers'.[38] Suddenly, Brenda remembered that Jean was alone downstairs; they had been talking for hours. She rushed down.

> Antoine was in the living-room, with a book in his hands. His face was white. He leapt up at the sight of us, saying fiercely:
> 'This is the end, the absolute end.'[39]

Brenda taken aback by the outburst, followed him upstairs as he shouted:

'You came downstairs, smiling happily, after being upstairs for two hours. I've walked round and round the wood. What do you think I've been feeling?'[40]

Eventually Jean did go downstairs to join them for supper, though he was still very moody. As they were finishing their meal, Hilde returned and went straight to bed. Her sudden arrival added to the tense atmosphere and that night Brenda was relieved to escape alone to her own bed.

The next morning, Brenda braved the worsening weather to go out into the fields to help harvest the Brussels sprouts. She wanted to be alone; her thoughts were confused and she was not looking forward to her departure the following day. Despite the uncertainty of their travel arrangements because of the heavy fall of snow, Brenda and Jean left Löhne on 2 February 1953. Fortunately, by the time they had reached the Hook of Holland, the storms had subsided a little and they were able to cross the Channel. Brenda was preoccupied with thoughts of Karl and as they crossed the stormy sea to England, she wondered whether her life could be quite the same again.

When they arrived home, Bardsey seemed cold and grey and without magic to Brenda. Long visits away from the island seemed to disrupt her life there, and she felt as unsettled now as she had after her trip to the south of France. In order to dwell a little longer in her memories of the trip, Brenda began to rewrite her journal into a manuscript for possible publication.

In the meantime letters arrived from Karl for both Jean and Brenda. To Jean he wrote that he was sorry to have been the cause of their quarrels and insisted that he had no intention of upsetting Jean or taking Brenda away. Her imagination had been overactive, he said, and he advised Jean to let his feelings subside and then apologise to her. To Brenda he wrote that she must forgive Jean for his jealous behaviour and appreciate his friendship once more: 'Often people think to be loved that is to be a prisoner. That's not true: love, flying over the hills and over the sea, to the sun and the stars, is like an angel coming from the good Lord; like a bird, winging in the trees, like the wind, blowing in Springtime'.[41] These words moved Brenda, and changing their order she made them into a poem which became part of *The Green Heart* sequence:

> Always remember:
> To be loved, is not to be prisoned.
> Love flies, over the mountains and the sea,
> To where the sun and the stars move.
> It is a bird singing in a wood
> Under the south wind of springtime.
> It is an angel from the hand of God.[42]

For the first few months after her return, Brenda concentrated on her writing. As well as revising her journals, she worked on two more cycles of poetry to complete *The Green Heart* sequence. As Karl's many letters arrived, Brenda incorporated his words and phrases into her poetry and the poems began to take shape. Part I was based on extracts from Karl's early letters. Parts II and III became more complex as, using her voice in some verses and his in others, she tried to show the deep level of understanding and communication between them.[43] However, her concentration was broken by the appearance of a feature article about her in *The Lady* magazine in April 1953. Entitled 'An Island Painter: One woman realises her dreams', it showed photographs of Brenda, Bardsey and her paintings and was particularly flattering about her work: 'Brenda Chamberlain is a painter in the great European tradition, profoundly influenced by Matisse, yet the works which are steadily gaining her an international reputation are produced on Bardsey Island, right out in the blue'.[44]

Praise always inspired Brenda and she stopped writing to turn to painting again. She decided to enter two of her paintings for the Fine Art competition at the Royal National Eisteddfod, held that year in Rhyl on the north Wales coast. They were *Carnaval de Nice*, a painting in gouache on paper, and *The Cristin Children*, an oil on canvas. Brenda missed these children whom she had often drawn and painted. They were no longer living on the island and that summer, their farmhouse, Cristin, became established as the base for the Bardsey Bird and Field Observatory.

When the Eisteddfod was held that August, Brenda won the Gold Medal for her painting *The Cristin Children*. *Carnaval de Nice* was also amongst the four paintings that received honourable recognition. She was delighted by the news, and, loving the drama of the occasion, she dressed in black with large black earrings and red shoes for the presentation, where she received a heavy medal designed by Sir Goscombe John. By happy coincidence, a past resident of Bardsey, Dilys Cadwaladr, the schoolteacher on the island in the 1940s, also won a major prize, becoming the first woman to win the Crown for Poetry.

Despite her winning the major art prize in the Eisteddfod, Brenda's paintings did not sell. Having exhibited in London, she had perhaps pitched her prices too high, between 45 and 85 guineas, whereas most of the other exhibits ranged from 2 to 25 guineas.

Jean at the Schäferhof, 1950s, ink on paper

At about the same time, Brenda had three of her paintings selected by the Women's International Art Club to be exhibited at the New Burlington Galleries in London. Her work was also selected for the British Romantic Painters exhibition held in Brighton. All this positive news acted as a tremendous inspiration and she began to work on new techniques in her paintings. Two paintings in particular epitomise this transition. In *The Doves* she combined the statuesque figures of her earlier works with a more abstract, decorative background created by collage letters cut out of newsprint and magazines. There was a return too, to the use of shading. The figures unlike the earlier stylised forms, now have depth and their clothes fall in draped folds. In *The Acrobats* Brenda placed her figures in a steeply raked room with a high balcony. Whereas most of her work had hitherto been two-dimensional, this painting allowed her to explore the arrangement of a composition in a three-dimensional space. In the foreground a solemn figure concentrates intensely on the small balls he is juggling while several other figures are involved in a variety of balancing exercises. One figure in the background balances the weight of another on one arm and all that can be seen of the balanced body is the inverted upper torso. Brenda cuts off the rest of the figure, leading the eye outside the frame, much as Degas used a ballet dancer climbing up the spiral staircase in *The Rehearsal*. Brenda found the painting disturbing and in a letter to the buyer, her friend Henry Mitchell, she reveals her feelings about it:

You are most brave: I could not bear to have the Acrobats in my bedroom! In fact I had to screw my courage up in order to paint it! It is of course the best of those paintings sent up. The Gimpels will probably have told you that they were pleased when they saw it. The Acrobats was a painting that came slowly and was abandoned several times towards the end. I became so horrified by the Juggler that it was with difficulty that I was able to complete the picture. The idea of a man obsessed with tossing balls into the air in a windowless room is quite horrible: IF HE DROPS ONE, THE DREAM WILL BREAK. HORROR! HE WILL COME AWAKE![45]

As the autumn arrived, Brenda's thoughts turned to the possibility of another visit to Germany. Karl had invited them both, but although she and Jean had reconciled their differences about Karl, it seemed more sensible for Brenda to go alone. Jean decided to spend Christmas with friends in Paris and they arranged to meet up in the New Year either in Germany or Paris.

Brenda left the island in early December and travelled to London where she spent a few hours with her mother before catching the night train to Harwich and on to the Hook of Holland. On 12 December she arrived in Löhne, where Karl was at the station to meet her. He rushed to greet her, kissed her hand and walked arm in arm with her to the horse and cart outside the station. Brenda felt relieved to see him in such good spirits. Some of his letters had been so sad that 'I had imagined him wandering through Europe, dazed and hopeless, wearing a ragged rucksack'.[46]

Karl took Brenda to Oberbehme where she was to stay this time. She had returned to Germany after only ten months and she was worried in case the intensity of her previous experiences had been illusory. In fact she was relieved to feel great warmth from her friends, particularly the children, and was once more able to draw inspiration from her surroundings. In her journal she wrote: 'this is my strong myth, in which poetry is rooted'.[47] Her visit proved to be stimulating in many ways. Going with Ulla to meet Frau Koenig, a friend of the poet Rilke, rekindled Brenda's interest in his work. From a published letter from Rilke to his wife, Brenda extracted the names 'Brita Sophie Hastfer' and 'Vivica Bonde' and used these names for some of her characters in *The Water-Castle*.[48]

Brenda wearing the Gold Medal for Fine Art won in 1953 at the
National Eisteddfod of Wales, Rhyl, with *The Cristin Children*

Brenda felt a sense of freedom when she was in Germany.

> At last the winter is here. I love the dark desolate vistas
> under the trees, the sense of space, the fact that I can be
> alone there and unknown, after the closed shallow life of
> the island where one cannot move without being
> observed.[49]

Spared from all the island chores Brenda found there were
more hours in the day to walk, sketch and write in her
journal. Everything here seemed to have a sharper edge, to
be vivid and well-defined, something which is reflected in
her journal.

We walked through the forest [,] on the one hand black fir trees; on the other, the white boles of silver birch. Behind us a white moon mounted the pale sky, before us the foreground was splintered against the fringe of the forest. It was utterly still, utter immobility ... [50]

As the days passed Brenda began to worry about Jean. He had not written and she did not know if he was in Paris, London or still on Bardsey. Each day she was disappointed when there was no letter. Despite her attraction towards Karl, she felt loyalty to Jean. Christmas Eve arrived and she still had no news from him. Brenda gave Karl all the new poems of *The Green Heart* cycle to read. She asked him not to show them to anyone else.

I was really afraid to give them to him, for there he could read everything I felt for him. He kissed my hand: suddenly, he took me gently in his arms and kissed me on the cheek. I kissed him in return on the other cheek. What happiness? for a few moments spent with my other self ...[51]

In her mind Brenda still intensified every moment and every exchange that occurred between her and Karl. Even as she sat alone in her room she tried to picture Karl reading her poems. When he returned on Christmas morning after reading them, Brenda confided in her journal:

This is the greatest agony I have to endure with him, to be alone with him, apart, unnaturally close. It makes me tremble; I must hide myself behind words ... we talk. I scarcely know what I am saying ... I talk only to hide my passion ... If I was to fall silent, what would happen? We should be in one another's arms.[52]

Karl had enjoyed these poems, which he found much easier to understand than the earlier ones of *The Green Heart*, part I. She had spent less time reworking these more recent ones and the language, apart from retaining freshness and fluidity, stayed closer to the wording of Karl's letters which had been her inspiration.

After some hours of intense conversation, they were joined by Ulla and Cef. That evening, Ulla and Karl asked Brenda if she would give them some painting lessons while she was staying with them. Brenda was flattered by their request and agreed to do so, and after making copious notes on painting techniques, she began the lessons at the end of December. She took them seriously and encouraged her pupils to explore different materials and techniques of drawing and painting. Inspired by the success of the lessons, she began to fill her notebooks with portraits of her friends and their homes. Sometimes the drawings were accurate and precise recordings, while others were looser and more carelessly observed. While in Oberbehme, Brenda felt an urgency to record as many thoughts and images as she could store for later use on Bardsey.

The New Year arrived and Brenda had still heard nothing from Jean. It was 6 January before a letter finally came, dated 22 December, much delayed by the holiday. In it, Jean invited Brenda to join him in Paris. Then a couple of days later another letter arrived. Brenda wrote in her journal:

He is dancing and going to parties in Paris: enjoying life. How absurd of me, that I worry about him when all the time he is perfectly happy without me.[53]

As Jean was enjoying himself, she decided to stay longer in Germany and she returned with enthusiasm to her painting lessons. She stayed with her friends until 21 March when she returned to Wales.

Although it was spring, a season Brenda normally enjoyed on Bardsey, she felt restless and yearned to be back in Germany. Despite having friends on Bardsey, she did not feel the same empathy with them and she missed being able to discuss art and literature. Also, in 1954 Jean began to do some teaching on the mainland and was away for long spells. As Brenda felt in need of company she encouraged friends to visit her on the island but by July, she was still feeling very unsettled and decided to go back to Germany. She found it:

> ... strange to look at Germany in high summer instead of under white snow. The corn is immensely tall, but most of the fields have been flattened by days of rain. The castle is enshrouded with leaves, the moat is bright green with scum.[54]

She stayed again at Oberbehme where there was much more room than at the Schäferhof. As the weather was much warmer on this visit, she was able to do more sketching outside. She made many drawings of the Water-Castle from all its different bridges and spent time at the Schwarze Moor, where the black and white farm buildings fascinated her. In particular she was attracted to the Tree of Life painted on the great doors of the barn there. During previous visits to Germany Brenda had grown very fond of Insea, the daughter of Karl's elder brother, Otto Justus, and who lived at the Schwarze Moor. Insea wanted to visit Brenda on Bardsey and plans were made for her to go over later that summer.

Brenda returned to Wales at the end of July. Insea arrived a few weeks later and Brenda went up to Bangor to collect her from the train. Brenda was in good spirits and delighted to be able to share the island with one of her German friends. A self-portrait drawn that summer shows a dark-eyed, calm Brenda with short-cropped hair, dressed in a favourite waistcoat embroidered with lions.

The Water-Castle, 1980s

She made little attempt to write that summer, and sent only a few poems to magazines. She felt her painting to be a priority at that moment and she had organised a retrospective exhibition to be held in Bangor in November. Her selection spanned twenty years and included a painting made when she was an eighteen-year-old student. She chose forty-seven works covering her experiences on Bardsey, in France and in Germany. The exhibition was held in the Powis Hall at the University College of North Wales, Bangor, and was opened on 10 November 1954 by Mrs Kitty Idwal Jones, who had been the first person to buy a painting by Brenda. The opening was quite grand and well attended. Jonah Jones, the sculptor, and Maurice Cooke, the art historian, were there to talk about the pictures, and a film made by Edgar Pritchard was shown.[55] This featured Brenda at work on Bardsey and while it was being shown, Leonard Tibbetts, a Bangor lecturer in Speech Therapy, read one of Brenda's poems, 'Island Fishermen'. Brenda, as always, revelled in the attention and was especially pleased that her first retrospective exhibition had been held in her home town.

As winter approached, Brenda's thoughts turned once again to Germany and she left the island in December to join her friends in Westphalia. Jean once again went to Paris to stay with friends of his and they planned to meet in either Paris or Löhne. On this visit Brenda had specific plans for what she wanted to draw. The Water-Castle was full of Persian and Indian patterned carpets, and their maze-like angular forms had intrigued her for some time. She was especially interested in the way the forms of fish, birds and flowers were woven together, joined by decorative line into a cohesive whole. The juxtaposition of colours fascinated her too:

Who could have dreamed such colours into the life of a carpet? The fresh juice of a pomegranate, blue of the summer Mediterranean, grey-white of goat hair, an unnatural blue almost black tipped with white on a tawny henna'ed ground. The trampling of feet only enriches the colours.[56]

At first she copied the carpet pattern designs, colouring them in with wax crayons, then began to develop them into her own angular form of expression. The earlier adaptations show echoes of the zigzag, and triangular blocks of colour, while later ones have Brenda's own interpretation of two-dimensional symbols and line. In a few she attempted to incorporate words with the image. *We dream of the desert sand* depicts an angular red dog sitting against a flat background decorated with irregular geometric red patches, with the following words written in red wax:

> We dr
> eam of t
> he desert
> sand
> and silence
> or of a classical
> island mute
> with fallen temples

Here Brenda's words are taken from a draft poem in her notebook:

> The dream sometimes of the desert, true
> desert built of sand and of silence;
> fallen colonnades, a bony rock in a bronze
> untravelled sea ...[57]

In the same series is a portrait of Sybille and a self-portrait *Free and with Wings*. This surreal image shows Brenda's disembodied head resting on a rock shape. There are two eyes in her hair and decorated wings attached to the back of her head. The whole image floats in front of a vividly coloured triangular patterned background. In other works, rams' heads are superimposed on geometric abstract designs. A pair of angular birds stand beak to beak on a patterned ground in *Begegnung* (Meeting) and in *The Rams of Carreg* the stylised rams' images have been decorated with lines, arrows, circles and crosses. To achieve the textured background Brenda used the technique of frottage which had been favoured by Max Ernst and some of the Cubist and Dadaist artists. She laid her paper onto canvas and rubbed a crayon across the surface so that the texture of the canvas came through onto the paper. Then, to achieve the sharper edged lined of the subjects, she placed the paper on a hard untextured surface like glass.

With this series Brenda began to find a new freedom from her usual representative paintings. Here, she attempted to express the content of her imagination rather than the world outside her. She explained that these designs '... are an attempt to forge a new pictorial meaning from a combination of music signs, a personal feeling from the colour and shape of words and universal conventions of linear draughtsmanship'.[58]

Brenda caught flu early in the year and wrote to Jean inviting him to join her in Germany, but there were floods in Paris and Jean suggested they both stay where they were until mid-February. She became miserable while she was trapped in bed by her illness and in her journal she wrote:

232

Self Portrait, 1954, ink on newspaper

I have an overwhelming desire to be BAD. It had become hateful to be moral. I long to do something positive, instead of drifting along in this fashion, merely suffering mental torture. 'Nothing happens'. Will anything 'ever happen'? Deep despondency.[59]

233

By the end of January 1955, however, Brenda had recovered and was able to return to her drawing. Then on a trip to the Schwarze Moor in the snows of February, she fell off the big horse-drawn sledge and broke her ankle. The accident did little to brighten up her spirits. On 25 February she wrote in her journal: 'Telegram from Jean: no need to be vaccinated. As if that mattered now. I wonder what he will do = return to England. Come here = or wait in Paris'.[60] Just a few days later, after hearing again from Jean, she wrote again in her journal: '... he returns with his "friend" to the island? She will use my air ticket! Speechlessly angry'.[61] Surprisingly, despite this upset, it was thought of Karl's situation which really bothered her.

> Nothing touched my heart, save the thought of him and of his children. One night I dreamed of his face: it was wet with tears; and the memory of the dream haunted me because I took it to be a sign or premonition of disaster, for the fact is that, knowing the children to be entirely in the care of their feckless mother, and that there is a mill-stream only a few yards from her rat farm, my mind is prepared for misfortune to overtake them.[62]

While she was trapped indoors with her ankle in plaster, Brenda had too much time to dwell on these thoughts and she became quite depressed.

> Quite emptied of imagination and emotion I pass the days in boredom. That inspiration can ever have visited me, seems impossible in this mood of negation.[63]

Because there were a lot of people living in Oberbehme, Brenda was never left alone too long but she often felt restricted and frustrated by her limited knowledge of the German language. Insea went to see her frequently and was always able to cheer her up: 'My greatest joy when K. is not here, is to be with Insea.'[64] Brenda attempted to carry on with her drawings which she wanted to finish in time for her next exhibition at Gimpel Fils in May, but she was feeling so low in spirits that her progress was slow. However, she did produce a striking portrait of Insea. It is a finely observed line drawing, making full advantage of the frottaged background. The elongated head and the lines of the coat collar are reminiscent of some of Modigliani's drawings. Although at first Insea had been a reluctant model, the resultant drawing pleased Brenda at a time when little gave her pleasure.

As the end of her stay in Germany neared, Brenda had to face her relationship with Jean. She sat down with Karl and talked about what she should do. He suggested that she should stay for a month in London, and perhaps rent a room and finish her drawings there before making any further decisions.

A few days later Brenda left Germany for London, where she stayed with Kaye and Charles Gimpel. They made her welcome in their busy flat, but Brenda withdrew into herself, and apart from going to see art exhibitions, she spent her days curled up in a chair, reading. The Gimpels introduced her to many of their friends and she took a particular liking to one couple, Sheila and Clement Mundle, who lived in Bangor, where Clement lectured in the Philosophy Department of the University. The Mundles took an interest in Brenda's painting and they invited her to visit them the next time she was in Bangor.

Brenda found it difficult to work in London and returned to Bardsey. Although she eventually forgave Jean for giving her air ticket away to another woman, her trust in him was broken and their relationship was strained. Since Jean had been teaching and Brenda had been spending more time in Germany they spent less time on the island together now, and Brenda relied more and more on her island neighbours to care for the animals in their absence.

Soon after she returned, Brenda heard that she had won a commission of £100 to paint a mural for the Wales Gas Board in Swansea. It was to be for a new building in the Kingsway and at 10 ft x 8 ft (about 305 x 244 cm) would be the biggest painting she had attempted so far. As Carreg Fawr was too small for the execution of such a painting, Brenda found a temporary studio in Dean Street, Bangor, and arranged to stay with her mother for the months it would need to complete. She spent a lot of time preparing her drawings and developing cartoons drawn to scale. Her brief was to paint a bright, colourful mural and she chose as her theme 'The Child Music Makers'. It showed a young man playing a stringed instrument, watched by a rather solemn young woman. Both figures were seated against a rather abstract background of building and stairway in distinctly Fifties style.

Because the mural was so big, Brenda worked on it flat on the floor. For weeks she planned the design in meticulous detail and her studio became cluttered with sheets of drawings and designs. There were small-scale drawings of the composition, full size studies of the heads of the girl and boy, and small versions in different colour combinations. Until she had every detail complete, Brenda did not want to begin scaling-up the design to its full size.

The Rams of Carreg, 1955, wax crayon on paper

Eventually she began painting, still working with the board flat on the floor. When she stood it upright, however, she was disappointed by the results. The shapes of the figures seemed distorted and much of the drawing needed readjusting. Unfortunately she had to leave the mural uncorrected and go to London for the opening of her exhibition at Gimpel Fils. Twenty-three of her German works were shown, but they were not particularly well received. Brenda's earlier figurative style had been popular, but this most recent work did not sell well and Brenda's work was no longer considered to be in keeping with the house style of Gimpel Fils. This was to be her last exhibition at the Gallery.

Despite her efforts to create a new pictorial language, she discovered that it was not one easily understood or appreciated by others. However, there can be no doubt that this work was significant in Brenda's development. It allowed her to break away from the confines of figurative painting and experience a freedom of line and image which she had not enjoyed before. Although her response to the exhibition was to review the direction her work was taking, Brenda suppressed any self-doubt and rushed back to Bangor to immerse herself in work on her mural.

Once she had realigned the drawing, Brenda worked quickly and completed the mural within a month. She was pleasantly surprised by the result and particularly liked the girl's head. The finished work – in deep reds, blues, brown and black – was mounted in place in December 1955 but has since been dismantled. Some studies for the mural are in private collections.

Brenda had been away from Bardsey for some time and now, despite the cold weather, she wanted to spend some time there. A distance had developed between her and Jean especially since he had been teaching on the mainland and spending time in Paris. Brenda was forty-three and Jean still an attractive man of thirty-two, and despite their recent separations, Brenda was shocked when she heard he wanted to leave her. Apparently Jean wanted to stay on Bardsey, and suggested Brenda should move from the island but Brenda was unwilling to leave and turned to her friends for advice. With their assistance, the matter was settled; Brenda was to stay and Jean to leave the island and take their dog although details of their separation are not clear as accounts from Brenda's friends are inconsistent. The outcome of the situation, however, was that Brenda found herself alone once more. In order to cope with the change of circumstances, she buried her feelings, spoke little about the incident to her friends and immersed herself in life on the island. She sought company by inviting her friends to visit and among them came Esmé Kirby, Sheila and Clement Mundle and her old friends from Bangor, the Daniel family, who regularly spent their summers on the island and who had recently converted to Catholicism. Because of its history, Bardsey attracted many religious people and it was around this time that Brenda considered turning to the Roman Catholic faith. Out of all the religions that she knew of, Catholicism appealed to her most although she never reached the point where she felt able to commit herself to it. She dabbled with some paintings of crucifixions. They were not painted in her style but were derivative of early Celtic art and it was not a theme she developed.

Since Jean's departure, Brenda had been finding it hard to settle into her creative work but the news that she had won a prize of £100 from the Arts Council of Great Britain for the typescript of her collection of poems called *The Green Heart*, gave her great encouragement. Her work had been selected from over seventy entries and the achievement both pleased and confused her. Receiving recognition for her literary talent raised once more the question of whether she was an artist or a writer. In the previous few years, she had settled with the idea that she was primarily an artist, but now she felt forced to think again. Once again she tried to work out her feelings by writing them down:

> Emotionally, I was always tempted to drop the writing, and to concentrate on painting, because, for some unknown reason, writing has always been for me an unhappy activity; while painting almost invariably makes me happy. But however hard I tried to discipline myself, sooner or later the other form would take over, dominate entirely for a time, then swing back again.[65]

Inevitably, after her literary success, Brenda turned her attention to her writing, spending time preparing her typescript of poems for publication. She also revived her interest in recording ideas and thoughts in her notebooks and spent many happy months working on her writing and enjoying her life on Bardsey. She was able to find adventure in simple everyday tasks such as collecting driftwood:

> The other evening, just before sundown I came to Ogof Hir and found it full of wood – Ogof Hir is a strange place, not steep but full of slime and treachery. It is fairly easy to get down, but coming up again with wood is quite a different matter.

It was so like a butterslide that I was obliged to come up on hands and knees, pushing and throwing the wood before me. I was glad there was no one to see me. I was soaking wet to well above my knees. After such a struggle and the faintest whiff of danger, comes a wonderful well-being. Then, it's good to drink a mug of fresh coffee and to eat a fresh sandwich filled to bursting with watercress.[66]

Brenda began to settle once more into the rhythm of life on Bardsey and for the first time in six years, stayed for the winter on the island. Frequently the sea was too rough to make a crossing to the mainland, the days were dark and it was often necessary to light the Aladdin lamps during the early afternoon. Brenda felt she could never take the weather for granted and found inspiration even in the heaviest storms:

I've been caught in a spectacular storm in Ogof Las, hail and thunder and darkness at noon – succeeded by limpid blue sea & sky towards Ireland – necessary to us, if only to convince us of our own being. Thank goodness, I love my neighbours.[67]

Two years had elapsed since Brenda had last been to Germany and in late March 1958 she went to see her friends there. She had missed their company and she found the trip happy and invigorating. In May she holidayed on the Baltic coast at Dahme and Grossenbrode with Ulle, Cef and their family. Brenda was amused to see so many storks' nests in the chimneys of the buildings there, and made copious drawings of them. Along the coast, there were huge

The Music Makers, 1955, oil on hardboard, [now dismantled], in position at the South Wales Gas Board Showrooms, Swansea

expanses of white sand which were littered with large bucket-shaped beach-chairs and fishing nets hung out to dry. These new sights inspired Brenda and she began to plan paintings to work on once she returned to Wales. She was still in the Baltic when her book *The Green Heart* was published by Oxford University Press. It was widely and positively reviewed, which delighted Brenda and gave her the confidence to return to her writing. She had also approached the Press with the manuscript of 'Silkie and Tide-race', her book about life in Bardsey, but they were not interested and suggested she try Hodder & Stoughton.

By the time she returned to Bardsey in early July, Brenda was bursting with ideas for her work. She immediately began developing a black and white painting called *Women in the Wind*. Two newspaper photographs of elegantly

THE GREEN HEART - IV

ON THE LAST NIGHT OF OUR PILGRIMAGE

On the last night of our pilgrimage
We come in darkness to a village
Beyond stream-linked marshes
Fringed by reed and iris
The sun and moon
Are water-doubled
At rising and setting
Where the wild goose speaks of you
You great armies asleep under water

Sound of the ocean follows us
From the shore where wave
Raises phosphorus fire
Like the body of Christ
Walking Gennesaret
In the fourth watch

House on the Baltic Coast, ink on paper, from
The Green Heart brochure published by Cidron Press

Women in the Wind, 1950s, ink on canvas

Cutting from newspaper used as inspiration
for several paintings

244

dressed women with their bodies curved against the force of the wind survive as inspirational material for Brenda's this work.[68] She copied the grouping of the three women as she had originally seen them in the newspaper, elongated and streamlined their bodies and placed them on a background of a large expanse of beach covered with handwritten prose, as she had in the earlier painting *Children on the Seashore* (1950). After finishing this work, Brenda turned her attention to her notebooks again and spent the autumn immersed in her writing about the island and revising her book about Bardsey.

[1] *WC*, p. 13.
[2] *WC*, p. 14.
[3] *WC*, p. 15.
[4] *WC*, p. 11.
[5] *WC*, p. 20.
[6] *WC*, p. 17.
[7] *WC*, p. 24.
[8] *WC*, p. 23.
[9] *WC*, p. 18.
[10] *GH*, part 1.vi, p. 44.
[11] *WC*, p. 18.
[12] *WC*, p. 23.
[13] *WC*, p. 23.
[14] *WC*, p. 26.
[15] *GH*, part I.vii, p. 45.
[16] *WC*, p. 26.
[17] *WC*, p. 37.
[18] *GH*, pp. 67, 35.
[19] *WC*, p. 36.
[20] *WC*, p. 28.
[21] *WC*, p. 41.
[22] *WC*, p. 59.

[23] *WC*, p. 21.

[24] *WC*, p. 60.

[25] *WC*, p. 81.

[26] *WC*, p. 62.

[27] *WC*, pp. 69-70.

[28] *WC*, p. 71.

[29] *WC*, p. 81.

[30] *WC*, p. 81.

[31] *WC*, p. 83.

[32] *WC*, p. 84.

[33] *WC*, p. 87.

[34] *WC*, p. 88.

[35] *WC*, p. 107.

[36] *WC*, p. 107.

[37] *WC*, p. 129.

[38] *WC*, p. 129.

[39] *WC*, p. 130.

[40] *WC*, p. 131.

[41] NLW MS 22494, f.6.

[42] *GH*, p. 76.

[43] Explanatory notes in notebook dated December 1953 in private collection.

[44] *The Lady*, 16 April 1953, p. 480.

[45] A copy of this letter was copied out in Brenda's handwriting in a notebook dated March 1955, private collection. The painting was bought by Henry Mitchell in June 1955.

[46] Notebook dated 5 December 1953, private collection.

[47] Ibid, Saturday, 19 December 1953.

[48] *Selected Letters of Rainer Maria Rilke 1902-1926*, trans. R.F.C. Hull (London: Macmillan, 1946). Names taken from letter to Clara Westhoff Rilke, 9 July 1904, p. 65.

[49] Notebook dated December 1953, private collection; entry dated Sun. 20 December.

[50] Ibid., 17 December 1953.

[51] Ibid., Christmas Eve 1953.

[52] Ibid., Christmas Day 1953.

[53] Ibid., 8 Jan. 1954.

[54] Notebook dated July 1954, private collection, entry dated 14 July 1954.

[55] Edgar E. Pritchard of Brownhills, near Walsall, made two 16mm films on Bardsey Island (one featuring Brenda Chamberlain), and made a detailed photographic record of the island in the 1940s and 1950s. Now Caernarfon, Gwynedd Archives, XS/2274/239-241.

[56] Notebook dated Xmas 1954, private collection.

[57] Ibid.

[58] Notebook dated March 1955, private collection.

[59] Notebook dated December 1954, private collection.

[60] Ibid.

[61] Notebook dated 3 March 1955, private collection.

[62] Ibid.

[63] Ibid.

[64] Notebook dated Dec. 1954, private collection.

[65] NLW MS 21501E, f. 56.

[66] NLW MS 21511C, f. 44.

[67] Ibid., f. 48.

[68] One in Germany, and one in private collection, Wales.

Chapter 8
The Eye of the Sea 1959-62

After a peaceful Christmas on Bardsey, the New Year of 1959 made a disruptive and noisy entrance. Early on Monday, 5 January the peace of the island was shattered by the sound of loud bellows and shrieks. The noise was first heard by Jane Evans of Tŷ Pellaf who was milking the cows in the field below Carreg Fawr. She rushed to the house to tell Brenda, who initially disbelieved her, as she had heard nothing and suggested that the sound had been made by the seals or the sea. Then, after a few minutes, Brenda also heard the noise and it became obvious that the blood-curdling wails were coming from Plas Bach, the nearest house to Carreg Fawr; Brenda was frightened. As the wailings grew louder Brenda began to think that her neighbour Bert must have gone mad.

Berthold Panek was a strange character, a young Pole who had come to the island in 1955 as caretaker of Plas Bach, which was rented by the Armstrong family. When he first arrived he was polite and friendly and had explained to his neighbours that he wanted to lead a life of prayer and meditation. Gradually he had become a recluse who avoided contact with all the islanders and left the house only at night. He developed an aversion to daylight, nailed blankets over all the windows and doors and even blocked up the chimney. Food parcels sent to him by Professor Armstrong were left in a tin box by the gate to be collected after dark, while Berthold would leave mail there to be posted and sometimes a shopping list. From time to time, the islanders would feel concern for him and try to talk to him through the closed door but he did not wish to communicate and was left alone.

Brenda and Jane felt too frightened to go to Plas Bach by themselves, and as all the island men had gone to the mainland earlier that morning, they decided to go to the lighthouse and ask one of the men there to come down and investigate. Brenda and Jane cautiously left the house together and while Jane stayed at Tŷ Pellaf, Brenda walked on to the north end. It took her half an hour to walk to the lighthouse in which time she had become quite agitated.

Bardsey Island, view towards the lighthouse from Cristin

She asked the men to send a message to the island men on the mainland for them to bring back a doctor and a priest for Bert. She also asked for one of the lighthouse keepers to go to Plas Bach to see what was happening to Bert. As Brenda's account of the dramatic events sounded so out of character with the normal peace of the island, the men took little notice. 'Two of the men there, laughed tolerantly, spoke of "women" contemptuously, and refused to send a message', but one of the keepers, Harold Taylor, agreed to go to see Bert.[1]

It was quiet at Plas when Harold arrived and he had to force open the bedroom door to see if Bert was alright. Bert was cowering on the floor with a crowbar in his hand. The floor was strewn with hundreds of cigarette ends and shreds of wallpaper torn from the walls, and there had been a fire in the corner where the Pole had smashed a paraffin lamp. Sitting amongst the rubble of the darkened room, Bert was a pitiful sight. Dishevelled and exhausted, he confided in Harold that he had been battling with the Devil all night and that for days all he had eaten was the water from boiled-up cabbage stalks. Harold went over to Carreg Fawr and asked Brenda for some food to take to Bert, before returning to the lighthouse to work his duty shift.

After his initial outburst, Bert seemed calm, but the islanders felt very apprehensive and that night they all locked the doors of their houses for the first time. No one really slept well. But there was no sound from Plas and Bert was not heard or seen till the following afternoon when he turned up at Tŷ Pellaf to ask Nellie and Wil Evans for some food and tobacco. He had appeared calm but as Wil was about to give them to him, Bert screamed, 'The Devil! The Devil!', prostrated himself on the floor and began to pray.

When he finally calmed down, he was taken back to Plas Bach while Wil went to the lighthouse to radio for a doctor. Bert was reluctant to go into Plas Bach alone for by then he was convinced it was full of devils. Harold later recalled that 'to ward off the Devil he wished me to sing hymns with him. It was quite an eerie occasion with thick mist and drizzle, a very black night with the fog signal moaning into the bargain'.[2] When he seemed more settled, Harold left the house and called in to Carreg to return a bowl in which Brenda had sent soup to Bert that morning. They were discussing his condition when they heard him bellowing outside and shouting for Harold. As Brenda wrote in *Tide-race*:

> Before we had time to do anything, Wolfgang [Bert] was screaming at the window; then he fell to beating on the door. The flimsy lock gave way, and the maniac was in the doorway. Throwing himself so violently upon Merfyn [Harold] that he was thrust back into the room, he cried hoarsely, 'Save me! Save me!'[3]

He could not bear the light and begged to hide in the darkness of the understair cupboard, then he asked for a gun and mumbled parts of prayers. Brenda recalled:

> We persuaded Wolfgang to sit before the fire, with his back to the lamp. He looked like an old man; his knees buckling under him. He shook uncontrollably, and was constantly on the verge of hysteria.[4]

As his behaviour became more unpredictable, it was obvious that it would be best to get him to the lighthouse where he

251

could be watched by the keepers. Harold persuaded Bert to go to the lighthouse and on the way they met Wil, who told Harold that a distress signal had been sent to Holyhead. At the lighthouse the men took turns to attend to the light tower and watch Bert, who alternated between moments of passivity and fits of screaming when he would thrash his arms around in an attempt to extinguish the tower's light. The keepers were greatly relieved when the relief ship radioed to say that it was on its way to the island.

Meanwhile Brenda had gone down to Tŷ Pellaf where she could be with Nellie and Jane. Wil had locked them all in before going up to the lighthouse. Brenda recalled how frightened they had been and how little they slept that night:

> We lay fully clothed on the beds, with lamps burning, listening to the dogs howling on their chains in the yard; to the roaring of the swell on the west side; imagining stealthy footsteps outside the window, listening to the beating of our hearts. We talked at random, to keep fear at bay.[5]

At about 3.30 a.m. on 7 January the Trinity House vessel, the Argus, arrived with two policemen on board. By that time Bert was even more disturbed, as Wil told Brenda:

> ... one whole side of Wolfgang's body was given over to the Devil, the other side to God. One side of his face was evil and twitching; the other side was smooth and placid. His legs shook convulsively; his hands were swollen; his eyes deeply sunken. He had stroked himself on the 'God side'; attacked anyone who approached the 'Devil side'.[6]

252

When the policemen arrived, Bert was handcuffed, and snarling and protesting, he was put in a straitjacket and carried on a stretcher to the waiting boat. On the mainland he was taken to a mental hospital for treatment.

Although the immediate drama was over, vivid memories lingered with the islanders for many months and the incident was soon woven into island folklore. Apart from the story being retold orally, Brenda decided that she must include a detailed account of the episode in her book about Bardsey. She revelled in telling the story with all its melodramatic flourishes. She traced Berthold's story from his arrival on the island to his attempts to reach his religious goals through prayer and fasting and his anguished battles with the Devil. Bert's religious fanaticism left Brenda distressed and frightened. She was particularly shaken as she had recently felt drawn to Catholicism and had been encouraged in this by the Armstrong family who were, in effect, Bert's employers. Brenda found herself questioning the need for religious commitment at all, especially if it could lead to madness, and decided against becoming a Catholic.

Soon after the drama of Bert, Brenda received an invitation from the magazine *House and Garden* to write an article on her life on Bardsey Island. It was to be included in a feature in April 1959 entitled 'The Islanders – 8 Famous People Define the Joys of Island Living'. Apart from the company of one other Welsh island-dweller, R.M. Lockley, who lived on Skokholm, the other locations were far more exotic. Nancy Luscher wrote about Dahu, Hawaii; Sir William Walton about the Gulf of Naples; Norman Parkinson on Tobago; Sir Compton Mackenzie on Jethou in the Channel Isles; Robert Graves described life in Majorca;

and Ian Fleming wrote of his north shore island home, Goldeneye, on Jamaica. Brenda was excited to be among such prestigious company. Her own account described the island, her house and the way she worked. Unlike many of the other islanders in the series, Brenda did not seek total isolation by living on an island and in fact she admitted that she worked best of all in company.

Brenda in Carreg with *On the Balcony*, 1956,
oil, gouache and charcoal on paper

I have been married but, alas, have no children. Fortunately for me, my friends often send their children to stay in the holidays. In summer-time the house and cottage are usually packed to capacity. Wet bathing costumes and damp, sandy towels hang out of the windows and on the clothes-line. It is when the house is full, and I have a fair amount of housekeeping to do, that painting comes easiest to me.[7]

Brenda rarely showed an interest in the art work of her contemporaries but when payment for her *House and Garden* article arrived she decided to visit St. Ives. It was then a lively centre for abstract art in Britain and apart from transient artistic visitors, the residents included Ben Nicholson, his wife Barbara Hepworth and the potter Bernard Leach. While she was there Brenda viewed the work of as many artists as possible and made numerous sketches, particularly of the fishing boats. It was a useful visit for Brenda if only to confirm her belief that she could not work with a group or school of artists. She saw her work as very personal and private, and felt no inclination to integrate and exchange ideas and techniques with other artists. Always needing to assert her individuality, Brenda wanted to be recognised for her distinctive style. She was in search of a new direction for her painting and hoped to find it in St. Ives, but apart from its obvious influence on the half dozen paintings completed on her return to Bardsey the impact of the visit was not lasting. In her painting *The Night Fishing* Brenda presented the boats in a two-dimensional manner with their hulls and masts creating curious shapes against the turquoise sea. It is a work which has echoes of the paintings of Alfred Wallis, a resident of St. Ives in the early part of the century. In *Seascape in Red*, the painting has become distinctly abstracted with an undulating cliff and hollowed out two-dimensional rock reminiscent of one of Hepworth's sculptures. But Brenda soon realised the trip was not leading to any exciting painting and she stopped working on these drawings.

Instead she turned her attention to a commission she had been given by the University of London Press to illustrate a children's story, *The Magic Journey* by Dora Broome, for their Dolphin Books series. Brenda made twenty-six drawings and coloured some of them with ink washes. All the drawings were vigorous and fresh and included studies of horses, and of children playing on the seashore.

Boy with horse from *The Magic Journey*,
1961, ink and wash on paper

Inspired by this commission, Brenda decided to write and illustrate her own children's story. It was based around a boy and a girl who lived on an island. They were called by the fishes and seals into the depths of the sea where they found the 'Salty Susan', a sunken treasure ship. Although Brenda tried out a variety of plots, she was unable to sustain the narrative and it turned into a rather weak story.

After making a few drawings based on her St. Ives fishing boats, she abandoned the project.

The summer of 1959 proved to be a disjointed time for work, and although Brenda attempted to rewrite passages of her book on Bardsey and experimented with new ways of applying paint, she found it difficult to settle to do anything. She had also heard from Jean van der Bijl's solicitor, who had sent a cheque for her from Jean and requested the return of some of his belongings. Although it was a relief that things had been resolved, Brenda still found the letter unsettling. Consequently, the arrival of the summer visitors to the island that year proved to be a welcome distraction and Brenda spent much more time socialising with them than normal. Some of the houses on the island were on long-term leases to families who spent their holidays there so each summer the island population would double and sometimes quadruple. Each summer there would be reunions with old friends and news exchanged over coffee and at mealtimes. In September a trio of visitors arrived and Brenda found their company particularly invigorating. In her journal she listed them:

The distinguished visitors to the Bird House comprised 'my friend Lambourne', 'Bill Badger Condry' and Kenneth Williamson, Chief Migration Officer [sic] of the BTO (The British Trust for Ornithology) at Oxford.[8]

Brenda was very pleased to see them and the lively exchanges they had on walks over the island improved her mood enormously and stimulated her to paint again. One morning soon after their arrival, she felt extremely pleased with herself for by lunchtime she had finished a painting with which she was happy. It was of three white birds and Brenda felt a little embarrassed about her choice of subject matter because of having three bird enthusiasts around.

Although she chose to live in isolated locations and frequently wrote of the importance of her imagination to the process of creativity, in fact she often needed an external influence to inspire her to work. On other occasions the boost of energy had been provided by a bundle of the *New Yorker*, a trip to Germany or the drama of Berthold Panek's madness. Brenda needed the two worlds of stillness and action, of writing and painting, of being alone and of sharing life with others.

Whereas the summer had been dry and hot, the autumn was very cold and wet and there were many days when the sea was too rough to make a crossing to Aberdaron. On one particularly stormy day when Brenda was painting, she attempted to express her feelings of fear and isolation:

It was blowing force 11 from the nor'west. I fixed the small canvas on the slate chimney breast, on the hook where my rosary hangs. On that terrifying day, it seemed the safest place in which to paint. My hand trembling under the onslaught of wind leaping the Sound. The storm had cut me off from my neighbours. I painted to keep up my courage. I had some months before built up the canvas with plaster which I had partially removed when it was thoroughly dry and stubborn to the knife. The remaining plaster became a black relief map of a frightened island, then I put in small red points of fire, signs of contact in the darkness. I thought the house really was going to be destroyed this time, the windows were creaking so. Those with cracked panes had already given way.[9]

This painting, *Bardsey Storm Force 11*, became the forerunner of a new style for Brenda, giving her the breakthrough for which she had searched. By expressing her feelings of the storm in paint, Brenda realised the possibility of achieving a more subtle and atmospheric treatment of her subjects. She turned her thoughts to the sea – the element which ruled the lives of all the islanders: 'Life on this, as on every small island, is controlled by the moods of the sea; its tides, its gifts, its deprivations'.[10] In all the years that Brenda had lived in close proximity to the sea she had never painted it, but it now preoccupied her, as she explained to Tom Cross of the Welsh Committee of the Arts Council:

> To paint at all is to be in the grip of an obsession, so it seems quite reasonable for an intenser obsession to arise from the first, by which I mean hammering away at one theme for a long time. I had been dreaming of a breakthrough – at last, after years of being surrounded by it, I felt ready to explore the sea (in paint) and the effects of light and sunshine and shadow on water, and on objects at various depths.[11]

Drowning had been a recurrent theme in her earlier poems and now she began to develop it in her painting. She became intrigued by the way a drowned torso could be transformed, imaginatively, into rock, shaped and sculpted by the action of the sea and the pull of the tides.

> I have lived for years in a world of salt caves, of clean-picked bones and smooth pebbles. I began to paint salt-water drowned man, never completely lost to view.

These are anything but abstract paintings. They are ledges of encrusted rock, an armoured leg braced in silt, the loins of a body changed gradually into a stone bridge, a wounded torso, flood-tide rising up the walls of a cave into the far corners of which a storm has embedded bones. In particular, there is the breast of the drowned, the man in rock, or the rock-man. A cloud crosses the breast, or a golden light strikes it in shallow water. Detached bones are set in violent motion by storm on the sea-bed.[12]

Brenda chose titles to suit these themes such as *The Eye of the Sea*, *His Thigh has become a Stone Bridge* and *Grey Breast*. For further inspiration she returned to her poem,

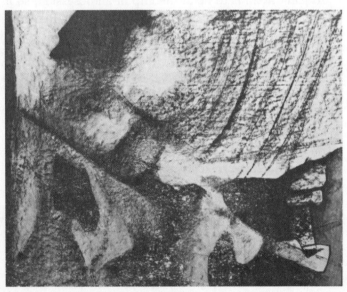

His Thigh has become a Stone Bridge,
1962, chalk and conté on paper

'Shipwreck Demeter', inspired by a news cutting from *The Times*.[13] Begun in 1953, it would be first published in its formative stages in *Tide-race*. The article described a bronze bust of a mourning mother goddess thought to be Demeter which was rescued from the sea off Asia Minor by Turkish sponge-fishers. It intrigued Brenda that although the base was thickly covered with encrustations, the beautiful face remained unharmed. The origins of the bust are unknown but it seemed likely that it had been lost in a shipwreck, possibly in Roman times. As she explained in *Tide-race*:

> For a long time, almost a year on and off, I was obsessed with the idea of a woman's archaic bronze head having been found by chance and raised from the seabed to strong southern light; theme, I suppose of death into life, darkness overcome by dayspring; the unity of our universe; under-water and earthly; the sponge-fisher and the goddess, the intact though shipwrecked woman's face, Aegean tears still wet upon her cheeks.[14]

This image influenced Brenda's exploration of the metamorphosis of human bodies in the sea and was one of the main inspirations of that period of her work.

She also returned to her stock of magazine and newspaper cuttings for source material to stimulate her imagination. For this series she worked with illustrations from scientific journals. As Maurice Cooke points out in his article 'The Painting of Brenda Chamberlain', her painting *His Thigh has become a Stone Bridge* is remarkably close both in pattern and format to a photograph in a German magazine showing a particular

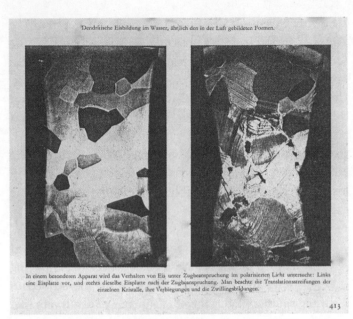

Dendritische Eisbildung im Wasser, ähnlich den in der Luft gebildeten Formen.

In einem besonderen Apparat wird das Verhalten von Eis unter Zugbeanspruchung im polarisierten Licht untersucht: Links eine Eisplatte vor, und rechts dieselbe Eisplatte nach der Zugbeanspruchung. Man beachte die Translationsstreifungen der einzelnen Kristalle, ihre Verbiegungen und die Zwillingsbildungen.

413

Source material for
The Wounded Torso of the Drowned Fisherman

kind of crystal, much magnified, and with special lighting.[15] Another pair of scientific photographs are obvious sources for her drawing *Study for Metamorphosis* shown in the exhibition Welsh Drawings (organised by the Welsh Committee of the Arts Council in 1963) and later developed into the painting *His Loins have become a Stone Bridge*, while a close-up of contours of a man provides an inspiration for *Violent Motion of the Sea*. Many more cuttings can be linked to whole or partial areas of paintings. Brenda had found a formula that worked and was squeezing as much out of it as possible. She was not scientifically-minded but obviously enjoyed working from these abstracted and textured shapes, combining them

The Wounded Torso of the Drowned Fisherman,
1962, ink on paper

with her themes of the sea and adding green-blues, grey-greens and brown-greens to develop depth and texture. Although the file of source material varied from photographic cuttings of clouds, to ice-floes, details of mouse-skin, aerial photographs of hurricanes and grains of crystal, she moulded them to express her theme of sea change.

Over the years, Brenda continued to keep a journal and had spent a lot of time working these writings into the manuscript of a book which she first called 'Silkie and Tide-race'. As she felt equally at ease with her writing and painting, she still remained uncertain on which talent she should concentrate. She longed to resolve her indecision:

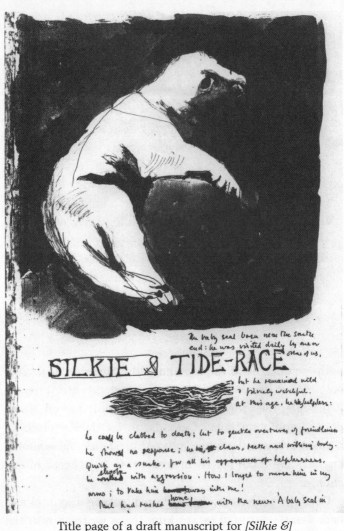

The baby seal born near the south
end: he was visited daily by one or
other of us.

SILKIE & TIDE-RACE

→ but he remained wild
& fiercely watchful.
at this age, he was helpless:

he could be clubbed to death; but to gentle overtures of friendliness
he showed no response; he bit, claws, teeth and writhing body.
Quick as a snake, for all his appearance of helplessness,
he shoot with aggression. How I longed to nurse him in my
arms; to take him home away with me!
Paul had rushed home with the news. A baby seal in

Title page of a draft manuscript for *[Silkie &]*
Tide-race, ink on paper

264

The struggle went on, a prose book on which I had worked for many years (in between painting) was to be the touchstone, the sign, long-looked for. If a publisher took it, that would mean the sign had come, showing the direction – writing was to be the dominant.[16]

In July 1961 she had a letter with an offer of publication, but it was not what she had expected. When Hodder & Stoughton agreed to publish her book, they also requested an exhibition of paintings to coincide with the publication. Brenda felt that the decision had been taken out of her hands. 'I was tempted to the belief that it was a sign from heaven; in fact, it was a wonderful feeling, to be wanted for both forms of expression'.[17]

As she had written several versions of many of the episodes in the book, she found it difficult to select which ones to include. In the end, it was only with expert guidance of her editor, Elsie Herron, in their long and profuse correspondence, that she was eventually able to make the necessary decisions. When all the illustrations had finally been selected, the publication date was set for September 1962.

Throughout the year Brenda worked hard on her book and her series of 'sea change' paintings, and stopped only for six weeks to travel to France with the sons of Charles and Kaye Gimpel. Brenda had been asked to draw the children in their French home and make a painting of them both. Compared to her earlier paintings of the same children in the 1950s, there was now greater freedom of line and composition in Brenda's work. *Charles at Ménerbes* incorporates the atmospheric handling of paint that Brenda had been using in her recent series of work. The sky is a

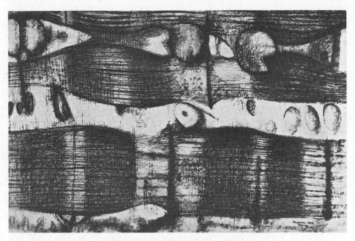

Flood Tide in West Cave 2,
1960, chalk and gouache on paper

blur of rough brushstrokes of varying hues of blue while the building and child's body are treated in the same textured style in ochres and soft greens. Brenda produced some exciting figurative work in France but this phase did not last long, as she felt anxious to return to her sea paintings and her writing.

On her return she spent the winter painting on Bardsey and then at the beginning of 1962 she went to Bangor to stay with her widowed mother who was now living in a flat in 6 Menai View Terrace. As several of Brenda's friends lived in this elegant row of houses in Upper Bangor Brenda felt relaxed and comfortable enough to stay for a few months. She was both surprised and pleased that she was able to paint there, as she explained in a letter to Tom Cross: '... apart from a brief period when I made a series of drawings there, it had almost been impossible for me to work in the "home town"'.[18] She went on to explain how

266

the 'sea change' paintings came to culminate her residence on Bardsey Island:

> In 1962, I had been forced to the realisation that life on Bardsey was coming to an end – but, these had been the formative years, and I knew that the island was in me for life and that wherever fate was to lead me thereafter, I should never lose the reality I had gained from it.[19]

Brenda felt a cycle in her life was ending and although she had no positive plans for the future she felt the need to move on.

> So it did not matter (creatively) too much that I was away from it = the body in the sea which eluded me for so many years had at last become partially visible, the surf-tormented caves so close to daily life were startlingly clear as mental image = all I had to do, was to paint and draw obsessively.[20]

Apart from a short trip to visit friends in London and Cambridge in June, Brenda stayed in Bangor working intensely. She had found a rich vein in her 'sea change' theme and she produced over seventy paintings and many drawings in the two-year period, culminating with her painting of *Man Rock* in 1962. Maurice Cooke gives a vivid description of the painting:

> ... we easily recognise that this curious shape symbolises a man's torso, and that the white which surrounds it, and through which one occasionally glimpses the red of the ground, is the sea ... The surface of the stomach is

fuzzed up as though the water above it has been disturbed by the swirling of the tide ... the sailor has become a rock, his form solid and immovable; but the flux of the water distorting the edges and surfaces gives the illusion of transformation in the act.[21]

An exhibition of Brenda's work had been arranged at Zwemmer's Gallery in London to coincide with the publication of her book, now entitled *Tide-race*. She felt the two belonged together as expressions of the sea:

Through the medium of paint and canvas I have in these latest paintings attempted (what I went after with words in *Tide-race*) to explore the 'theme of death into life', darkness overcome by dayspring; the unity of our universe; under-water and earthly. The 'gold-encrusted, bronze-breasted' man and stone, the furnishings of the ocean.[22]

In September Brenda went to London for a few weeks to set up her exhibition which opened on the 17th, to coincide with the launch of her book *Tide-race*. She showed eight of her drawings and seventeen of her 'sea change' paintings which were received with great interest but it was her book that received the most acclaim. It was finely produced and illustrated throughout with figurative line drawings which vividly portrayed the atmosphere of the island. Drawings of rocks, seals, fishes, boats, shells and the islanders themselves were placed within the text and there were colour plates of four of Brenda's paintings. For the dust-jacket, Brenda chose of her 'sea-change' paintings, *The Eye of the Sea*, a green whirlpool with the eye at its heart.

The book is hard to categorise, being neither fact nor fiction but a blend of the two. It is written not as a single narrative but as a collection of events and experiences taken out of chronological order and context and woven together as one story. Many extracts had already been published in magazines and much of the prose, poetry and drawings can be traced in some of Brenda's notebooks which cover the years 1947-51. It is a painter's book full of compelling images and poetic prose. Her characters are rich portraits painted with both humour and drama. Cadwaladr ('Bullneck') Tomos, one of her finest characters, is shown as wilful and independent, in open conflict with many of the islanders, as Brenda had discovered herself when she first moved to the island.

He could be cunningly aware of the feelings of others; he could show a grudging admiration of other men if they were tough-fibred and had proved themselves. He was primitive and self-reliant, with the qualities of an old race driven back on itself along the sea-margin.[23]

With the same vigour Brenda wrote her account of the Polish hermit's madness, the trauma of being storm-bound on the island for five weeks, the on-going feud over the island boat and much more. The book was reviewed widely both in Britain and abroad as far afield as South Africa, in *The Cape Times*, and in the *New Zealand Woman's Weekly*. In Wales, *the Western Mail* serialised sections of it in four parts and Brenda was interviewed for BBC radio. Although the critics admired her book, some of the residents of Bardsey Island felt hurt and disappointed by the way Brenda had portrayed them. It had never been her intention to give a factual account of life on the island, but although she had deliberately changed the names of all the people and places, the characters could still be recognised and it was obvious that the island was Bardsey. Despite their criticisms, Brenda remained pleased with the book.

Once the exhibition had opened and all the interviews were over, Brenda accepted an invitation from John St. Bodfan Gruffydd to go on a driving holiday from Switzerland to Athens. She names him as 'J' in her journals. From the start she had misgivings about travelling with him as she did not know him very well. He had been a close friend of John Petts and John had stored his belongings with him when he moved out of Tŷ'r Mynydd, but the temptation of a trip

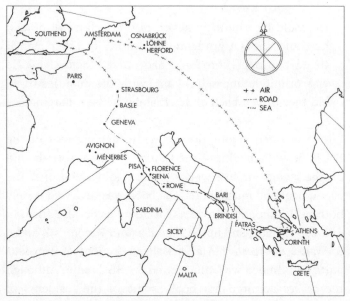

Map of Europe showing the route ending in Athens,
20 October 1962

through Europe was too great, and impulsively she went along.[24] In fact the journey seemed doomed from the very first day. They had planned to fly from Southend to Basel but arrived at the airport too late to catch the plane and were offered the alternative of a flight to Strasbourg the following morning. It was late September and the airport was fogbound. Brenda's journal records her nervousness:

> Plane delayed its take-off for hours. Pilot could not decide whether it was safe to leave the ground or not. This is my first flight. Ah me! At last, we taxied off into dense cloud. Was sure we would collide with another plane coming into land. The Channel was invisible, but I was soon relieved to see glimpses of fields, then the earth, then the whole land mass of Europe, thank God! [25]

In contrast to the cold winds of Southend, in Strasbourg the earth exuded heat and there were figs, grapes, and colourful flowers in bloom. After staying overnight they drove to Basel pausing at Colmar for Brenda to see some paintings by Grünewald and then on through the Alps to Geneva.

> The road became more and more sensational, on the brink of the precipice, a sheer drop into a gloomy gorge. I recognised les Diablerets in the distance, from the photograph they sent me after Peter P[etts] was killed there, knowing it must be that particular chain of snow-crested alps.[26]

By the time they reached Italy Brenda found that '[a]t last, I have got back into my rhythm of writing on a journey'.[27]

271

She had been given a notebook by a man she called 'M' and Brenda had promised to let him read her travelogue when she returned home. The knowledge that she was recording her experiences for a specific reader gave her an added impetus to write an exciting account of their travels. As the journey progressed, however, Brenda grew increasingly unhappy with her choice of travelling companion. He was constantly quarrelling with waiters and shopkeepers and Brenda found it a strain to be in his company. She confessed in her journal that she had made a mistake, she should have followed her initial instinct and had the courage to say it was not a good idea to set out on the journey with 'J'.

> It is bad for the mind to be exclusively in the company for whole days at a time with someone who is on another beam or wave-length or however one can express these things. It must be just as depressing for J to be with me, me with my superstitions and fetishes and myths, he with rationalism and an attitude of 'no show of temperament'. The truth is that he is a smouldering dangerous volcano while I sound off harmlessly.[28]

Brenda felt that it was now too late to turn back and as she became more distant from her fellow-traveller, she turned more frequently to her journal. She released her emotions into her writing as well as recording her impressions of the countryside through which she was travelling. As they drove south and it grew hotter, Brenda's descriptions became more colourful.

> The dark hours at Nervi are filled with the cloudy perfume of burning, of chocolate. Red-ochre walls and

blue shutters in the sleeping town. The warmth of the Mediterranean under the moon. Lapping of water against the rocks.[29]

Her writing was its best in her journals where pared-down words and images captured the essence, colours and smells of the places she visited. She was entranced by Tuscany and at Sienna she wrote:

Blue-white oxen grazing the Sienese [sic] earth in the evening after the day's work. An old woman who clutched a stick, and is wrapped in a shrill viridian shawl, guards her swine below the road.[30]

They moved on every day and Brenda found the constant travelling very gruelling. When they reached Viterbo, Brenda felt too ill to move and while 'J' went to explore Rome, Brenda stayed in bed for a few days to recover.

The people of the hotel visit me frequently, the women clutching their stomachs and crooning sympathetically over me, the men full of solicitude. The patrone came, shook hands twice with enormous vigour and asked if I'd like another pillow. Would I please take my temperature at five o'clock and write it down. Old women with brooms stand in the doorway, eager with sympathy. Outside the activity of the villagers is tremendous.[31]

While bedridden Brenda was able to catch upon her letter writing and to write longer entries in her travel journal. She was feeling concerned about her writing style. 'It must be good to write flowingly and with detachment. It[']s always by massive bounds and blank pauses with me, passion, boredom, despair; flutterings of happiness, memory and anticipation'.[32] In a review of *Tide-race*, a critic had accused her of not showing a 'blob of passion'. Brenda reacted hotly in her journal:

> Damned idiot, if I didn't produce that work out of passion I'll eat my only pair of good shoes. Particularly the drawings. I'd like to meet him someday when I'm in a diabolical mood (full of salt air and sunshine and general all-round satisfaction with things) wearing dark sun-glasses and my new green Italian velour, and ask him how the hell he knows they were not painted etc etc. This mood of spite and malice must mean I'm going to recover soon ...[33]

She ended her entry with a passionate cry: 'I hate to be thought of as sweet and gentle – I'm bloody-minded and obstinate and terribly sad and seething-wild underneath'.[34]

When 'J' returned Brenda was feeling better and so they continued on their journey towards the south-east coast. On 12 October they reached the Abruzzi, which Brenda loved. It was

> ... a riot of herbs and flowers, and trees with leaves turning to flame. Peaks, perched towns, the great plain it has taken 1000 years to drain. The road incredibly tortuous, to each town a climb, then a mad descent. Brown bears, chamoix [*sic*], eagles, wolves. The Wolf of the Abruzzi. Lunch in the village where Benetto [*sic*] Croce was born, a thrill for me – Croce one of my great heroes.[35]

They encountered rain as they travelled, the first rain on that land for four months. There were thick mountain fogs and although it was dangerous driving around the hairpin bends at night, they travelled on. As the days passed 'J' became even more argumentative and difficult and Brenda was relieved when they finally reached the coast and caught the ferry from Brindisi which would carry them to Greece. The boat journey took almost twenty-four hours, but despite the rough seas Brenda was relieved to be out of the car and away from the noise of Italy. As they drew closer to Greece, she felt increasingly excited: 'It seems unbelievable to be entering Greek waters, but the other passengers seem to be taking it quite calmly.'[36] She felt both exhilarated and nostalgic:

> The mainland of Greece – a dolphin leapt! Homesick for my own island at sight of the first small fishing-boat passing us, the men standing as they do in the Enlli boats, easily balanced and full of pride.[37]

Brenda was instantly attracted to the Greek people. She felt they were more dignified and thoughtful than the Italians who made her feel ill at ease. In her journal she wrote:

> The drive form Patras to Athens was like a frieze or an early classical poem. Transylvanian Gypsies and ancient sybils, old women in black, always in the shade of olive trees and looking calmly out of their wisdom and many years ...[38]

In Athens, she found the Acropolis breathtaking and spent hours in the museum admiring the treasures. A visit to the

British School of Archaeology brought much pleasure as there were letters waiting for her. 'The relief of having two letters from my mother was quite enormous', she noted.

> Having the home news at last was like getting the mail on Bardsey after bad weather – the same old clammy feeling in the palms of the hands, and an unwillingness to read the long-awaited words; because of a complex of expecting bad tidings or harsh words.[39]

In her notebook she explained to 'M':

> You will probably never be able to understand the basic insecurity from which I suffer – it is ingrained, a mental coal-dust in the skin – so that when 'J' handed me a letter addressed in your hand, the relief was not to be described. I simply clutched them and did not open them for a long time. It was enough that you had written as you said you would.[40]

Later that same day, Brenda and 'J' had a car accident. It was something that Brenda had feared throughout their journey. They were both bruised and shaken but not seriously hurt and the car, although damaged at the front, was repairable. Three days later, on Saturday, 20 October, Brenda flew to London leaving 'J' to continue his journey alone. Despite openly admitting her terror of flying in a jet, she found it far preferable to riding in 'J's car again. The great sense of relief that she felt about leaving, together with the unexpected stability of the plane allowed her to relax and enjoy the flight. As the plane left Athens airport:

The sea came up like a soup-plate spilling blue soup, then we levelled, and Italy lay on one side, Greece on the other. Elba, Corsica, Vesuvius under a blanket. The Alps, before, around, under. Mont Blanc and the rest, peaks black-purple, silver glaciers, crevasses, cruising at 22,000 ft at a speed of 425 mph. Blinding light, searing sunshine. After the Alps, solid cloud over the whole of Northern Europe. To come in to land, we glide dreamily round and imperceptibly through the cloud into dry autumn air. Made it![41]

Thankful to be back, Brenda spent a few days in London and then travelled up to north Wales. Amongst her post which had been forwarded to Bangor from Bardsey Island was a letter dated 3 May from her landlords at the Glynllifon Estate. It asked if she was prepared to surrender her tenancy of Carreg Fawr and Carreg Bach as it was clear the islanders were unhappy with the contents of *Tide-race*. Choosing to ignore the letter, Brenda decided that she did not want to stay in Bangor or return to Bardsey so began to plan her next move.

Before allowing 'M' to see her travel journals Brenda spent a couple of weeks tidying them up and adding her afterthoughts. She was convinced that her regular writing in the journal had kept her sane through the trip. As she looked back over her journey, it became clear to her that she wanted to return to Greece: 'A big part of me still lingers behind with the stones, the beasts of burden, the people: wonderful, wonderful humanity and patient pack-animals.'[42] Long before she had gone there, Greek themes had begun to affect her work. As she explained in an autobiographical essay:

I wrote most of the poetry with sea-connections whilst living in the mountains, but the next thread of movement in my life was already being formed, in such a poem as 'Shipwrecked Demeter'. The Mediterranean washed my dreams ... For a long time, the theme of a book had haunted me. It had to be set on a Greek island, in a peasant community.[43]

On her next move. Her mother provided the answer. One evening, while attending a social function in the town, Mrs Chamberlain met a lady who had a house on the Greek island of Ydra or Hydra. On learning that Brenda wanted to spend more time in Greece, this lady, Mrs Didi Cameron, suggested that she could stay in her house which was empty for a few months. With the promise of a place to stay, Brenda began to plan her return visit.

[1] *TR*, p. 205.
[2] Harold Taylor, letter to the author, 31 Jan. 1987.
[3] *TR*, p. 207.
[4] *TR*, p. 207.
[5] *TR*, p. 208.
[6] *TR*, p. 209.
[7] 'Brenda Chamberlain's Bardsey', *House and Garden* (April 1959), p. 71.
[8] NLW MS 21512B, f. 48, dated 6-9 Sept. 1959.
[9] Original draft in NLW MS 21515B, f. 48, of Brenda Chamberlain's catalogue essay in *Two Painters: Brenda Chamberlain and Ernest Zobole* (Welsh Committee of the Arts Council of Great Britain.
[10] *TR*, p. 14.
[11] Brenda Chamberlain, letter to Tom Cross, 12 May 1963, and draft in notebook NLW MS 21515B, f. 100.
[12] Ibid.

[13] 'Bust of the Age of Praxiteles', *The Times*, 5 Nov. 1953, p. 8.

[14] *TR*, pp. 197-8.

[15] Maurice Cooke, 'The Painting of Brenda Chamberlain', *Anglo-Welsh Review*, 20 (1972), 3-16 (p. 7).

[16] 'The Relationship Between Art and Literature', NLW MS 21501E, f. 57.

[17] Ibid.

[18] Brenda Chamberlain, letter to Tom Cross, Welsh Committee of the Arts Council, 11 Aug. 1963.

[19] Ibid.

[20] Ibid.

[21] Maurice Cooke, 'The Painting of Brenda Chamberlain', pp. 8, 11.

[22] Brenda Chamberlain, letter to Tom Cross, Welsh Committee of the Arts Council, 14 May 1963.

[23] *TR*, p. 94.

[24] Later, it was through John St. Bodfan Gruffydd that John Petts heard that David Lloyd George's widow, Countess Frances Lloyd George, was looking for a designer to assist in the memorial museum in Llanystumdwy. In the summer of 1947 John Petts moved into the house next door to the museum with his new wife, Kusha, and continued to run the Caseg Press from there. See Alison Smith, *John Petts and the Caseg Press* (Aldershot: Ashgate, 2000), p. 83.

[25] NLW MS 21499E, f. 2. This section of the journal, part typescript and part handwritten, contains many deletions and corrections.

[26] Ibid., f. 4.

[27] Ibid., f. 5.

[28] Ibid., f. 20.

[29] Ibid., f. 6.

[30] Ibid., f. 9.

[31] Ibid., f. 9.

[32] Ibid., f. 12.

[33] Ibid., f. 12.
[34] Ibid., f. 12.
[35] Ibid., f. 16.
[36] Ibid., f. 17.
[37] Ibid., f. 17.
[38] Ibid., f. 18.
[39] Ibid., f. 19.
[40] Ibid., f. 19.
[41] Ibid., f. 26.
[42] *AW*, p. 52.
[43] *AW*, p. 52.

Chapter 9

The Sound of the Ocean Follows Me
1963-64

Brenda was overjoyed at the prospect of a visit to Greece and planned to go at the earliest opportunity. As she had various projects to complete, she was not able to leave before May 1963. She spent Christmas with her mother in Bangor and began to prepare paintings for two exhibitions which the Welsh Committee of the Arts Council was holding later that year. Eight of her drawings had been selected for a group exhibition, *Welsh Drawings*, and she was to hold a joint show with Ernest Zobole, *Two Painters*. In the midst of the preparations, she heard from Hodder & Stoughton that they had accepted the manuscript for her second book, provisionally entitled 'A Winter Visit', based on Brenda's trip to Germany in 1952-53. This news increased Brenda's workload and before she could go away, she had to select drawings for inclusion in the book, and discuss revisions with the publisher.

It was a busy time for Brenda's mother too, as she was elected Chairman of Caernarvonshire County Council in March. She had been a member of the Council since 1940 and an Alderman in Bangor since 1959. In many ways,

Brenda and her mother were alike: they both had a creative inclination and a tremendous drive and enthusiasm for everything they did. But the way they applied their energy could hardly have been more different and while Elsie Chamberlain felt a sympathy towards her daughter's work, Brenda found it extremely difficult to appreciate how her mother could possibly enjoy all the committee and formal gatherings that her mother attended.

Once Brenda had selected all the work for her exhibitions, she began to make arrangements for her visit to Hydra. She learned more about the island from Henry Mitchell, the friend who had taken her on her first trip to Bardsey Island. By coincidence, it transpired that he too had a house on Hydra and would be able to travel with Brenda as far as Athens. As she did not enjoy travelling alone, Brenda was relieved to have his company on the journey. They met in London on the rainy evening of 24 May 1963 and flew to Athens, where the night air was balmy and heavily laden with the scent of herbs and flowers. Shortly after leaving the airport building

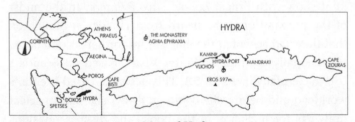

Map of Hydra

A near disaster happened – my case, and the case belonging to an English couple placed on the ground near the bus ready to be put away inside, were both picked up by a peculiar Greek with his belongings in the boot of a taxi. The man leapt out, and so did I, and we managed to make him give them up. He made a dash for them once more and had to be beaten off. The air flight must have confused his brain.[1]

It was dawn by the time they reached the city centre. Henry had to continue his travels elsewhere, and left Brenda in a café in Omonia Square, where she enjoyed a leisurely breakfast before catching a taxi to the harbour at Piraeus. The journey to the island of Hydra took two and a half hours across a calm sea. As the boat approached the island, Brenda wrote in her journal

At last, the port of Hydra was reached, a tight cluster of white houses on a long completely barren island, back-boned into naked rock. Barren except for a monasteri [sic] or two perched up there, far away from the town.[2]

View of the Harbour

As soon as she stepped off the boat, a man came forward and took her suitcase. He seemed to understand where she was going and went rushing off through the twisted lanes and steep steps towards the mountain. As Brenda followed her guide away from the port, she was almost running to keep up with him. By then it was very sunny and Brenda was becoming very hot and sticky in her winter clothes. She noticed that

> ... there was no road, only cobbled stepped alleyways between the huddled cubes, white and pale ochre, with the flat, red-pantiled roofs. We came out onto a dusty track covered in mule-dung, beside a water-course now dry and full of house-refuse.[3]

Brenda heard a woman's voice shouting 'Varvara! Varvara!' and realised that she must have arrived at the famous wells of Kala Pigadia. Brenda saw a young woman come out of the house and stand in the doorway at the head of a flight of stairs. It was Varvara Lembessi, a neighbour of Mrs Cameron's, and the person who was to look after Brenda's needs during her stay. Varvara showed her Spiti Cameron (the house of the Camerons) where she was to stay and introduced her to her daughter, Popi, and to Varvara's husband, who stood by the wells with his donkeys loaded with water tanks. Brenda was delighted with the house which she described as

> ... lovely and quite near the top of the mountain. The air is thick with the smell of blossom, there is a lemon tree just over the wall. It is a curious mixture of luxurious flowers, arid mountainside, and prickly pears.[4]

Spiti Cameron and the Good Wells, Kala Pigadia

The whole island is still one of contrasts today. Down in the port, affluent shops sell gold jewellery and fashionable clothes to the day-tourists and the wealthy yacht owners who anchor their expensive boats in the deep harbour, while the rest of the island lies virtually barren and uninhabited apart from isolated monasteries and convents. The island is about twelve miles long and varies in width between one and two miles. There is little agriculture or industry on Hydra and therefore most supplies have to be shipped from the mainland and in contrast to the affluence of the port, the islanders tend to live simply and frugally. But that kind of life suited Brenda and she was pleased that the Camerons' house was on the edge of the mountains away from the port and its 'unreal international set'.[5]

Brenda at the Good Wells, Kala Pigadia

Spiti Cameron was in the higher village of Hydra and directly overlooked the two wells of Kala Pigadia or 'The Good Wells' as they were known. They were a meeting place for the local community: the women did their washing there, the children played, gossip was exchanged and there was a constant procession of people leading their mules to carry their daily water supply in jugs and metal containers.

> ... the life of the wells went on almost round the clock, for the first water-buckets were let down with a clatter and splash from 3.30 in the morning until comparatively cool midnight.[6]

For the first few days Varvara helped Brenda to find her way through the maze of narrow alleyways, all without name or number and few with distinguishing features. As Varvara spoke no English and Brenda no Greek, verbal communication was limited to hesitant phrases which Brenda found in her phrasebook but soon they settled into a way of communicating and began to spend a lot of time together.

From her house Brenda had a clear view of Ere, the highest peak on Hydra, and she found the bare rocky hillsides bore an uncanny similarity to the rugged mountains of north Wales. She could see two of the island's monasteries perched among the high rocks and it was not long before she persuaded Varvara to take her up to visit one of them. Varvara explained that it would be a hard climb in the heat, and that it was best to go on mules. The following morning they waited by the wells for the mules to arrive. As they climbed up the mountain Varvara held a screaming conversation with the donkey man. Brenda was surprised how steeply the land fell to the port. 'It was wonderful going up the mountain, with the island unfolding, the harsh landscape, the herbs and flowers, and occasional clumps of trees'.[7]

On their arrival a nun greeted them and showed them the workroom where cloth was woven, before leading them to the sitting room where they were offered quince jam and a glass of water. Brenda found the monastery very soothing; the nuns were unveiled and looked happy, and she was attracted by the air of simplicity about their life. From the workroom she bought a fine white stole with a gold thread woven through it. The nun who had been looking after them spoke perfect English and invited Brenda to visit them again.

They returned to Kala Pigadia on mule-back and in the evening Brenda walked down into the port with Varvara and Popi,

> ... to parade like everyone else along the harbour front. Three tourist cruisers anchored outside the harbour. Many immaculately-white sailors. Varvara purchased her meat from her brother's shop – it looked unspeakably foul – hot Saturday night, with the meat exposed to the flies. She smelt it suspiciously, as well she might; but finally bought whole chunks of it. Then we sat at a café table and watched the world go by, Varvara greeting many friends.[8]

Brenda was introduced to one of the locals, Yanis Dragonou. He was a friend of Mrs Cameron who had written to tell him of Brenda's arrival at her house and asked him to make her welcome. They liked each other immediately and began chatting like old friends. According to the notes she made in her journal, Yanis had been an active member of the Greek Resistance in the Peloponnese,

288

helping Allied soldiers out of the country through Asia Minor to Palestine. Eventually he had been captured and imprisoned for five months by the Germans. Now, old and poor, he painted a little and spent most of his time in cafés and tavernas. Brenda discovered that Yanis had spent time in both Scotland and Wales and that they had been to many of the same places. They began to meet regularly and spent many hours talking and walking together and from him Brenda learned about the history of the island.

Unlike many of the other Greek islands, Hydra has very few archaeological remains and there is little evidence of early settlement there. The main influx of population seems to have been in the fifteenth century when the island became a refuge for Orthodox Albanian soldiers escaping from the Turkish occupation of the Peloponnese. In order to survive, these refugees from the mountains learned to sail, and before long, Hydra developed a strong fleet. The Russo-Turkish treaty signed in Bulgaria in 1774 allowed the Hydriot fleet to sail under Turkish and Russian flags at will. With this freedom and with the arms they carried as a defence against pirates, the Hydriots achieved a high reputation for nautical skills, especially in battle. During the Napoleonic Wars and England's blockade of Western Europe, Hydriot ships engaged in blockade-running during which some of the ships' captains amassed their wide fortunes. They built large mansions on the island and for a few years Hydra enjoyed great prosperity. Much of this wealth was sacrificed in 1821 to pay for the fleets which took part in the War of Greek Independence. There were many Hydriot heroes associated with the revolution and Yanis explained their stories to Brenda as he showed her their names on memorials, statues and streets that they passed by on their walks.

In its days of power, there were over 16,000 people living on Hydra, but when Brenda visited in 1963, the population had fallen to 3,000, not enough to keep all the 366 churches and monasteries in regular use. Hydra no longer had its fleet either, and there were only a handful of families who had their own boats, used for fishing on a small scale. By the twentieth century there was virtually no industry on the island and Hydra began to depend heavily on tourists to support its economy. Over the years, the beauty of Hydra had attracted many artists and writers and Brenda was surprised to find so many foreigners who had settled there. This international gathering of creative people excited her and she looked forward to meeting some of them and seeing their work.

Brenda found it too hot to wander far in the afternoons and so she tended to explore the island in the early mornings and evenings, allowing herself the rest of the day to write, sketch and take a siesta. There was little need to venture down to the port as tradesmen brought bread, fish and fruit up to the Kala Pigadia. Brenda used to look forward to their arrival.

> My favourite among the vendors is the old man who shelters from the sun. He is old and wrinkled and almost hidden by a straw hat, from under the brim of which his eyes glance up fearfully at the cruel sky.
>
> In my ignorance I had dreamed of a classical Greece, but in fact, this is already the East, another world than that of Western Europe.[9]

Brenda wrote down her experiences in her journal, as she had decided to gather material for another book.

It will be called 'Letters from Hydra' but it will really be an attempt at autobiography, nothing very factual, but I had to come if only for a short time to gain nourishment from my roots, snarled and twisted into the rock of Greece, deep in the red-eyed sea.[10]

4

Mist hung around the mountain-top and a chill penetrated into the weaving room where three nuns were working. Two were weaving, and the simple-minded Wrinkle-face was wool-carding in a corner, muttering and laughing to herself. From time to time she approached

the weaving-frames and put out a hand to touch the threads, but each time she was ordered to return to her own work.

In the middle of the morning, Rosy Pie-face went out for a few moments, and returned with the present of an apple for me. A clammy coldness grew over me as I sat in the sunless room, but I

87

Aghia Ephraxia, A Rope of Vines, p. 87

Originally Brenda had planned to stay for three weeks and that time was almost over, but as there were still many things that she wanted to do and see, she extended her stay for a few more weeks. This meant she would have time to re-visit to convent of Aghia Efpraxia where she had felt such a sense of peace. Once more she went up the hillside, this time alone, and with the intention of staying for several days. Normally visitors stayed in the guest house outside the walls of the monastery and Brenda felt honoured to be invited by the nuns to stay in one of the cells.

> I shall not easily forget my arrival, being taken to a cell, and feeling the inrush of air when the corridor windows and that of the cell were thrown open, and it was possible for me to lean out into the singing air towards the lower mountain ridges, the sea and the islands.[11]

She found the monastery extremely peaceful and even at 4.15 in the morning when the rising bell rang there was 'only a mouse-rustle, and a muted sound of water being run into a tin basin'[12]. Between prayer times the nuns tended the hens and the garden and carded, spun and wove wool.

Brenda [centre wearing a headscarf] with friends
at a café in Hydra harbour, July 1963

'There is no sense of constraint here. All is cheerful busyness, with spells for rest and gossip. It is a hard life which shows itself plainly in the faces of the nuns'.[13] Brenda spent her hours busily too and each day she wrote and drew. She felt able to relax and work well in the religious atmosphere and it was with great reluctance that she took her leave. 'These few days have given me an extreme happiness', she noted.[14]

Back at the Kala Pigadia, Brenda began to meet more of the English-speaking residents on the island. Many were artists or writers and Brenda felt very drawn to their company. The island seemed to offer her so many of the things she wanted and already she could feel herself establishing roots there. On July 14 she wrote in her journal:

> Following naturally the inevitable course of my life in Greece, as I knew already would happen last autumn on the first day on Hellenic soil, I am now part of a Greek peasant household having graduated from the solitary state in someone else's home, through retreat for nearly a week in a mountain monastery until I am at last in a strange cottage built half on the rocks with my dear Varvara who looked after me in the big house; her silent husband, her madly gay and temperamental child, Popi, and the grandparents. And the canary, and the cats and the goat Narita.[15]

Brenda did not want to leave Hydra but already she had stayed three times as long as she had planned, and now she was receiving anxious letters from Wales. The touring exhibition *Two Painters*, which she was sharing with Ernest

Zobole was due to begin, and she was needed to make some of the final arrangements. Reluctantly she left Greece at the end of July and went straight to Bangor. The exhibition opened on 5 August 1963 at the Royal National Eisteddfod in Llandudno, and then toured to Newport, Penarth, Bangor, Welshpool and Swansea. Brenda and Ernest Zobole showed twenty-five canvases each. Brenda's paintings spanned the years from 1938 to 1962, concentrating largely on her work from Bardsey. Soon after the exhibition opened Brenda accompanied her mother to a large society party in Bangor where she met the writer, Michael Senior, who had seen her work in the National Eisteddfod exhibition some years earlier. Michael Senior was a frequent visitor to Greece and when he realised that Brenda was about to return, he arranged to visit her on Hydra. She stayed only a few weeks longer in north Wales before returning to Greece, for as she wrote about herself in her preparatory notes for the exhibition catalogue, ' ... in Ydra, she has found once more her true element, where a proud and vigorous race inhabits bare-based mountains that plunge into the classical sea'.[16]

Soon after her return to Hydra, a friend of Brenda's, whom she calls 'Leonidas' in her notebooks, was arrested for the manslaughter of an English tourist in the port of Hydra. Her friend Yanis broke the news to her. She made him tell her every detail of the incident, which she later fictionalised in her book, *A Rope of Vines*:

An Englishman with a big dog, an Airedale, was sitting at a table in the port. In passing Leonidas tripped over the animal. You know how he walks with his head in the air. You know how nervous he is, how violent in his reactions. He flashed out sharply, shouting something about the dog, and the young Englishman leapt to his feet and struck Leonidas in the face. They began to fight, Leonidas pressing the other man towards the water's edge. Having his back to the harbour, the Englishman did not realize how close he was to the kerb of the paving. In fending a blow to his body by Leonidas he tripped over backwards and fell on the gunwale of one of the moored boats. He died soon after he was taken out of the water.[17]

In reality, 'Leonidas' had indeed been arrested for manslaughter, but the events leading up to it had been quite different. He had been on the Greek mainland, driving with three Swedish friends to see a play in the amphitheatre at Epidavros. As 'Leonidas' was driving quite fast along a straight road near Argos, an old woman suddenly walked out into the middle of the road ahead of him. On seeing the car, she moved back, then leapt out in front of the car and was killed. 'Leonidas' reported the accident to the police in Argos where he was arrested and held in custody.

Brenda was shocked. She had met 'Leonidas' on her first visit to the island and had grown fond of him. Suddenly, the tragedy of the event had intensified her feelings. She looked back to every exchange that she had held with 'Leonidas' and dwelt on every moment they had spent together. She desperately wanted to help him, but while he was in prison she felt helpless. A few days later, 'Leonidas' was allowed to return to the island on bail pending his trial. Brenda was shaken by his appearance.

Leonidas's house [on the left], *A Rope of Vines*, p. 105

Grey-faced and tense, he was standing alone in the bow of the white ship. He could have been naked, so vulnerable appeared his face. With staring eyes and puckered mouth, he stretched out his neck for a first view of a friend on the quayside. His shirt was dirty and crumpled, he explained that it had been borrowed from a fellow-prisoner in the jail-house. He, accustomed to appear each day on the waterfront as a handsome hero, had now a tarnished look, a kind of grey stubble seemed to have grown all over him like moss.[18]

Brenda walked up to Kala Pigadia to clear the jumbled thoughts from her head before meeting 'Leonidas' for lunch. She felt determined to stand by him in his ordeal. She decided that if she could not help him in any practical way, she would withdraw from the world, return to the monastery and pray for him. To Brenda this seemed the most appropriate action as 'Leonidas' had encouraged her to re-visit the monastery and spend more time with the nuns.

The day after having lunch with 'Leonidas', she returned to the convent where she was granted permission to stay as a guest for three days. The nuns gave her a simple cell equipped with a bed, chair, table and one cupboard with a sink outside the door. With her sketchbook, her journal and a few clothes, Brenda felt she had all she needed.

> If living and praying with the nuns leaves Leonidas unmoved and unhelped, then I make my care and prayer and offering to God, from the cell (my flesh) within the cell of plaster and wood, within the cell of the island within the cell of the sea.[19]

In her journal, Brenda was more self-analytical than ever. She began to question her own need for attention and her ability to give freely of her time to others. In a heavily crossed-out page she wrote:

> ... It can so easily be overcome or thrown about by one's emotions in response to another's disaster, a kind of neurotic vying for equal attention sets in, a sort of saying 'Yes, how terrible for you, but look, so and so has happened to me, me, me. I am a figure of tragedy too'. One tries/can try to deflect the glare on to oneself, one tries to use it for one's own selfish reasons, often of a tortuous, subtle kind too ignoble for examination.[20]

Rarely had Brenda looked so honestly at herself and this second stay at the monastery allowed her to do so calmly and without upset. In fact, surrounded by the dedicated nuns, Brenda found herself being attracted to their way of life.

> I am drawn equally by the two worlds, the sophisticated Agora and the mountainside moved by prayers. Now one, now the other draws me – whichever one chooses, it leads to a form of self-indulgence. It is only the safe middle way which calls for sacrifice and a life-denial.[21]

Several times while on Bardsey, Brenda had felt an attraction of Catholicism but had not succumbed, and once more here on Hydra, the balance tipped in favour of 'the world': 'I am too dedicated to life as it goes on in the world, to tempt myself into thinking I could make a nun of me'.[22]

About this time another letter from the Glynllifon Estate, dated 19 September 1963, was forwarded to her. This time, the letter was more formal and issued a six-month notice to quit Carreg, the outbuildings and garden on Bardsey Island by 25 March 1964. She tried to put this to the back of her mind while she was worried about 'Leonidas', but it obviously troubled her.

The journal entries of this time are lengthy, and as in earlier periods of stress, Brenda found it calmed her nerves, and allowed her to worry less.

> It is so much of a relief to put down even a page of words each day, it eases a little the trembling of my hands. I have always been pulled many ways at once, pity has had too great a call on me, but here in Greece I have found strength to stand hard-fast to a decision. How far can I bend before I break, how much salt water covers my head before I drown?[23]

A few days after Brenda returned, 'Leonidas' was summoned to Athens for his trial. Brenda called him 'a harried ghost' who 'flits from his home to the Post Office and back, hoping for news from his legal advisers in Athens'.[24] In a letter, he told Brenda that he had been found guilty of manslaughter and had been sentenced to either nine months imprisonment or a heavy fine. He had decided to appeal. Brenda, determined to stand by him, wrote him a letter every morning before breakfast. In them she told 'Leonidas' the daily news about his friends, the exchanges she had had with various Hydriots, the walks she had been on and the flowers and birds she had seen. Several of the letters were copied into her journal under her daily entries.

There was no exciting news to relate until the beginning of November when the Greek elections took place. In the run up to election day, police and marines armed with rifles arrived on the island. Brenda found the tension unbearable as she explained to 'Leonidas':

I am afraid of the police-state, of ships with loudspeakers that come to tell the people what way they shall vote, I am made afraid by the fear of the people. At night, in the deserted port, the police are much in evidence.

We were peaceably eating our dinners at Graphos'. Two policemen came in, one behind the other. For whom were they looking? We were the guilty, we were ready to be led away and interrogated. We were guilty because we dared to be individuals, to be free to walk about. He flushed, the man at the next table, frowning in concentration at his plate. He hoped the policemen would not see how his hands were shaking. He was on bail, we were, every one of us, on bail for nameless crimes.

Here within the house-wall is security, down there is fear and honesty. I try to digest fear and honesty. From my neutral vantage-point, I can see the how and the why of human behaviour conditioned by local circumstance.[25]

Despite the involvement of Brenda's mother in politics for many years, Brenda had not considered its relevance to her as an individual. On Bardsey, she was unaware of any restrictions upon her and was ignorant of political events in Britain and the rest of the world. She soon realised that in Greece, politics affected everyone, even her. In her journal she wrote:

The island of decisions? There can be no half measures on this rock, no poetic dreams, no charm. Beauty or ugliness, love or hate, you break down and leave it before it is too late for recovery, or you grit your teeth, clench your fists and hang on to what the sea has to offer and to what the mountains hold out in promise.[26]

The elections were held on Sunday, 3 November. From noon on Saturday until Monday morning no intoxicating liquor or coffee was allowed to be sold in any public place. Brenda found this unacceptable and in order to prove that she was a free person not restricted by the situation, she deliberately requested coffee at Graphos' Taverna, where coffee was not usually sold anyway: 'it was worth the danger, to see the pleasure of the two ancient campaigners in the sweet Turkish coffee served in fine cups'.[27] Later that evening, Brenda was delighted when her friend, Yanis, forgot about the proscription and ordered cognac from another taverna. Without comment or fuss, the proprietor served them cognac in coffee cups.

On the Sunday, the men went to vote in the library and the women at the school. At both sites, Marines were on guard with rifles at the ready, and Brenda was surprised that all the voters wore their Sunday clothes. 'There is an air of half-suppressed festivity, the peasant women are in high clackety heels and tight skirts. Lipstick, perfume, handbags'.[28] With the unusually tight restrictions on the island that weekend and the oppressive presence of the armed Marines, there was naturally a tense atmosphere among the islanders. Nevertheless, Brenda was horrified to learn that Yanis had been accused of bribing the electors. 'Yanis, one of the saints of this world, to be charged with bribery and corruption – what a bitter joke'.[29] Apparently, Yanis had been standing in the queue to cast his vote when he saw his landlord and without considering the consequences took out some money to pay his rent. Someone saw him and he was accused of bribery. Fortunately, it came to nothing.

They did not hear the results of the election until Monday when the ship brought the newspapers. Brenda and Yanis went down to the port to hear the news. The change of government from right-wing to the Democratic Party caused a great deal of excitement in the crowd that gathered and Brenda was surprised that there were no demonstrations when the results were announced. As soon as the news became public the crowd scattered, the police and the Marines returned to the mainland and life on Hydra resumed as peacefully as before. News came from 'Leonidas' that his appeal had been successful and his fine had been reduced. He would soon be able to return to the island.

Meanwhile, Brenda's book *The Water-Castle* was nearing publication and her publishers, Hodder & Stoughton, wanted to see her discuss the final decisions for the dust-cover illustrations. But Brenda found it very difficult to leave the island.

> For some years, I have been on the fringe of other people's lives. Now, on this island, I have found my way of life again, having my own table at Graphos', with my friends, my guests. I am sometimes in control of the situation. Often, alas, the situation controls me.[30]

Eventually Brenda did leave Hydra and she travelled to London where she spent some time with her publishers before going on to Bangor to see her friends. She returned to London for the publication of her book in February 1964 She decided to call *The Water-Castle* a novel and stated at the front of the book: 'The characters in this book are entirely imaginary and bear no relation to any living person'.[31] Despite this statement, the book is clearly autobiographical and the people and places do indeed exist: it is only their names that Brenda chose to change.

Unlike her first book, *Tide-race*, which took Brenda fourteen years to write, *The Water-Castle* was written quickly and based very closely upon her detailed journal recording her first visit to Germany from 23 December 1952 until February 1953. The story revolves around the triangular relationship of Elizabeth Greatorex (Brenda), Klaus (Karl von Laer) and Antoine (Jean). The action begins in Klaus's home in Westphalia, the tension mounts as they go on a skiing trip to the Hartz Mountains and the story continues and ends in Westphalia. Elizabeth's strong feelings for Klaus become apparent, which inevitably cause jealousy in both her husband and Klaus's wife. Written in the first person, *The Water-Castle* is a very personalised and emotional account of Brenda and Jean's visit to Germany. It has all the ingredients for a lively novel, but because Brenda adhered so closely to the pattern of the events as they originally happened, the narrative lacks an overall structure and there is no real climax to the book.

While she was in Germany Brenda seems to have been in a continual state of heightened awareness and many events and exchanges were seen by her to have a profound significance which they did not really warrant. In *The Water-Castle* she places great emphasis on details. When Klaus offers Elizabeth the choice of a red or white cyclamen plant as a gift, Elizabeth chooses the white. She justifies this by thinking of Klaus's wife, 'of her dark, heavy maternal aspect, and it seemed the red blooms were more suited to her than to me'.[32] White for purity, for innocence, for the memories of youth perhaps, for the young girl who met the German boy twenty years earlier. Perhaps because of this over-emphasis, Brenda's portrayal of her characters is uneven, with some of the minor ones such as the couple, Hans and Anita, and Kurt Hastfer being more fully developed than the main protagonists. The book was widely reviewed but was not as favourably received as *Tide-race*, and although the critics were bemused by the lack of storyline, they had praise for her 'lucid economic prose' and 'her artist's eye for detail'. It was because of the highly visual quality of the writing that Brenda was approached by the National Library for the Blind for the permission to transcribe *The Water-Castle* into Braille. Brenda was thrilled by the request, as she explained in an interview for the BBC Welsh Home Service when she returned to Bangor after publication.[33]

Knowing that she could not return to live on Bardsey, Brenda needed to remove her belongings from Carreg Fawr. On 27 March 1964 she crossed over to the island for the last time with two friends who stayed with her for a few days to help pack up her belongings. It was an emotional time, as she explained in a letter to the publisher and bibliophile, Alan Clodd: 'It was all rather upsetting. Saying goodbye to a house that had been home for many years – also saying goodbye to a way of life'.[34] Alan Clodd had written to Brenda at her mother's house in Bangor after reading *The Green Heart* and had expressed interest in purchasing an original set of the Caseg Broadsheets. His letter was waiting for her in Bangor on her return from the island and she read his request about the Broadsheets with particular interest. In her reply she wrote:

It was rather strange to read one item in your letter about the hand-coloured prints of Caseg wood engravings and lino-cuts, since we had just thrown the blocks in the sea, off Bardsey![35]

With this one action, Brenda had closed the chapter on her life in Llanllechid as well as her life on Bardsey Island. Brenda so looked forward to the future in Greece that she had no wish to hold onto the past.

[1] NLW MS 21516B, f. 3.
[2] Ibid., f. 5.
[3] Ibid., f. 5.
[4] Ibid., f. 7.
[5] *AW*, p. 52.
[6] *AW*, p. 52.

7 NLW MS 21516B, f. 10.

8 Ibid., f. 13.

9 Brenda Chamberlain, *A Rope of Vines* (London: Hodder & Stoughton, 1965), p. 24. [Henceforth *RV*].

10 NLW MS 21516B, f. 25.

11 NLW MS 21517B, f. 99; *RV*, p. 79.

12 *RV*, p. 80.

13 *RV*, p. 83.

14 *AW*, p. 52.

15 NLW MS 21516B, f. 129.

16 Typescript draft dated 19 July 1963 of Introductory Notes, in National Library of Wales, Welsh Arts Council Archives A/E/47/1.

17 *RV*, p. 70.

18 *RV*, p. 73.

19 *RV*, p. 13.

20 NLW MS 21517B, f. 3. What 'It' in the first line refers to is unclear.

21 Ibid., f. 93.

22 Ibid., f. 113; *RV*, p. 65.

23 *RV*, p. 71.

24 *RV*, p. 120.

25 *RV*, p. 154.

26 NLW MS 21517B, f. 59.

27 *RV*, p. 133.

28 *RV*, p. 135.

29 *RV*, p. 134.

30 *RV*, p. 133.

31 *WC*, p. 4.

32 *WC*, p. 16.

33 Brenda Chamberlain interviewed by Wyn Williams, 17 March 1964.

34 Letter to Alan Clodd, 30 March 1964, NLW MS 23381D, f. 30.

35 Ibid., f. 30.

Chapter 10

This Island Burns Me 1964-65

A view from the mountains, *A Rope of Vines*, p. 87

306

On 29 May 1964 Brenda returned to the Aegean and to the rigours of life on Hydra. A Greek island might sound a more exotic home than one in the Irish Sea, but the climate was equally harsh though so different. On Hydra, the summers were uncomfortably hot and the land scorched and barren, the winters were cold with the dust-bearing Sirocco sweeping across the island. The winter rains were torrential, pouring off the parched land, swirling down the stepped streets and filling the river-beds, which were dry for the rest of the year. Slime and mud washed down the hillsides making the steps and alleyways slippery, dangerous and sometimes virtually impassable.

Apart from the climate, it was a much more challenging place for Brenda to live than either Llanllechid or Bardsey as she had no means to make a living. There was no land for her to farm, no means of catching fish easily and no outlet for her to sell her paintings. The market for both her painting and writing still remained in Britain.

She returned to the island knowing that Hodder & Stoughton had accepted her third book, which she provisionally called 'The Pelican', based on her first two trips to Hydra in 1963. She had also received her second advance payment of £75 on *The Water-Castle*, and so financially she felt quite secure. Although Brenda still had to work on the drawings for her new book, she knew that the text needed little alteration and she decided not to work on it straight away but to make some more drawings of a dancer, Robertos Saragas, who was on the island that summer.

Before she had gone to London, she had seen him dance in the moonlight on a terrace and had been entranced by his vigour and energy. He was a close friend of the Greek Cypriot artist, Marios Loizides and the Canadian writer, Roger

Robertos Saragas rehearsing

Maybank, who had befriended Brenda on the island. She
persuaded them to introduce her to Robertos because she felt
a compulsion to draw him while he was dancing. Robertos was
flattered by her attention and agreed to let her watch him
rehearse. He was preparing some new choreography for a
dance recital which he had been invited to perform at The
LAMDA Theatre Club in London that autumn.

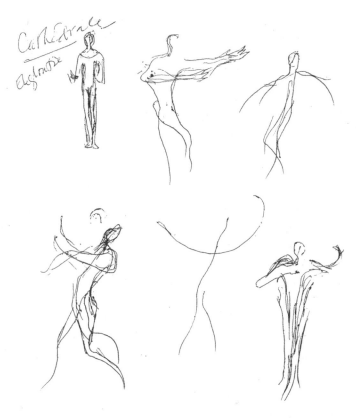

A drawing of Robertos dancing to *La Cathédrale Engloutie*
by Debussy, ink on paper

Robertos was a handsome man who had been trained in
the Central European style of dancing by Mary Wigman in
Berlin. Brenda joined him at rehearsals where she sat in a
corner and drew his rapid movements. At first she was
tentative, and because she was accustomed to drawing static
objects, her approach was naturalistic. When she first tried
to capture Robertos's movement in her drawings, Brenda

realised that she was trying to freeze the action into one position and make it static. Gradually, she relaxed a little and allowed her hand to move more freely over the paper. She tried to draw Robertos so that 'someone looking at them could, with a little practice see what position the dancer had moved from, and to what position he was approaching.[1]

Brenda found this challenge very demanding and was absorbed for hours, drawing the same movements over and over as Robertos rehearsed. Inevitably, she became more involved with Robertos's project and suggested that she write some poems which could be read while he danced. They tried this and were both excited by the effect. Very quickly, the performance evolved into a multi-faceted performance. Marios Loizides suggested that his friend, the actress Dorothy Tutin, might agree to read the poetry and Michael Senior, a friend of Brenda's who was visiting from Wales, offered to write some new poetry for the performance. Many long conversations took place in candle-lit tavernas, plans were made and rehearsals went ahead with great enthusiasm and dedication.

Robertos shared his enthusiasm with a friend:

> This madwoman with whom like two mad birds from morning till nearly dawn I engage in thoughts and in rehearsal and I am very happy indeed with all the results I have had up to the moment. I am glad to say she has written some wonderful poetry adapted to the choreographies, apart from some new dances, we made directly inspired poetry and movement together after midnight in this wonderful blue sky of the Aegean.[2]

Many of their mutual friends have said how alike Brenda and Robertos were, although the pair would always deny it. As a mutual friend, Roger Maybank explained:

> They both claimed to be straightforward. They both thought they were, but really they worked like snakes, never moving in a straight line and always taking a roundabout way of doing things. They were both spirited, loved dramatic actions and would often get angry with one another. Brenda was always running to me or Marios to say, 'He's impossible! I'll kill him! ... but he is a charming man and such a genius!' Robertos likewise would do the same about Brenda, 'I'll kill her! ... She's impossible! ... but such a lovely lady'.[3]

Despite their clashes, in those spring and summer months, Brenda and Robertos were virtually inseparable and rehearsed together for hours every day. Some days they worked indoors, sometimes down on the terraces or up on the mountainside, always searching for the right space and atmosphere in which to work. The place where they spent most of their time was the house of Janette Read who lived in the Kaminia area of the island. While she was away Brenda and Robertos rehearsed in a large room in her house. Brenda described it as 'a huge sort of barn, snowy-whitewashed rough stone walls, almost bare, rough wooden floor and a Byzantine chandelier hanging'.[4]

At that time Brenda was working on a new poem, 'The Cock, which had been telling of dawn', to accompany a dance choreographed by Robertos. Brenda experienced difficulties working in this new form but reassured herself:

Of course, when Dorothy Tutin takes over the words, they will come to life – I can't believe that what I now see taking shape, above the night-sea, among the harsh rocks, will eventually be a performance on the London stage.[5]

It was a period of great stimulation for her:

It is the happiest summer of my time on earth! No time can be happier – or more human, more pagan, or more difficult at times almost impossible to bear.[6]

When Janette Read returned, she was so intrigued by the progress of their work that she suggested that they continue to rehearse there. Sometimes they would work into the early hours. One morning, Janette found a note from Brenda: 'Today, he's danced superbly', and discovered two large drawings of Robertos painted directly onto the walls.[7] They are vigorous free drawings full of energy and feeling. In one, Robertos crouches with his head thrown back and arm outstretched. The other shows him with cleft feet and an angular extended head-dress. Apparently Robertos had declared 'I feel like I am dancing like a goat. I have goat's feet', and in her exuberance Brenda added them in this second drawing.[8] Fortunately, Janette liked the drawings and they are still in place in the house.

In between rehearsals Brenda busied herself with the task of correcting the typescript of her third book and sketching the local people and houses to illustrate it. She wanted to finish it in November so that she could take it with her when she went to London for the performance of *The Dance Recital*. Some days the rehearsals flowed smoothly but on other days Robertos would be tired, moody and

Drawing of
Robertos on the
wall of Janette
Read's house,
Kamini,
Hydra, 1964

totally un-cooperative. By the end of June they had begun
work on a new dance called *Apollo*. It was based on a series
of poems written by Michael Senior and Brenda had the
idea that Robertos could recite the poetry as he danced.
Three poems were used out of a cycle of five based on the
traditional five Pythian songs sung at the games which were
held every four years at the sanctuary of Apollo at Delphi.
At first Michael read the words over and over as Robertos
danced and then gradually Robertos began to speak the
words with Michael. It was an arduous process as Brenda
describes in her journal:

It begins, with pluckings at the sky, fistfuls of air drawn on an O of breath, for the rock has need of oxygen, the blue is grasped at, the feet stamp, the god is being invoked. The words come haltingly, with passion and difficulty, and very slowly, the gestures grow, are abandoned, returned to, modified, made concrete. The god and the identifying man fuse, leaving only a strong loneliness outside Arachorn [sic].[9]

Robertos was very obstinate and often provoked Brenda. If he sensed opposition in her he would deliberately mispronounce the poetry. They began to argue about the interpretation of the piece and Brenda described him as 'spoilt boy bastard worst in Athens' in the same breath as 'pure vibrant dancer'.[10] The creativity of the one fed off the mood of the other. Brenda's ragged badly constructed sketches mirrored Robertos's fits of bad-tempered stamping and shouting. When he moved with all the magnificent, exuberant energy of a brilliant dancer, a fluid, vigorous drawing would result.

They were preparing ten pieces to perform in *The Dance Recital*, four of which would be performed with poetry. Brenda was particularly sensitive about the interpretation of these, and at times felt oppressed by her involvement. So whereas she found *Apollo* both arduous and rewarding to work on, the piece *Cathédrale Engloutie*, danced to music by Debussy, caused her no conflict at all and the rehearsals for it were smooth and free of arguments. She felt the freedom just to sit and record the movements. By that time she had developed her own form of dance notation which blended words with drawings to capture the movements. Her notebooks became filled with this dance shorthand. For *Cathédrale Engloutie* her words began:

314

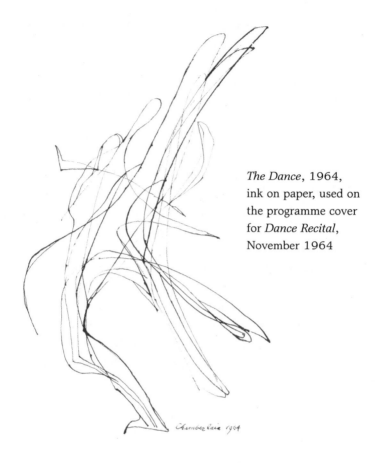

The Dance, 1964,
ink on paper, used on
the programme cover
for *Dance Recital*,
November 1964

opens as it finishes
positive and negative electricity
the rigid body, the vibrating hands

Interspersed with drawings, it continues:

The great swinging of the bell and the throwing down of
the body and rising up to full stretch and then round and

round to fixed position on raised heels. the grieving
body, one hand to earth, the other to heaven raised –
Back to door – and out, with outstretched wings of
purple cloth, to kneel and sway clutching and then
benediction!
back to start.[11]

During that summer Brenda was introduced to the Egyptian
composer, Halim El-Dabh, who was staying on Hydra for a
short time while composing a piece of electronic music,
'Theodora in Byzantium', for the Athens Festival of 1965.
He had previously composed the music for three of Martha
Graham's dance works including 'Clytemnestra', and was
interested to hear how Brenda and Robertos had been
combining dance and music with poetry and drawing.
When Brenda showed him her dance drawings, Halim felt
immediately drawn to them and asked if she would like to
take part in an experiment with him. He wanted her to
sketch freely as he played his own composition on the
piano. A similar experiment with the Japanese-American
sculptor, Noguchi, had not produced very good results but
he felt keen to try again with Brenda.

On the evening of 1 October 1964 they sat drinking ouzo
while Halim outlined the story behind 'Theodora in
Byzantium'. It was the early hours of the morning before
they began the experiment. Halim played a simple short
earlier composition on the piano while Brenda scribbled in
her notebook but the results were not very interesting.
However, when he began playing from 'Theodora in
Byzantium', Brenda felt a direct response, 'as though I was
a machine recording each individual note'.[12] Afterwards,
Brenda felt very tired but was intrigued when Halim placed

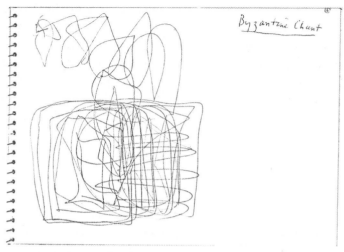

A page from a music notebook showing
Byzantine Chant, ink on paper

her notepad on the piano and was able to play passages
from her notations. She was excited with the results, but
because she could not follow his reinterpretation of her
notations she was not fully convinced that the results were
valid. She asked Halim if they could repeat the experiment
and they met again two days later.

This time, Brenda was more relaxed and found herself much
more responsive to the music: 'I can almost but not quite
anticipate what notes will fall from his hands – *there* is the
tension probably – I am like an electric wire waiting to be
vibrated'.[13] Halim began to play the Overture, then on
through Byzantine Chant, Bells, Chorus, Love Duet and other
parts of 'Theodora in Byzantium'. Brenda recorded each piece
over several sheets of her small notepad indicating with
arrows in which direction the music flowed. With these works
the line flowed continuously interlocking and criss-crossing

across the page. When he had finished playing Halim looked at the drawings and without hesitation he wrote the titles in the corners of the pages and went to the piano and played from Brenda's notation. Brenda was now convinced that the experiment was working and wanted to do more.

She arranged to meet him the following day in Athens at the apartment of Madame Mylana. She was a friend of Halim's and he often used her music room. On this occasion the line Brenda produced was less continuous as she herself noted:

A new form of staccato codation = I am striking notes on the paper. On some of the papers, a few musical notes are concentrated, passages being worked over and into.[14]

With some pieces she felt the pen moving quickly off the edge of the sheet while with others, it slowly pushed deeper and almost through the paper. Brenda was thrilled with the results of this session:

Thus far, the experiment seems to be successful. I had felt an absolute participation in the music; my whole body had vibrated with the notes. *It* was the most direct form of communication I could imagine.[15]

She kept a separate notepad for each of the three experiments in which she wrote more about her experiences. Although she wanted to develop the ideas further with Halim, she had to leave for London with Robertos, Marios and Michael for the final rehearsals of *The Dance Recital*.

The three arrived in London at the beginning of November

and began working with Dorothy Tutin. As almost half of the ten dances in the programme were presented to the spoken word alone, it was important to rehearse the poetry with the dance in order to maintain the correct rhythms. Robertos was temperamental, frequently arriving late for rehearsals and often unwilling to work on the dances to poetry. Brenda felt extremely tense and everyone was worried how Robertos would behave in the actual performances. At its best his dancing was breathtaking but his moods could make him wooden and awkward.

Eight of the dances were choreographed by Robertos and the other two by Nahami Abell, who had also studied with Mary Wigman in Berlin. The music ranged from Bach to a Judaic folk song, the costumes were designed by Marios Loizides and the verse in the first part of the programme was spoken by Dorothy Tutin. *The Dance Recital* was performed at The LAMDA Theatre Club on 14 and 15 November 1964, and although Brenda felt it was under-rehearsed, the performances were well received.

When the project came to an end, Brenda went to see her editor, Elsie Herron, at Hodder & Stoughton. Because of the distraction of working with Robertos and Halim on Hydra, Brenda had neglected her book about Greece and was behind schedule. Elsie encouraged her to make the final selection of drawings and they agreed to change the title from 'The Pelican' to *A Rope of Vines*. Brenda still needed to design the dust-jacket and she took the work with her to Bangor, where she planned to stay with her mother. Although pleased to see her mother and her friends, she felt distracted. Her mind was in Greece but she knew it was wiser to stay in Britain until she had corrected the galleys and checked the page proofs for her book.

The galleys arrived in December and Brenda worked on them over the holiday. By February, the publishers had pulls of the line blocks for her to see and – wanting to discuss another project with them – she made a short trip to London. She asked Hodder & Stoughton if they would photostat a limited edition of her three notepads of music notations. They agreed to produce fifteen copies which Brenda thought she might be able to sell. For a set of the 5 x 7 in. (about 12.5 x 18 cm) photostated sheets of paper, Brenda charged thirty guineas (£32.12s, or £32.60 today) which was an exorbitant price at the time. Without the corresponding music, it was hard for an observer to appreciate their worth and the initial attempts to sell them proved fruitless. Brenda left a few sets in the Times bookshop for them to sell on a commission basis, but they were not optimistic. Returning to Bangor, Brenda wrote to the Welsh Arts Council to ask for a bursary to develop the music notations but no money was forthcoming. Disappointed by the poor response to what she considered important work, she fled back to Greece determined to continue her project despite the lack of artistic and financial interest. Although beset by disappointments, Brenda always retained a strong belief in the quality of her own work, which gave her the courage and determination to see it to its conclusion.

On her return to Hydra she started work immediately on larger works based on the music notations. As she wanted to recreate the immediacy and vibrancy of the originals, she played a recording of an orchestrated version of the music while she worked. Although this helped, she did not feel the same energetic response and concluded that the most successful work would depend on her personal collaboration with Halim.

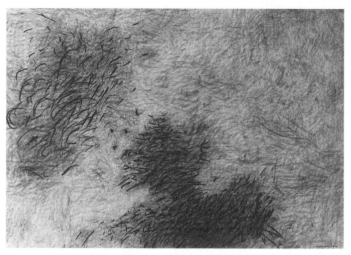

Untitled, December 1965, wax crayon on card

She was most satisfied with the results when she drew 'blind'. This involved drawing on a large card placed in front of her while looking solely at the original notation. Against a grey wax background she drew with an empty biro using it almost as a stylus to engrave the surface of the card, then drew over it once more with a wax crayon, describing the movement in a darker line. Finally, the drawing was polished with an old woollen sock. Although she worked through all the notations in the little notepads, she was not able to transpose them all into this larger size of 29 x 38 in. (about 74 x 96.5 cm) and was surprised to find 'that what appeared and still appear the most promising drawings never came to anything'.[16]

Although they are abstract in appearance, it is easy to see how Brenda had related her marks on the paper to the sounds. They are not merely doodles or careless scribbles as some critics have suggested, but reflect rhythm even though the musical source may be unknown to the viewer. Crescendos were represented by short erratic lines building up to shapes like mountain peaks and cliff edges to establish the increase in volume and excitement. More gentle and repetitive sounds were depicted with a softer, undulating line. Brenda varied the technique to suit the nature of the music. Some drawings are composed completely of short erratic lines, others are long and curved. There are dots, smudges, patterns and combinations all in monochrome. She felt this was as a result of living in a land that was 'drenched in whiteness' by the sun and the reflected light off the sea. She was convinced that everything in Greece was reduced to the bare bones and tried to produce this effect in her work by taking away all the excess colour and decoration. As she put it, 'I was not at all interested in colour because I was trying to make pure form'.[17]

After the initial rush of work on her return to Hydra, Brenda's output decreased. She felt vulnerable and clung to the company of her friends, spending more time visiting and chatting than working. She sat in cafés having conspiratorial conversations with Yanis and went for walks with Marios and with Janette. Halim and Robertos were abroad and she missed their creative company and for weeks she could find no inspiration for new projects. Finally, the idea came to her to write a film scenario. This would allow her to blend her literary and visual talents, and could incorporate dance, poetry and music.

Slowly her urge to work returned as she began to write on the theme of Orpheus and Eurydice. In the Greek legend, Orpheus went to Hades where, by playing his lute, he charmed Persephone to release his wife, Eurydice, from

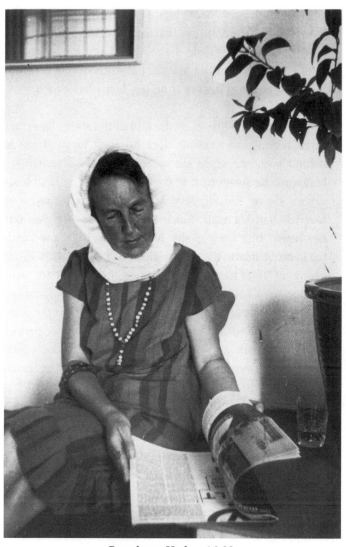

Brenda on Hydra, 1963

the dead. On the way back, he lost her for ever because he failed to obey the condition that he must not look back at her until they had reached the world of the living. In Brenda's version Orpheus rescues Eurydice from a taverna. As he departs, he is unsure if he has lured her away:

> He can bear it no longer, at the mid of the steps, he at last turns because so near his door he must know if she is behind him. She stops her ascent as his face recognises hers and she sways as if to come on, or fall, or run blind-driven down the slippery stairs. His arms come out towards her, his head snakes back; she too stretches out her arms, but slowly; she feels her way by toe-touch backwards down the steps, slowly at first, then in an agony of retreat, throwing herself from wall to wall, coming up a stair or two then going down. Going down. And he, the lover, does not move his feet from the stair where first he turned and saw her, only the upper part of his body, neck and shoulders, head and arms yearn downwards towards the darkness of the grave. 'The leaves of the tree wither from the weight of my desolation.'[18]

Brenda had great difficulty with this film script. Although it was a form of writing which allowed her to combine visual imagery, dance and drama, she found it impossible to combine these aspects simultaneously. She tried rewriting the theme in different ways but was never satisfied with the results and felt unable to give the storyline the dramatic structure it needed. This frustrated her as she had cast Robertos as Orpheus and was anxious to finish the script so she could work with him again. But the more she struggled to write, the more her enthusiasm

324

waned and she found it a relief to allow the celebration of Easter to interrupt her work.

On Hydra, Easter is the most celebrated festival in the year and it was impossible for Brenda to ignore the preparations and the expectant atmosphere. The island looked resplendent: many of the houses were freshly whitewashed and flags and coloured lights were hung in the port. The atmosphere, however, was solemn. In the first service on Good Friday evening in the church at Kamini, the whole of the island population was in quiet mourning for Christ's death on the cross. At the end of the ceremony candles were lit from the altar and the congregation followed the decorated Epitafios or image of Christ, carried by the School of Merchant Marine down to the sea. The men waded into the sea and blessings were made for the waters, fish and safety at sea, followed by a symbolic deposition of Christ's body into the sea. The congregation began singing as they followed the bier-carriers back to the church which they re-entered by passing beneath the bier held high across the doorway.

Brenda was stunned by the power and drama of the occasion.

Immediately after, shrieking with pent feelings, the women fell upon it, and tore off the flowers made holy by ceremonial (dividing his clothes amongst them, confused with the flowers made sacred by having being on the bier). Almost all followed the priest and the bearers, with one or two others, I turned off for home, and was able to reach the house-door with my candle still alight. Firecrackers and people passing home with their candles, loud explosions went on throughout the night.[19]

325

By Saturday morning, the atmosphere was more festive. People decorated their houses and bought red Easter eggs and long white candles. To recognise the slaughter of the Lamb of God, many lambs had been killed and were being killed and roasted over wood fires in tavernas. The festival was taken very seriously by the islanders and sometimes the hundreds of tourists who flocked to watch the festivities upset the Hydriots with their unseemly behaviour. As Brenda observed:

> A foreign woman in the pharmacy, wearing a green dress cut so low at the back, the cleft at the top of her buttocks was plain to see, shocked an old woman waiting for a prescription. She said 'Curse you, Curse you – and Christ not yet risen'. The young woman smiled at her, thinking she was being congratulated for her dress.[20]

Late on the Saturday night, everyone gathered at the church of Panagia Paneromeni at the port. Aromatic herbs and palm fronds were strewn in the white courtyard and the crowd, clutching their candles, waiting expectantly. Just before midnight, the priests, cantors and deacons came out singing and stood on a raised platform decorated with herbs and greenery. From a light inside the church each person's candle was lit, then, on the stroke of midnight, the Bishop called out 'Christ is risen'. At this moment Brenda recalled that

> … hell burst in the port. Sirens hooted, guns blazed, cannons were fired, fireworks, shouting, kissing – 'Christ is Risen. He is indeed Risen!' The chanting priests were demented, all rushed into the streets which were

becoming hazy with gunpowder smoke. The feasting could begin – 'Christ is Risen. He is indeed Risen'.[21]

[1] NLW MS 21520B (vol. 40), f. 42.
[2] Letter from Robertos Saragas to Norman Ayrton, copied by Brenda Chamberlain into her notebook, NLW MS 21518C, f. 56.
[3] Roger Maybank in conversation with the author, Oct. 1985.
[4] NLW MS 21518C, f. 76.
[5] Ibid.
[6] Ibid., f. 70.
[7] Janette Read in conversation with the author, Oct. 1985.
[8] Janette Read in conversation with the author, Oct. 1985.
[9] NLW MS 21518C, f. 51.
[10] NLW MS 21520B, f. 6.
[11] NLW MS 21519C, ff. 42-43.
[12] Draft letter from Brenda Chamberlain to Isabel Hitchman, Welsh Arts Council, 7 Feb. 1970, NLW MS 21520B, ff. 118-19, fair copy, ff. 120-21.
[13] NLW MS 21520B, f. 116, 6 Oct. 1964.
[14] NLW MS 21520B, f. 113.
[15] NLW MS 21520B, f. 113.
[16] NLW MS 21520B, f. 119 (draft letter to Isabel Hitchman).
[17] Brenda Chamberlain interviewed by Gareth Jones for BBC Welsh Home Service programme, 'Spectrum', Oct. 1968. Transcript in NLW MS 21501E, ff. 50-54 (f. 54).
[18] NLW MS 21518C, f. 81.
[19] NLW MS 21521D, f. 43.
[20] NLW MS 21521D, f. 43.
[21] NLW MS 21521D, f. 56.

Chapter 11

Love in a Private Garden 1965-67

The result of having experienced my first Orthodox Easter is a feeling of exhaustion, of having being caught up in a battle zone, of having been for days under constant fire, explosions of dynamite sometimes far, more often near, by day and night. In lulls between explosions, a terrifying silence, foreboding of tragedy. The weather also erratic: now hot, now shivering, dead calm becoming suddenly raging wind from the southwest. No escape from the tension caused by the reality of Christ's passion. Thunder, donkeys braying, cats screaming.[1]

In an attempt to transfer these feelings of tension to a productive purpose, Brenda returned to her drawing. She rose early, worked intensively until lunchtime and spent the rest of the day socialising and walking. Often around 5 o'clock she went to Janette's house for a chat over meze and a glass of ouzo. It was a creative period and while retaining the ink and wax techniques that she had used with the music notation, Brenda now turned to other subjects. Taking phrases she had overheard in the street or tavernas, Brenda attempted to interpret them in line drawings and compositions with titles such as *Cry like a Wolf*, *There's Been an Accident* and *They've Come to Take Me Away* began to emerge.

In May 1965 she moved to a house further into the interior of Hydra. It was small and very low with few windows and tended to be very dusty, but Brenda was happy there and found it easy to work. The following month

Brenda's house [on the left]

she began a series which she called *The Black Brides*. There were ten in all, featuring the Bride in an identical stance: the face was a black silhouette contrasting against the white of the bridal dress and a wide-brimmed hat. Brenda worked quickly on the series, which was finished within a month. Each afternoon when she went to see Janette, Brenda would discuss the progress of her day's work. She admitted that she did not know where the image for the series had originated, but that she found it disturbing and was bothered by many sleepless nights. During that time Michael Senior came on a visit and although he too asked about the Brides, Brenda felt unable to explain them. When he asked why the Bride was black, Brenda merely replied, 'Because she is'.[2] In each of the ten images the Bride is surrounded by an irregular shape representing the bridal veil, which changes in form throughout the series. Brenda added a cryptic commentary to them which hints at the reason for the subtle changes. In an illustrated notebook and on the back of photographs of the work she included more explanation.[3] Throughout the series she refers to images of fishing and the sea. *The Black Brides* are numbered in a different order to the way they were originally created, but the reason for this is not known.

The 10 Black Brides as displayed in the
Island Artist exhibition at Oriel Mostyn, 1988

'The Black Bride 1' is a black line-drawing with washes of blue-black and an area of purple crayon above the hat.[4] Falling from the hat is a bridal veil decorated with flower-like shapes. Although Brenda may not have originally intended it, this Bride is a self-portrait: the profile and the proportions of the body are her own. She calls this one 'La femme en cage' and adds 'On ne peut pas embrasser la mariée'.

The veil in the second 'Bride' has become more solid. It resembles a fishing net and begins to surround the figure. There is no colour, the profile is more pronounced, but the figure now bears no resemblance to Brenda. On the back of a photograph of it she wrote: '"C'est un hasard". She is entombed, must always look before her'.

In 'The Black Bride 3' the figure is drawn in black wax crayon. Her hand is raised to her face and a magazine cutting of a man's face is attached to the drawing in front of the Bride: 'The Bride confronts the Bridegroom and is surprised to see that he is the Prince Regent. La Mariée! Le Mari!'

'The Black Bride 4' is entitled 'The Bride Enmeshed' and is inscribed with: 'children have been menaced (before now) by nightingales, so why should not the Bride be made uneasy by a web of lace and artificial roses?' There is freedom in this line drawing, and while the hat and veil remain, the dress has become transparent.

The fifth Bride is called 'Anonymous in a Fishing Net' and is drawn in black ink and red chalk on white paper. The slender figure is once more in her dress and the hat has become more solid, almost resembling fingers on either side of the net, poised as in the action of wrapping a porcelain figurine.

The Black Bride No. 7, 1965, gouache, ink and crayon

Bride 6 is 'The black woman in a white shell'. There was something she did not like about this one and although she personally rejected it, it was kept in the series. For Bride 7 she wrote: 'The Bride enters the sepulchre of green Mediterranean light and roses grow from the sterile node.' In this free line-drawing against its heavily waxed background, the veil has now become a solid wall. 'The Black Bride 8', called 'The Bride entombed', is a collage of newspaper overlaid with wax crayon. The Bride's now rather pregnant figure and the solid veil have almost blended into one. 'She became entombed but the Bridegroom pressed close', wrote Brenda. The ninth Bride was called 'La mariée en cage des pieds à la tête' and in her notebook she adds 'yellow, bronze, dark blue, white rock'. In style and shape it is almost identical to Bride 7.

The final Bride is called 'Voyage sans passeport'. It is a newspaper collage and the most abstract of the series. Against the dark blue and red wax background, the Bride has been reduced to a white mass cut out of paper. She appears encased by newspaper shapes at either side and at the head. It is possible that the Greek and French headlines in the newspaper cuttings may give further clues to the meaning of this last enigmatic picture. To add to the mystery, Brenda signed it on two sides, leaving a choice of which way it could be viewed. The Bride has become one with her wedding dress. The veil which appeared in Bride 1 has now metamorphosed into a shroud of Bride 10.

The Black Brides is a melancholic series which Brenda found unsettling as it evoked memories of her past relationships, with its references to fishing nets like those used on Bardsey, and to Blodeuwedd as in her early poems, as well as its use of French words as a reminder of her romance with Jean van

333

der Bijl and her visits to Ménerbes. At fifty-three Brenda was alone and dearly wished she was not.

While working on the Brides series, Brenda also began a series of four drawings which she called *Love in a Private Garden*. In contrast to the figurative treatment of the Brides, this series is completely abstract, consisting of combinations of red, grey and black spots on a crayon-textured background. As the series progresses, the spots become fewer and move from geometric to more random arrangements. It is a curious series made between June and August 1965 and although it offers no immediate meaning, the drawings have a certain power and presence which is compulsive. How they relate to *The Black Brides* – if at all – is unclear, and as Brenda wrote no notes about them, their significance for her is not known. The series, like that of *The Black Brides*, stands alone, seemingly unconnected with the work that she made both before and afterwards. In fact, shortly afterwards, Brenda returned enthusiastically to her work based on music notations.

Early in August 1965, when her third book, *A Rope of Vines*, was published, Brenda received a cheque for £75 as an advance on royalties. Although she was adept at surviving on little income, the money was very welcome and allowed her a few luxuries. Life in Greece was proving hard – she had no outlet for her poetry or paintings and she relied heavily on royalties from her books. It had been two years since her last exhibition and the arrival of the cheque prompted Brenda to consider her financial position.

Sometimes, though not often, I wish I had a lot of money. Tonight in a cold wind, sitting with Yanis, to warm ourselves we drank chamomile tea laced with cognac, I

334

should have liked to have gone to the emporium, 'a thousand and one delights', and return with a thick sweater and a tweed suit for him, but then he would give it away to the first man he met. It warms one, to be in the company of a saint. He thinks only of other men's misfortunes, never his own.[5]

A Rope of Vines was subtitled 'Journal from a Greek Island' and included vignettes taken from her notebooks written during her first visit to Hydra from May to November 1963. Unlike in *The Water-Castle*, here Brenda did not date the entries or present them in chronological order and she made no attempt to weave them into a novel. They exist as vivid memories written in short lively sentences. It is not a relaxing book. Brenda portrayed the constant tension of Greek life including the domestic arguments which flared up. When her neighbour, Sophia's house was being renovated, it affected everyone in the area.

Sophia's cottage has been transformed with the maximum of drama and upheaval, in which we at the wells were somehow involved. The noise and the passion aroused was [*sic*] beyond belief.[6]

Compared with the virtually unspoken bitterness invoked by the family feuds on Bardsey which Brenda had described in *Tide-race*, the arguments on Hydra seemed to be louder, more flamboyant, much more public and were over far more quickly. But fundamentally their lives were very similar, as Brenda had quickly discovered. Both sets of islanders wanted to remain independent from the mainland, they struggled to make a living, and they had their joys and sorrows. Unlike J.M. Synge, in his well-known study of the Aran Islands, she was not interested in the anthropological story behind the island cultures. She was intrigued by the more universal issues of human drama and struggles, of myths and human exchanges, which affected people wherever they lived and whatever their cultural background. Brenda loved gossip. It broke down barriers and allowed her immediately to feel part of a community. To be able to offer a tit-bit of information gave her a sense of belonging. Whether it was in the house of her friends in Upper Bangor, amongst the islanders of Bardsey or at the wells or tavernas on Hydra, she very quickly picked up the local gossip and often recorded it in her journals and many letters to friends. She enjoyed the way stories were exchanged and dramas were elaborated and all her books are coloured with such incidents.

Brenda's selection of line drawings is an outstanding feature of *A Rope of Vines*. There are over fifty interspersed in the text and with her free, confident line Brenda takes the reader to some of her favourite corners of the island. The drawings capture the atmosphere of the tightly-packed houses and their steeply stepped alleyways, the nuns at the monastery of Efpraxia, a cat sprawled in the sun on a terrace, the bay at Vlichos, the rocky landscape and some of the many island churches. Brenda showed the bare bones of the scorched Greek island in these images. The book was described as a travelogue and did not attract as large a readership as *Tide-race* and *The Water-Castle*, but it was well received by the critics. Brenda was not tempted to go the London to promote the book but left that aspect to her publishers. At the time, her painting was going well and she didn't want to lose momentum by leaving the island.

Cat on the Terrace, *A Rope of Vines*, p. 88

Monks on Muleback, *A Rope of Vines*, p. 26

Throughout the autumn Brenda enthusiastically continued her work on the music notations. Still using the scratchy quality of the early music drawings, Brenda now gave the forms more solidity and texture. In *Genesis* she developed the line to depict a vibrant dance by a group of Greeks, while in *The Beast* she depicted a wild hairy creature. However, much of her work remained untitled and she concentrated on producing abstract forms with a strong sense of movement. Her work was now mainly in grey and black wax crayon with touches of rust. Living in Greece had greatly affected Brenda's approach to both her art and literature. In her writing, Brenda's sentences had become pared down and more concise, while in her art the colour was bleached out and the forms had become simpler and less cluttered.

The Beast, October 1965, wax crayon on card

She worked steadily throughout the winter on drawings until 8 January 1966, when the entry in her diary reads: 'I think the major effort (inspired by Halim's graphic impulses) is now almost completed'.[7] But with the work finished on the music series, Brenda felt very low. On 23 January she wrote: 'This is the spring, my depressed spirits sense it, lassitude, melancholy. The great effort of these wild months is over. What now?'[8] She was exhausted and as soon as she relaxed from her constant work pattern, she became ill. She felt very weak and at night became delirious with a fever which disturbed her sleep. In her journal she wrote:

Same dream, repeated endlessly, of leaving home for ten minutes (fish on the stove frying) going too far, unable to find my way back always through barns, farmyards, fields ... I dream too much, anxiety nightmares, always lost, crowds of alien people, vast town or landscapes in which I wander seeking. Roses, narcissi, eucalyptus, mandarin oranges, anemones the exact colour of my nightdress.[9]

A few years later, Brenda looked back at the entry in her journal and used the words as the basis for a poem:

I dream too much, over and over: I
Wander far from home, and am unable
To find the way back
Through farmland and empty barns:
Lost, among alien people, in unbounded landscape

Against night-hauntings, an evocation:
Narcissi, eucalyptus, fritillary.[10]

She had lost inspiration and felt at a loss.

> What I look forward to when I am overworking, is a time of doing nothing in good health, but what inevitably comes, is a sense of exhaustion and sterility. I am deeply depressed, having come to the end of about eight months' constant painting. I long for respite: then, when the fountain dries, I cannot bear life on these terms. Everything becomes reduced to greyness.[11]

But despite Brenda's despondency, there were two high points for her in January. Three of her poems from *The Green Heart* had been translated into Greek by Georgia Proteios and were included in the Christmas edition of the *Athens Literary Review*. The issue contained a section of work of eight foreign writers living on Hydra, and Brenda was delighted to have been selected. She was also excited by a group of four photographs that an American, Kitty Crapster, had taken of her using a Brownie camera.[12] In a letter to Michael Senior, Brenda wrote:

> They are the first photos I've seen that capture Ydra, the claustrophobic steps and stairs, the whiteness, the labyrinth.
>
> One set is concentrated on a steep flight of stairs, she standing quite high above, with me in black coming up, moving slowly so as not to blur the picture, but nonetheless in motion, a little foreshortened lost figure, the other set is done also from above, on the roof, using my figure against the tar-lines drawn in the cracks opened up in the cement in the heat of the summer sun. One of them is a beauty, a marvellous design.[13]

Brenda, January 1966

Brenda's enthusiasm proved just a brief respite from her gloom, however. The nightmares continued, she was still weak from fever and had a persistent cough. Although it was festival time on the island Brenda felt very detached from the celebrations. On Saturday, 18 February she wrote: 'Lunched alone at Graphos'. I needed to be alone. A crowd of acquaintances came and sat with me, I suspect because they sensed I did not need their company'.[14] Nothing seemed to cheer her for long and she realised that she was sinking into self-pity. On 1 March she admits in her journal:

To feel ashamed of the blackness of one's own moods helps not at all: to say to oneself, Look, you fool, the sun

341

shines every day, it is almost summer. Who wants summer?... I lag behind the days, in the past of that other island, another bad sign.[15]

Then, later that week, the rains came, and after the torrential downpour, the island burst into flower. Marios took Brenda up to the mountains to see them:

> ... exotic varieties I only knew before as colour plates in books of flora, rarities that on Ydra grow almost like daisies ... There are deep purple vetches glowing out of the yellow blooming gorse, palest lemon vetches, Venetian red vetches and other flowers so exquisite small, fragile, one can scarcely believe they have power to break earth so stubborn.[16]

The sight of such splendour seemed to help raise Brenda from her gloom and by the end of the month she was beginning to feel better, but still found it hard to settle down and work. She visited Janette, Marios and Roger, tried to learn more Greek, sat in tavernas with Yanis but still felt homesick for Wales.

It was May before her mood lifted on the day of a total eclipse of the sun:

> The earth gradually bleached ... As shadows moved from left to right, coldness came and a body-lightness. Shadows of foliage, surreal, sun-moonlight. Intensity of cypress tree green. Very cold. We were on the roof, separated from one another by a small zone of iciness; stars were faintly visible. Our shadows shortened, became more precise.

The neighbours were indoors, there was no sound from dog or donkey. As shade passed and life returned to our world, firerockets soared up from the port – the lifegiver had returned.[17]

Life seemed to return to Brenda as well and, inspired by the elongated and shadowed shapes she saw during the eclipse, she was inspired to draw again. She immediately rushed back to her house, recorded the event in her journal and pulled out the stack of work she had produced with the music notations. She also pulled out a reference file of *Scientific American* magazine. She had last used these cuttings to inspire some of her late Bardsey sea-change drawings and paintings.

Looking through these magazines, Brenda noticed that several of the black and white photographs had a similar texture and shape to some of her music notations. Excited by the similarity, she looked more closely at other photographs in the magazines and became particularly fascinated by the simple form of cells and nuclei and the watery character of their textures. She decided that she must incorporate these simple cell-like shapes in her drawings. She tried drawing sweeping circles and ellipses freehand but was not happy with the ragged lines that resulted. Instead she took a length of string, tied the ends together and laid the string circle flat on a piece of card. By moving the string around, Brenda could form smooth fluid ellipses. When she found a shape she liked, she followed the line of the string with a bold sweep of black wax crayon. Using this technique, Brenda drew large pebble shapes onto a grey textured background, and they became the basis of a new series of drawings.

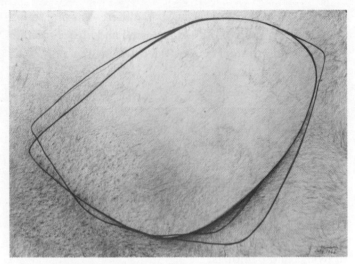

Pebble (Genesis), July 1966, wax crayon on card

At first Brenda drew one large single pebble at a time on a large card. She allowed some pebbles to have their shape echoed, as in a shadow, or the effect she had seen in the eclipse. Against one of these pebbles Brenda placed a poem, 'Rose of Lima'. Twenty years earlier she had presented this poem in *Tide-race* and she now rewrote it in a new minimal form:

> Rose of Lima! Rose of Lima!
> perfumed with myrrh aloe and cassia
> the fragrance of your passing
>
> reminds me of the island
> which like a bride wears
> a jewel at the breast's hollow

Barbar-coloured wave-worn pebble
burnt with sea-light in a dark cell
clasp exotic rose.[18]

After the single pebble images, Brenda gathered groups of
pebbles together, arranging them in patterns similar to the
composition of magnified grains of quartz she had seen in
the *Scientific American* photographs. She became intrigued
by the similarities of the shape of quartz grains, rocks,
islands, and the sun and moon. In the new drawings she
attempted to capture the essence of all these different forms
of matter in one image.

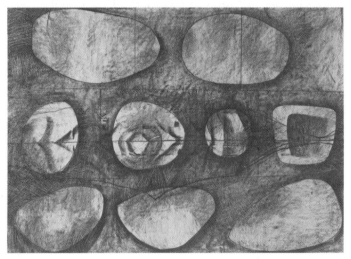

Untitled, 1966, wax crayon on card

The concept of metamorphosis had arisen in her work
before. In the 1940s she had written a poem about
Blodeuwedd, the woman who was conjured from flowers
and then transformed into an owl. In the sea-change

paintings made on Bardsey in the 1960s Brenda had attempted to show a transformation of human bodies into rocks on the sea bed. Now the challenge of exploring the same concept from a new angle excited her.

Once again she used the frottage technique to create an overall background texture. Then she covered some areas in thick black crayon and scratched marks with an empty biro to reveal the white card beneath. Finally, to seal the surface, Brenda polished the finished work with an old woollen sock until it was smooth and shiny. Sometimes whole sheets of card were completed in this manner, then cut into various shapes which pleased Brenda and were stored for use in future compositions. They would appear in collages, stuck onto more grey, textured sheets, often arranged against a geometric grid drawn in wax crayon on the base card. The majority of the series remained untitled and were merely numbered i, ii, iii, and so on. Titled works indicated their subjects, for example *Atoms, Chaos, Order, Eclipses, Stone*, with a touch of nostalgia in a few collages named *Enlli*. Now she was drawing again, Brenda felt much happier, and continued working in this style from June to December 1966.

See-Saw, August 1966, collage, wax crayon on card

In the middle of this creative period, Brenda's old friend, Esmé Kirby, visited her in September. Esmé was disappointed with Hydra as it did not match up to Brenda's descriptions of it. While Brenda had described the island as having a fascinating colony of serious writers and artists, Esmé saw a bunch of promiscuous foreign immigrants whose days seemed to revolve around a lazy café life where drug-taking was a fashionable activity. The island also appeared unattractive. After the summer drought the land was completely scorched and the only vegetation was the remains of thistles and the prickly stumps of cacti. Brenda had always described the island in glowing terms and even at this time of year, she could see beauty in it:

> ... the world had lost its eyebrows in a white-hot wilderness of thistle, stone and derelict wheat-terrace. The land was the colour of wet salt and there was a beautiful nakedness about the harsh soil. The sea was bare, no other land or island or sail or even puff of distant funnel-smoke marking it. The cliffs and man-made terraces fell away into the red-blue eye of the Aegean, but for a few yards out from the cliff-foot, the water was jade. Where the jade ended, the fire-shot blue began, and continued to the horizon.[19]

Brenda defended the island against Esmé's criticisms but when Esmé spoke of the lush green valleys and mountains of Snowdonia and of friends in Bangor, Brenda began to feel homesick for Wales. She resumed her drawing after Esme had left, but felt unsettled. Her thoughts were continually wandering to Wales. It had been a year and a half since she had last been there and she decided that she must go for a visit.

She left Hydra in December, stopping off in London to stay briefly with Janette who was staying there for the winter. While there, ironically Brenda met and fell in love with a Greek man whose identity is unclear. They spent each day together and Brenda, impetuous as ever, declared that he was the perfect man for her and they planned to live together when they returned to Greece. Brenda was ecstatic and told all her friends that she would be getting married when she returned to Hydra.

Meanwhile, in Bangor, Brenda's mother was suffering quite badly from arthritis. It was decided that as Brenda was now living abroad and her brother, Neville, was living in the Midlands, it would be best for Mrs Chamberlain to move into a residential home where she would be properly cared for. She chose to live in Plas Maesincla, a home in Caernarfon with which she had been involved in her capacity as Chairman of the County Council. Brenda helped her mother to move and settle into the home while she was in Bangor. Although Mrs Chamberlain was upset to leave her own flat in Bangor, she was happy that Brenda had found another man with whom to share her life.

Although Brenda had a tendency to over-romanticise her relationships with men, she convinced her friends that this time it was serious and she made plans to leave Bangor behind forever. On the eve of her departure for Hydra in spring 1967, the Daniel family held a farewell party in their flat in Menai View Terrace. On the following day, Brenda left Wales in high spirits.

1   NLW MS 21521D, f. 41.
2   Michael Senior, letter to the author, 9 Sept. 1983.
3   National Library of Wales, PE 1668. See this notebook for all references in this chapter to the *Black Brides* series.
4   NLW PE 1668, dated Ydra, 1965.
5   *RV*, p. 153 (all references are to the first edition, 1965).
6   *RV*, p. 31.
7   NLW MS 21500E, f. 4.
8   Ibid., ff. 5-6, and 'A Total Eclipse of the Sun', *Mabon* I, v (Spring 1972), 6-13, (p. 9).
9   NLW MS 21500E, f. 4, and 'A Total Eclipse of the Sun', p. 7.
10 Brenda Chamberlain, *Poems with Drawings* (London: Enitharmon Press, 1969), p. 18, and 'The Protagonists' (typescript; Hydra, 1967), f. 60, private collection. [Henceforth *Poems with Drawings* will be *PD*].
11 'A Total Eclipse of the Sun', p. 10.
12 These photographs would later be published in the *International Herald Tribune*.
13 Brenda Chamberlain, letter to Michael Senior, 21 Jan. 1966, private collection.
14 NLW MS 21500E, f. 10; 'A Total Eclipse of the Sun', p. 12.
15 NLW MS 21500E, f. 11.
16 Ibid., f. 14.
17 Ibid., f. 21.
18 *PD*, p. 3.
19 *RV*, p. 40.

Chapter 12
The Tide Turns 1967-68

Brenda returned to Greece on Monday, 17 April 1967, catching a boat from Piraeus to Hydra. All was peaceful, but within a few days the situation changed radically. On Friday, 21 April, right-wing army officers staged a coup, King Constantine II fled to exile in Rome, and Georgios Papadopoulus headed a new military government. Civil liberties were immediately curtailed and every hour radio bulletins announced the restrictions. A curfew was set for 6pm, assemblies of more than five people were forbidden, strikes were proscribed and criticism of the government was stifled, and there was strict censorship of newspapers and magazines. The penalty for disobedience was either immediate arrest or to be shot at sight. Greece, a land where Brenda had found freedom and a love of life, was now in chains and she found it very disturbing. There was suddenly a feeling of secrecy and conspiracy, people spoke in whispers while constantly looking over their shoulders. The prospect of informers made neighbours suspicious of one another. It was reported later that during the first forty-eight hours after the coup, about 68,000 people were arrested and herded into sports stadiums, the Athens Hippodrome and a few large hotels. Most of those arrested were suspected Communists and political opponents, but some were councillors, journalists, and anyone who spoke out publicly against the Junta. In order to prevent the opposition having an effective leadership, about forty top political and military figures were detained. After being held for a few days in Athens these people were sent to various islands including Leros and Aegina.

As a foreigner, Brenda felt she had to be particularly careful. On one occasion, when she was shopping, she felt that the locals were reassessing her:

> ... I did actually hear one man say to another, 'She's alright.' You see I heard that; I mean they were just chatting; it was like going through an examination of some sort. It was obvious as a foreigner you should just stay quietly at home, naturally they were terribly disturbed, and as a foreigner you were nothing to do with it. It seemed rather necessary to keep as quiet as possible and definitely not to talk publicly.[1]

The situation was very tense and for the first time in her life, Brenda began to understand the persuasive power of politics. It frightened her. Because of the distance between the Greek islands, there was a real threat that they could be cut off completely from one another. It would be all too easy for the authorities to prevent the movement of ships and to control all radio bulletins which would mean no mail, no news and no means of travelling between islands.

Before the situation became too restricted, Brenda decided to go and visit her friends who were living on the island of Leros. In a small pocket diary (now NLW MS 23382) she logged her visit: leaving Hydra on 7 June 1967 for Piraeus, where she caught a boat to Leros arriving the next day. Unlike her daily journal writings which were often a mixture of fact and fiction, here the events are factual, naming people who are not recorded elsewhere. Her entries were brief and cryptic. It is clear that she wanted to see a man called Meric but he was away in Beirut so she spent time with other friends. Was this the man she had hoped to marry on her return to Greece?

Brenda returned to Hydra, where she felt oppressed by the restrictions imposed by the army officers. They seemed to apply to everything: 'For instance, if you rested your leg on a chair,' explained Brenda in an interview with Alan McPherson, 'you know they have these very hard seats in Greece – and rest your leg on another, you would be hauled up by the police for that. If your dress was slightly transparent and could be seen through, that was another thing.'[2] Beards and long hair were banned, as was the Greek custom of breaking glasses to express particular feelings. In her breathless style, Brenda explained her sympathy for the local people.

The poor men, the peasants! They're an incredibly exuberant people and very noisy, and if they shouted or laughed or sang they were told to shut up. You know every Greek breaks glasses – the breaking of glasses is phenomenal – but suddenly this was a barbarous thing and must not be done. This breaking of glasses was either an insult or a congratulation, you see – it's a tricky business – you can be mortally offended or congratulated – if you've done a marvellous dance they break a glass at

your feet, or if they want to insult you, they break a glass
– and that was suddenly not allowed.[3]

Brenda found life on Hydra dull without the lively chatter
and arguments of the local people, and the six o'clock
curfew prevented any social visits in the evenings. Most
of the foreign artists and writers had left Hydra and
Brenda was beginning to feel rather lonely. She was
particularly pleased, then, to meet a young couple from
Britain who had come to the island for their honeymoon.
When Brenda discovered that Barbara Stafford, the new
bride, was from Aberdaron in North Wales, she was even
happier and was able to hear news of old friends and
acquaintances. She found it reassuring to hear about
Wales and to know that she could return if the situation
became too oppressive in Greece.

Brenda at the Villa Papandi, Hydra, 1967

Since the coup, Brenda had felt unable to paint and had only occasionally written. The entries in her notebook were expressions of her fears and frustrations and first appeared as fragments of overheard conversations. She showed them to an American friend who declared, 'My God, how strong, this is a play!' He spoke with such conviction that Brenda believed him and went off to write it.

I just went home; it was as though a key had been turned or something. I just saw the whole thing come, it just began and every day it never stopped after that. At 8 o'clock every morning I just sat and put it down – it came so fast that I always had one of those little blocks, those little Greek notebook things and when I went down into the port or anywhere, I had one of those with me, and it was just coming the whole time, people were speaking, it was direct speech. I never wrote any happenings, any direct description; it just happened through their voices. It was terribly exciting.[4]

She was constantly amazed by the statements she overheard and found it hard to believe the effect the military regime was having on the way of life of people. In order to gather more material for the play, she decided to visit a detention camp. There was one on Leros and as her friend, Meric, was due to return to Leros from Beirut so she used the excuse of visiting friends to make a return visit to the island in August.

This time, Brenda made a point of going to see one of the detention camps on the island. At the time, Leros was not a tourist island. It had had a turbulent history in the twentieth century. It had been seized by Italy in 1912 and had been established as a naval base. Later it was occupied by Germany and later Britain. After it returned to Greek rule in 1948, the abandoned Italian military camps, which housed over 3000 soldiers, were utilized for various purposes including a large mental hospital which became renowned for the primitive conditions in which it kept people suffering from a range of psychosocial conditions. There were thousands of inmates, no trained nurses and few doctors. The inmates were looked after by 'guards' who tended to be local fisherman and shepherds. Both adults and unwanted children were housed in filthy conditions with compounds surrounded by wire cages. Some aggressive inhabitants were often chained to trees.

Many of the people arrested in the wake of the coup were shipped to islands such as Leros and were kept in similar conditions to those in the mental hospital. Brenda was appalled at what she saw and what she heard about from the island's residents. She found it hard to believe that human beings had been imprisoned for what seemed to her such unimportant offences.

Because of the delicate situation, Brenda was advised by a Greek friend not to talk about her visit and certainly not tell anyone she had been interested in the political prisoners there. 'Well, I'll just say there were lovely flowers there', was Brenda's ironic response.[5] In her notebooks she made drawings of the caged prisoners and continued writing the play, but she was careful to hide it in the bottom of her trunk whenever she went out. Although she was being a little more careful, Brenda's Greek friends still felt she did not truly appreciate the seriousness of the material she was incorporating into her play. Brenda found it difficult to accept that it could be constructed as anti-Greek propaganda by the authorities and at times behaved rather irresponsibly. She described one such incident to Alan McPherson:

> I had to break out in some way – one night everybody thought I was completely crazy, the play was finished, I don't know why but I had it on me one night in the port and I was with old friends who had come from Cyprus and I very rarely go to a Taverna; we went to a Taverna and I suppose I'd had too much retzina; I started reading from it at the top of my voice – this was crazy but there was this feeling, you had to break out.[6]

Brenda hoped things would return to normal, but when they showed no sign of doing so, she decided it would be best to return to Wales. She had completed her play, which she called 'The Protagonists', and wanted to take it back to Britain where it could be publicly performed. She was convinced that people from other countries should be made aware of the devastating effect the Colonels' Coup was having on the Greek people, and she hoped her play would have repercussions in the world outside. It was, of course, an offence not only to write such a play, but even to be caught in possession of such writing and Brenda was aware she would have to smuggle it out of the country. She persuaded her friend, Janette, to take a copy of the play out of Greece via Cyprus and Brenda decided to hide another copy in her own hand luggage.

By now money had become a major problem for her. Normally she managed to eke out a meagre living but she found she did not have enough left for the fare back to Britain. Friends in Bangor came to her rescue and sent her enough money to pay for the journey home. She still had a small group of faithful friends in the town to whom she could turn for financial as well as emotional support. Several of them acted as her patrons, buying her paintings when they knew she was in need of money and in the process they gathered fine collections of her art.

It was not easy for Brenda to return to Bangor. Having left in high spirits, assuring everyone that she was going to settle with her new man in Greece, it hurt her pride to have to return and admit she had been wrong. She also knew that she had no base to go back to since her mother was now living in the home in Caernarfon. In addition, she had no money at all. However, her friends – as always – extended their hospitality and gave her a warm welcome. Several of the families that Brenda knew lived in Menai View Terrace, and Brenda first stayed with Sheila and Clement Mundle and their family. After a few weeks she moved further down the terrace to stay with Catrin and John Daniel and then when the Mundle family went off to America for five months, they let Brenda stay in their house. As Brenda was almost penniless, Sheila arranged for a lodger to stay in the house with her so that she could have some money, but Brenda did not bother to follow up the arrangements and missed this easy income.

Although she should have been concentrating on making a living, Brenda's main preoccupation was to try and arrange for her play to be performed and published. Among the people she contacted was Jeremy Brooks, at that time literary advisor to the Royal Shakespeare Company. In his reply to her letter, he wrote:

I've just finished reading *The Protagonists*, and want to write at once to tell you that I think it is a most distinguished and powerful piece of writing. I don't quite know *why* it is so compelling to read, since so many of its effects are virtually subliminal, but I do know that I did not want to stop reading and that I laid down with that feeling of satisfaction one gets after encountering a fully-achieved work of art.[7]

He also said he would ask the company's artistic director, Trevor Nunn, to read it and that he would have copies made for others to read. On the strength of his response, in mid January, Brenda decided to go to London to try to stimulate interest in her play. She also arranged to meet her publisher friend, Alan Clodd, who had expressed an interest in publishing the letters of Alun Lewis concerning the making of the Caseg Broadsheets. On her return to Bangor, Brenda arranged a reading of 'The Protagonists' by students of the University in Bangor. This was held in February 1968 at John and Catrin Daniel's house, where Brenda was staying at the time. Soon after this reading, the BBC contacted Brenda and asked if they could record an interview with her plus excerpts from the play. There was a long recording session in the BBC studios in Bangor and the resulting tape was broadcast on 4 April in the 'Spectrum' programme on the Welsh Home Service.

The programme generated a great deal of interest especially as the Welsh Drama Studio had decided to stage the play in Bangor in the autumn. This company had been formed under the auspices of David Lyn, its director, to produce new plays by Welsh authors and to present them in exciting and experimental productions. Although the play was not due to be performed until October, the company met once a week to rehearse and exchange ideas. The whole of

September was set aside for rehearsals which allowed Brenda about four months to put her energy into other projects.

Meanwhile, Alan Clodd had visited Brenda in Bangor in order to see the Alun Lewis letters concerning the Caseg Broadsheets, and he wanted to discuss the format of the book with Brenda. He asked her to place the letters in chronological order, to edit them, and to write an account of how the Broadsheets came into being. He also suggested that the book could include photographs of Brenda, John Petts and Alun Lewis as well as illustrations of the Broadsheets. The book was to be published in a limited edition of three hundred hardback copies by Clodd's Enitharmon Press and would sell for 45 shillings. He gave Brenda an advance of £30 and offered her a royalty fee of fifteen per cent.

While he was there, Brenda showed him all the work she had done in Greece and discussed the possibility of another book. Alan Clodd was interested in her work and suggested that a book could be designed to display her poetry alongside photographs of her drawings and paintings. Brenda was particularly enthusiastic about this idea as it would give both aspects of her work equal importance, and they agreed to publish this second book too.

Brenda was now almost too busy, and found it difficult to work on so many projects at once. She was transcribing and editing Alun Lewis's letters, revising her Greek poems, and rehearsing 'The Protagonists'. In addition, she had returned to the play begun in Greece, 'A One-Legged Man takes a Walk', and added new sections. She flitted from one project to another, never really concentrating on any of them for long and consequently found it an unsatisfactory and unproductive time.

The need for money bothered her too, because although she was extremely busy she had no income at all. The £30 advance for her second book for Enitharmon Press soon disappeared, and no more money was due until the books were published. As far as she could see, none of the other projects with which she was involved guaranteed any income either, and it began to worry her. She wrote to Meic Stephens, Literature Director of the Welsh Arts Council, describing both her current projects and the work she had produced in Greece. She asked him for a bursary or award of some kind to keep her '… in the modest way in which I am accustomed to live, so that for the next year I can work without the ever-present nagging of financial worries.'[8] Among the projects for which she wanted finance, she listed the play, 'A One-Legged Man takes a Walk', which she wanted to complete, 'The Protagonists', which she wanted to publish, and a proposed book about the sea '… in the abstract sense, not the scientific, like that marvellous work, 'The Sea Around Us', but something written out of my life's experience of living with the sea.'[9]

In his reply, Meic Stephens asked Brenda to send him the photostat copies of the three notebooks of automatic music drawings which she had mentioned and also suggested that she might consider selling some of her original manuscripts to the Welsh Art Council for their collection of manuscripts by Anglo-Welsh writers. But Brenda had little time to consider this proposal before she had to direct her energy towards selecting drawings and paintings to be exhibited in Bangor Art Gallery in July. Maurice Cooke was in charge of the gallery at that time and worked with Brenda to select the work and prepare the exhibition catalogue. Of the forty works in the exhibition, called New Works, most were

Brenda in front of *Clashing Rocks* at
the *New Works* exhibition, 1968

collage with some drawings. The Bangor audience found
these monochrome abstract works unexpected and so
unlike Brenda's colourful figurative work that they failed to
excite their interest. To make matters worse, Brenda had
overpriced the works, partly because she was desperate for
money and partly because she had a high regard for the
value of her work. The majority of the work was priced
around £200 with one piece as high as £600, far higher
than current prices and more than most local people could
afford.

Not only did most visitors find the exhibition difficult to
understand and appreciate, they also thought the lack of
colour dreary. In a second BBC interview for the 'Spectrum'
radio programme Brenda explained why there was no
longer any colour in her work.

Well, I was not at all interested in colour because I was trying to make pure forms. I mean the ultimate thing, I was trying to achieve as pure a form as I could and colour simply did not come into it. And I suppose living in a land which is drenched with whiteness you see. With light, but it is also colour but it's principally looking through. You feel you can look through solid marble for instance. There is a lot of transparency that is probably what I am subconsciously trying to get.[10]

The lack of interest in the exhibition depressed Brenda, especially as so little had been sold. She was still struggling to keep all her projects ongoing. Normally, Brenda enjoyed being busy but she found having to divide her attention between so many different projects both frustrating and draining and this began to show in the quality of her work. The book on the Caseg Broadsheets seemed to suffer most and because she was continually picking up and putting down the Alun Lewis letters, she found it hard to place them in order. Not having a flat of her own made her unsettled too, and when the Mundle family returned from their trip to America, Brenda moved out of their flat and into the Daniels' household once again.

At the beginning of September, rehearsals began in earnest for the Welsh Drama Studio production of 'The Protagonists', which was to be performed for two nights in October, and Brenda had to stop working on the books altogether. A Greek actress, Sophia Michopoulou from the Carolus Coun Company in Athens arrived in Bangor to play the woman's part in the play, and excitement began to mount in the company. In all the publicity given to the play during rehearsals, Sophia refused to give her surname for fear of persecution when she returned home. Her arrival and her statement added to the intensity which Brenda had already tried to inject into the cast. Apart from Sophia, there was another Greek involved in the play. He was Vasilis Politis who had left Greece at the time of the Coup and had moved to north Wales. The awareness of the Greek problem felt by Brenda and the two Greeks gave the rest of the company an acute sense of the loss of freedom expressed within the play.

'The Protagonists' is set in a cell-block where six political prisoners are held by a Guard and an Edict Maker. In Bangor, the play was performed on a scaffolding set built on four levels with the audience seated on three sides of the cells. The play opens with five of the six prisoners in cages and being closely observed by the Guard. The prisoners have no names but are known by letters: A, L, J, O, Z and N. Throughout the action, the Edict Maker enters from time to time to issue reminders of the restrictions:

IT IS FORBIDDEN:
FOR CHILDREN TO PICK WILD FLOWERS ON SUNDAY MORNINGS: to break glasses and plates; arms, legs and other bones, in places of public entertainment: TO COMMENT ON THE PREVALENCE OF POLICEMEN: to criticise the man with the briefcase: TO PUT MESSAGES IN BOTTLES AND COMMIT THEM TO THE SEA: to read, write or think without reference to the authorities: to complain of cockroaches in the rice.[11]

The dialogue is sometimes disjointed as each individual speaks out his and her thoughts, feelings and memories. At other times it is intensely focused, as when prisoner Z goes

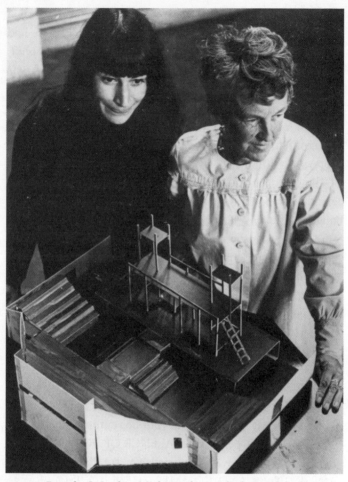

Brenda & Sophia Michopoulou with the model of
The Protagonists set, 1968

into a frenzy. This particular character is modelled directly on Berthold Panek, the Polish hermit from Bardsey. Brenda originally told the story of his fight with the devil and his ensuing madness in her book, *Tide-race*, and now she reused it in a different context. As Z begins to go mad, he babbles and prays in Latin, smashes the light bulb and believes everyone to be in a league with the Devil. As with Berthold, Z believes God was on the right side of his body and the Devil on his left, and leaps away when the Edict Maker tried to touch him on the left shoulder: 'Aaah! Aaah! The Devil, the Devil! I burn, I burn', Z babbles about the Devil and darkness until the end of the play when he is strapped into a straitjacket.[12]

Although the play is a protest against the new regime in Greece, Brenda felt the problem was a universal one which applied to all countries. In it she questions the power of the freedom of the individual and the capriciousness of those in positions of power. Throughout the play there is uncertainty as to who actually is prisoner and who is in control. For example, the Guard, who at the beginning guards the prisoners, later appears to be plotting an escape with them, then near the end finds himself imprisoned by one of the prisoners. Brenda wanted to make the point that in any situation power can be established and overthrown at any given time and the state of individual liberty is subject to the whim of whoever happens to be in authority.

The rehearsals for the play were exciting and demanding, and Sophia was certainly the most exuberant member of the cast. There were frequent fiery clashes of temperament between her and Brenda as they argued over the interpretation of the play. The two women had a mutual respect for each other, but because Brenda was particularly

Alan McPherson as the Guard in *The Protagonists*

tense and serious during the whole rehearsal period, she was easily roused by Sophia, who also revelled in dramatic exchanges. Because it was the first performance of the play there were many things to discuss and Brenda was

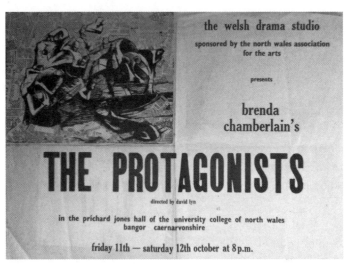

Poster for *The Protagonists*

constantly on hand throughout rehearsals to contribute her ideas. She found the process nerve-wracking but was driven by a conviction that only she knew how the play should be staged and a desire to be involved in all aspects of the production from costume and lighting, to the way the words were spoken. Some of the text was changed and with Brenda's permission, David Lyn, the director, changed the order of some sections of dialogue so they would flow better on stage. Brenda was delighted by the improvement.

The play was performed for two nights in the University's Pritchard Jones Hall in Bangor on 11 and 12 October 1968, and there were plans to take the show on to the Belgrave Theatre in Cambridge. Unfortunately, the company did not make a profit from the Bangor production which meant there were no funds to finance the visit to Cambridge. Brenda was very disappointed. The whole company had put so much energy and enthusiasm into the production and after receiving the encouraging letter from Jeremy Brooks, Brenda had hopes of the play eventually transferring to London and being acclaimed a huge success.

Many people labelled the play political propaganda, but Brenda insisted continually that there was no direct political message in the play. 'I know nothing of politics and I suppose I'm not interested. I'm just interested in how people react, in what people do and feel and think.'[13] She was adamant that her motive for writing the play was simple:

> I did it for Greece – I wrote it for Greece – I didn't know positively at first what form it would take, but as soon as it began to come out like this, I realised it was a play which isn't political propaganda in any sense but I suppose an emotional reaction to the situation.[14]

News of the performance of the play had reached Greece. It had been reported as being anti-Greek propaganda and her friends on Hydra were worried in case there were any repercussions. When Brenda wrote to her friend, Janette Read, saying that she wanted to return to the island, Janette was very surprised and realised that Brenda had still not grasped the seriousness of her position. After seeking the advice of their mutual friend, Henry Mitchell, Janette wrote Brenda a strong letter indicating that it would be unwise to return to Hydra under the present regime as her name was bound to be on the black list. She advised Brenda that if she really did want to return then she should bring enough money for the return journey in case she was sent back at the border. For a long time Janette did not hear from her and was afraid that Brenda may have been upset by the forthright letter. She had indeed found the letter disturbing, and felt frustrated that, having written the play for Greece, she was unable to safely re-enter the country.

In the inevitable lull after the staging of 'The Protagonists', Brenda felt tired and run down. Two of her dreams had been dashed. The play had not reached London's West End theatres and she was not able to return to Greece. She had deliberately not settled in Bangor because she thought she was just visiting, with the purpose of using her play to make a public statement about the Greek situation. Brenda was forced to accept that she had to stay in Wales for a while, at least until the fall of the present regime. She felt that she could no longer impose on her friends' hospitality and with the little money she had left over from the sale of paintings from her last exhibition, she decided she must rent a flat of her own.

[1] Brenda Chamberlain interviewed by Alan McPherson in *Forecast* (UCNW Bangor, April/May 1968), 18-19, p. 18.
[2] Ibid., p. 19.
[3] Ibid., p. 19.
[4] Ibid., pp. 18-19.
[5] Ibid., p. 19.
[6] Ibid., p. 19.
[7] NLW MS 20809E, f. 4a, copy of part of a letter from Jeremy Brooks to Brenda Chamberlain, 17 April 1968.
[8] Ibid., f. 4, 26 April 1968.
[9] NLW MS 20809E, f. 4^v.
[10] NLW MS 21501E, f. 51, transcript of 1968 BBC Radio interview by Gareth Jones for 'Spectrum' programme, 1968.
[11] Acting script for 'The Protagonists', p. 19.
[12] Acting script for 'The Protagonists', p. 21, with reference to *TR*, pp. 203-10.

[13] *Forecast* (April/May 1968), p. 19, interview with Alan McPherson who played the part of the Guard in the production of 'The Protagonists', Bangor, 11-12 October 1968.
[14] Ibid.

Chapter 13
Alone she faces darkness 1968-69

On 11 November 1968 Brenda moved to flat 7, Plas Rhianfa, Glyn Garth, across the Menai Straits on the island of Anglesey. It was part of an unusual building as Brenda described in a letter to Alan Clodd:

> I moved over the water last evening to this romantic spot, the former residence of the Verneys of Anglesey. It is an architectural aberration, nightmared out of memories or fantasies of the Loire chateaux.
> Not 'me' at all. BUT, there are marvellous panelled cupboards with drawers spare for all my papers, a luxury I never had before. And the view is heavenly, straight into the mountains opposite the Straits. It is precisely over the water from my mother's old flat in Bangor. My kitchen is in a little tower off the living room. This tower has slit windows overlooking the gardens and the sea. The bathroom is at the other end of the flat, also in a tower. The whole Plas is a madman's dream of the Loire Chateau.[1]

Plas Rhianfa, Anglesey

Brenda hoped that in the peace of the Plas she would be able to work on the two books that Alan Clodd was going to publish. In reality, she felt very lonely and cut off in her towers and turrets. She knew no one on that side of the

Straits, and as she could not drive, it was impossible for her to see her friends as often as she was accustomed. Lack of money still bothered Brenda and she began to consider Meic Stephens' suggestion of selling some of her manuscripts to the Welsh Arts Council.

Initially, she gave them the opportunity of buying the three books of automatic 'music' drawings made in Greece, the first typescript of *Tide-race*, and the first typescript of *The Water-Castle*, complete with original drawings. Meic Stephens found them interesting and asked Brenda how much she wanted for them. He said he would have them priced by experts and then approach the Literature Committee to consider their purchase. Difficulties arose over the price. The Welsh Arts Council consulted experts at the National Library of Wales and the British Library and the figure of £250 was recommended but Brenda refused this offer as she considered £1000 to be a reasonable amount. She then suggested that the Welsh Arts Council should give her £250 for fewer items and it was arranged that the administrative assistant of the Literature Committee, Ann Griffiths, should go to Bangor to discuss the situation with her. After the meeting, Brenda seemed confused about what they were interested in buying and wrote to Meic Stephens for clarification. He explained that as her manuscripts included both art and literature, they had to be presented to both the Literature and the Art Committees to consider their purchase.

Brenda was beginning to grow tired of exchanging so many letters and failed to understand why something that had begun as a simple negotiation had turned into such a complicated affair. She received another letter from the Welsh Arts Council saying that the joint Literature and Art

Committees also considered the sum of £1000 too high and could Brenda decide which items she would consider selling for £250. She replied saying that they could have the typescript of *Tide-race* for that amount. At this stage, Brenda thought the deal was assured and was very upset to hear that when the offer went before the joint committee, they recommended not to make the purchase.

Meic Stephens then suggested to Brenda that she might have more success if she offered a manuscript without drawings solely to the Literature Committee. As the correspondence had been drawn out over four months, and she had been under the impression they wished to buy some of her work, Brenda was now finding it all very distressing. In a letter to Alan Clodd, she wrote:

> I just wonder what they are playing at, and I am completely fed up and depressed by their rotten behaviour. Being uncivilised and totally lacking in culture doesn't excuse anything – and they call themselves the Arts Council! Sorry – I'm feeling bitter.[2]

By April, Brenda had had enough of the negotiations and ended a letter to the Welsh Arts Council with 'I think this totally pointless correspondence should now cease'.[3] In response, Meic Stephens made a further attempt to smooth out the problem and clarify the facts.

He explained that as an officer, he was not in a position to make an offer and that neither he nor the Council had agreed to buy the typescripts. of *Tide-race* as the figure Brenda had requested was far higher than independent experts had valued it.

He concluded by stating that they would still like to consider purchasing literary items and suggested she asked the Council to consider buying one item for £250. Brenda could not bring herself to reply. She had put so much effort into selling the manuscripts, she felt confused and exhausted and had not gained any money from the process.

By this time, she was feeling run down and was prescribed a course of tablets for the day and sleeping tablets for night by her doctor. The tablets made Brenda want to sleep at odd times, which she found disorientating. She could not concentrate on her work and frequently had to lie down and rest. In between writing letters to the Welsh Arts Council, she had been trying to select the material for the two books. While she enjoyed working on *Poems with Drawings*, her progress with the letters of Alun Lewis was slow. They needed to be dated accurately and carefully edited and in her present state Brenda found the task laborious. Although Alan Clodd offered to help she was convinced that she could manage and refused to part with the letters. She did enlist his help in contacting John Petts whom she knew had some letters from Alun Lewis. She wanted Clodd to ask him if these letters could be loaned for inclusion in the book and if letters from Alun to John which Brenda had in her possession could be quoted.

Alan Clodd wrote to John Petts on two occasions and was puzzled when he received no reply. Petts, on the other hand, was equally puzzled to receive the request for the letters:

Frankly (and I think understandably) I was appalled and surprised and annoyed to observe that Brenda had forged ahead and completed the book without any consultation with me as one of the three partners who developed the whole project. The first I heard of the book was when the publisher wrote saying that the work was ready for publication, but would I send him Alun's letters for inclusion. I'm afraid I was so infuriated by Brenda's behaviour in this matter that I could not bring myself to reply.[4]

Brenda, however, was surprised that John had not responded to Clodd's letters. It had not entered her mind that it would be useful to have John's view of the project to give a more complete account of the venture. Although Brenda had been at the hub of the Press during wartime, she had in fact only met Lewis once and it had been John who had set up the Press and developed a working relationship with Alun Lewis.

At the end of March, Alan Clodd let Brenda know that Alun's widow, Gweno, had returned the draft of the book: 'She has approved it as it stands and not suggested any alterations except to query our dating of four of the letters'.[5] In the same letter, he told Brenda that he had still not heard from John Petts: 'His silence seems to imply he has no objections but if he changed his mind when the book was half printed, I would have to take them out and run into a lot of expense'.[6]

To play safe, it was decided to include only letters addressed to Brenda and to Brenda and John and to exclude any letters written to John alone. As a result, Brenda had to reconsider the arrangement of the letters in the book and she struggled on with the task. She was still taking tablets but was finding the side-effects demoralising and did not feel comfortable taking the medication. Her reply to Alan Clodd's letter reveals her fragile state: 'Thank heaven,

Gweno Lewis approved of the script. I am still in such a nervous persecuted state by means of the Welsh Arts Council, that I expect anything to happen, however irrational ...' [7]

In March 1969 Brenda moved back to Bangor, to a small flat on Glanrafon Hill. She was relieved to leave the isolation of Plas Rhianfa and be back amongst her friends. Trouble with her back prompted her to spend a couple of days in bed and she felt much better after the enforced rest. During that time, she had read an article in *The Sunday Times* which moved her very deeply. It was about the politically active Greek composer, Mikis Theodorakis, who had been imprisoned for two years because of the Colonels' Coup. For the last nine months, he, his wife and two children had been held in heavily guarded exile in the remote village of Zatouna. He had recently managed to smuggle out of Greece two documents which had reached *The Sunday Times* and aroused widespread interest. One was an appeal for help addressed to U Thant, Secretary General of the United Nations, and the other was a formal offer to the European Rights Commission to give evidence against the Greek regime. *The Sunday Times* sent a journalist, John Barry, to Greece to discover more about Theodorakis. Since reporters were not allowed to visit Zatouna, Barry hiked for two days over rough terrain, managed to evade police patrols and was eventually able to make contact with Theodorakis, even though they were unable to meet.

The composer, who was a Marxist deputy in the last freely-elected assembly, had been labelled a dangerous Communist by the regime. But as John Barry wrote in his article: 'The more potent reason for his banishment is that, above and beyond politics, Theodorakis and his music have become a symbol of resistance to the military rule'.[8] The constant pressure of being exiled from everyone and being under constant surveillance was wearing the composer down: he was not well and suffered from tuberculosis and heart trouble. He was a charismatic character who had a strong influence on modern Greek culture, having written more than two hundred pop songs, ten symphonic pieces, two oratorios, three ballets, a folk opera and several film scores, including the famous *Zorba*. Now he wrote the occasional melancholic song and his music was banned in his own country. He was allowed to go out for four hours a day, no further than the village, and could only speak to certain people. Even at night, wrote Barry, '… guards floodlight the house from all four corners. This, of course, makes it hard for the family inside to sleep, but, illuminated, the house looks like some strange monument'.[9] The article touched many chords for Brenda. It rekindled all her strong feelings about Greece and about her desires to return there. She too, had felt in exile since the coup, but certainly in much freer conditions than those of Theodorakis. The image of the floodlit house lingered in her mind and she decided to write a play about Theodorakis, to be called 'The Monument'.

In May, another article appeared in *The Sunday Times*.[10] This was Theodorakis's own account of his exile and gave a more graphic description of his situation. Using these two articles and various other news cuttings, Brenda began work on her play. She wanted it to be based on accurate facts and quoted freely from the two *Sunday Times* articles in her dialogue.

Although Brenda poured a lot of her energy into writing the play, it was never completed to her satisfaction because

North Wales Hospital for nervous and
mental disorders, Denbigh

she began to feel guilty about neglecting her other books. She knew she must go back to work on them but found it difficult to raise the enthusiasm. Lack of money weighed heavily on her, and her failure to sell any of her manuscripts still upset and annoyed her. She could not see a way out of her money problems and became depressed by this. Thoughts of Greece haunted her too, and she could not imagine when she would be able to return. As she struggled with her work, all her problems and worries seemed to increase and she felt less and less able to cope. There came a point where she could not take any more. In early July she suffered a nervous breakdown and was taken to the psychiatric hospital in Denbigh. 'I could not believe it', she wrote in her notebook, 'that my body was in such a predicament, that my mind should receive such a shock'.[11]

At first Brenda was put in a general ward and was horrified at the state of the patients there. She did not see herself as one of them, and wrote in her notebook to keep her mind clear:

It was a large ward, my bed was not clean and there was a smell from the woman in the next bed. The Sister had my bed moved to the opposite side under a window. A woman nearby began muttering against me, never meeting my eye, but looking just past me. She was accusing me of being in her bed. On the other side of the ward an old woman muttered darkly against me whenever I passed to and fro from the bathroom. A young Swiss girl about seventeen years old, totally withdrawn, sleepwalked between the beds, reaching out to hold the hand of any passer-by.[12]

Brenda sensed the despair and futility in the lives around her: 'The *wife* will kill herself because the husband had deserted her, *he* will kill himself if she will not take him back, the *mistress* will kill herself if he returns to his wife'.[13] There was a feeling of hopelessness, of problems with no solutions:

To this place we have come as to a refuge from impossible problems. Rather than face bankruptcy, one dives into the smooth white bed in the orderly ward. Our problems are insuperable, we cry. The story is told over and over to the point where one could scream.[14]

Brenda wrote in her notebook for the duration of her stay in hospital. She described her feelings, thoughts, observations and dreams, and decided to rework the writings into an article which she hoped to have published in the magazine *Mabon*. In a letter to Alan Clodd, she wrote: 'Am completely disgusted with myself for getting into such a state. I've been working a bit here, to get things out of my system'.[15] She was determined not to allow herself to sink down into the state of some of the other patients: 'This is where I hit myself on the back of the head. This is the bin, the tunnel of echoes, the sick place. The corridors are filled with distorted faces, faces without magnetism, bodies without fire'.[16]

She compared the situation with Greece where

> ...at this moment the island boys are throwing themselves into the foaming sea, knowing exactly where they are, and where they are going. Here, nobody has a purpose, slow tears like those of the birth-giving turtle, run on many faces. Mouths lack mobility; despair rides high and low. Everyone is at a standstill, though they make the motions of walking about and sitting down, even of conversation.[17]

In all her descriptions Brenda saw herself as an observer rather than as a patient. As she improved, she felt even more out of place amongst the patients and asked to be moved to Gwynfryn, the convalescent centre at the hospital. Brenda's observations are acute and focus on her horror of being out of control and misunderstood:

> A doctor came to examine me. I mistook him for an inmate, he looked so disturbed, hideously ugly, with a harsh voice, lacking in sympathy.
> 'Do you want to kill yourself?'
> 'I most certainly do not.'
> I turned away my head. He examined me.[18]

Brenda tried to convince the nurses and the Sister that she needed to be transferred to Gwynfryn but no one took any notice and it was some time before she was able to speak to another doctor. After a long discussion and an examination a bed was arranged for her in Gwynfryn that afternoon.

> At about 2.30 suitcase in hand, in nightdress and dressing gown, I was escorted by the sister through the same nightmare corridors, aware that the floors were slightly tilted towards the outdoors. A taxi took us uphill towards Gwynfryn.[19]

To Brenda it was like being transferred to another world and back to sanity:

> G. is a long, low building. The ward was tranquil, in a sunfilled garden. A pot of flowers stood at the foot of each bed. It was enough to break one, the sudden enfoldment, the peace. I lay down, began to relax.[20]

In Gwynfryn, Brenda found refuge and was able to escape temporarily from the worries of work and money which had tormented her. Although there was an occupational therapy room where patients could paint and do handicrafts, Brenda stayed away from it.

> I had thought to find a few inspired paintings. The externalising of phobias and inhibitions to release tension. Instead, hideous trays, more hideous coffee tables... I have rebelled finally against occupational therapy. It is the bitterest joke to see everyone so cowed and subjected, making hideous embroideries and trays,

382

planning coach outings to Llandudno and social evenings. For the common mean I suppose this is justifiable; it is the way most people function.[21]

Instead of participating and mixing with the other patients, Brenda spent most of her time alone, writing, and thinking back with fondness to her life in Greece: 'I close my eyes, and there is a translucent sea full of swimmers and puttering benzinas, white chapels, the overwhelming breath of resin'.[22]

After a week in Gwynfryn Brenda was allowed to go home for the weekend. Initially, she was excited and on Saturday friends took her to the International Eisteddfod at Llangollen. By Sunday, 'I was neither here nor there, and did not know in which place I wanted to be. It is difficult to orientate myself now that I am back, the sense of a new place having worn thin'.[23] In retrospect she realised that she had found the weekend a strain and was relieved to return to the security of Gwynfryn. When she went home the following weekend, she felt more at ease and was unhappy to return, which was seen as a good sign. After another week at Gwynfryn, she was discharged and she returned to her flat on Glanrafon Hill.

After a month at the hospital, Brenda felt more stable and better able to cope with life. Her previous worries now seemed manageable. She had been able to proofread her books at Gwynfryn, and *Poems with Drawings* was due to be published within two months. She received a letter from David Tinker, then Head of Art at the University College of Wales, Aberystwyth, inviting her to exhibit her work there in December, and she was also planning an exhibition for the spring with the Welsh Arts Council. The latter would

Brenda at Fron Dirion, Bangor, August 1969

incorporate her Greek writings with her drawings and tie in with the theme of her book, *Poems with Drawings*. Having found the art classes at the psychiatric hospital Denbigh so uninspiring, Brenda offered to teach art therapy there and each Thursday, she had a lift with her friend, Sheila Mundle, who worked at the hospital. Teaching the classes helped Brenda regain her confidence and she began to feel much better. Her anxieties about money had been alleviated too, for since her breakdown, she had been receiving some state benefit payments.

In September, Brenda's spirits soared when friends from Greece, Roger Maybank, Marios Loizides, and Robertos Saragas came to visit her in Bangor. She was particularly overjoyed to see Robertos as they had not spoken since *The Dance Recital* in London in 1964, when they had argued after Robertos was late for a performance. Brenda felt happier than she had for months. She took them on trips to see the mountains and beaches around her home and constantly pressed them for more news about Hydra. While they were in Bangor, Robertos became involved with a student production of a play, *Staircase*, by Charles Dyer[24] and decided to stay on after his friends returned to Greece. He spent a lot of time with the students, instructing them in ways of moving and projecting life into their work. He stayed until they had finished the production. Brenda was sorry to see him go, he made her feel she had something to give, and she missed his energy.

Although she had previously declared her correspondence with the Welsh Arts Council to be at an end, her new self-confidence led her to write once again to Meic Stephens offering various manuscripts for sale. She suggested a proof copy of *The Green Heart* with book-jacket and original drawings which had not been used by Oxford University Press; a red notebook from Bardsey dated April 1950 containing poetry and prose; and a green notebook, dated Spring 1953, London, containing the first draft in long-hand of *The Water-Castle*. Meic Stephens told Brenda that the Literature Committee would consider the first draft of *The Water-Castle* and the proof copy of *The Green Heart* and asked Brenda to state clearly how much she wanted for them. After consulting Alan Clodd, she asked £100 for *The Water-Castle* and £150 for *The Green Heart*. A gap in their correspondence followed, as the Literature Committee did not meet until November.

In October, when *Poems with Drawings* was published, Brenda went to London to sign the two-hundred-copy limited edition. The book was well-designed with poems and drawings placed alongside each other on opposite pages. It included seventeen poems which varied in length from three to twenty-three lines and spanned the period from 1947 to 1967. All sixteen drawings were from the Greek period. Although the book was well subscribed, it was greeted with a mixed, and on the whole, noncommittal response. Most people wanted to make the connections between the words and their corresponding image, and were perturbed when they failed to do so. There were in fact only a few pages where the drawing and poem did obviously complement each other and while for Brenda each arrangement of word and image held a vital significance, her work of late had

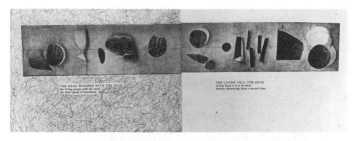

A double page from *Poems with Drawings*, pp. 8–9

became so personal that those connections were not easily communicable to others. A straightforward link could be seen between one of Brenda's pebble drawings and a fragment of her poem, 'Rose of Lima', which speaks of the 'Barber-coloured wave-worn pebble', and was originally written during the 1940s on Bardsey. She noted in *Tiderace* that the poem was inspired by phrases from the Masses of the Saints in the Catholic Missal and dedicated to St. Rose of Lima.[26] It was a poem full of nostalgia, evoking images of sea-rock of Bardsey and the religious soil which houses twenty thousand saints.

All the poems included in the collection held strong memories for Brenda and three related to particular men who were important to her. The dedicatory poem, taken from her book *The Green Heart* is to Karl von Laer, and 'The Dawn-Foretelling Cock' was written for a dance by Robertos Saragas. In her book Brenda places it alongside a drawing called *Genesis* which was sometimes known as *Greek Dance*, a work which emerged from her sessions of automatic drawing with Halim El Dabh. The third man was 'Leonidas', whom Brenda evoked in the poem on page 22 of the book. Throughout *A Rope of Vines* (which she had originally called The *Pelican*), Brenda had used the image of

Genesis/Greek Dance, wax crayon on card, September 1965,
reproduced in *Poems with Drawings*, p. 29

the pelican to represent 'Leonidas'. She described him as
the persecuted bird who was harried out of the sea by a
crowd of Greeks, and

> ... was borne along, hemmed in midst of craven
> persecution towards the police-station, a bloody-breasted
> bird, to be accused of what? Of simply being the axe-
> beaked pelican, the self-wounder destined to be mob-
> wounded. This bird has been tried and found guilty by the
> people of Chalkis long before it had reached the law courts.
> What sore place in my consciousness is touched by the
> memory of the pious bird? Leonidas on the waterfront at
> Ydra! The bird has taught me what the man suffered
> when he was taken by the people.[27]

388

Since being in Greece Brenda felt more attuned to myths and symbols and here compares Leonidas' fate with that of the pelican known to be both a symbol of atonement and of Christ's sacrifice on the cross. She also adapted this in the following poem, which appears in *Poems with Drawings*:

A sore place in me is probed
by the agony of a pious bird

On Sunday morning,
it is the townsmen's amusement

to harry the pelican,
to persecute the fish-gobbler

the bloody-breasted, axe-beaked pelekan [*sic*],
the self wounder

is tried and found guilty
before it has reached the law courts.[28]

Of the remaining poems, eight were extracted from the text of 'The Protagonists'. These were stark and imagistic and thought by some to be incomplete. In her attempts to simplify her work, Brenda tried to eliminate what she felt to be unnecessary words and lines, but she was sometimes too ruthless and took away a little too much. While for Brenda, the book was full of memories for the reader, it leaves many unanswered questions.

When Brenda returned from signing the books in London, she went to stay on Anglesey for a week to look after the children of Norma Fulford who had rented Henry Mitchell's house on Hydra the previous summer. Brenda found it strange to be on the other side of the Straits again and she was glad it was only for a week. It brought back bad memories of her last stay on the island, as she told Janette in a letter: 'Since last night I am in this large house almost next door to the awful haunted palace where I suffered so much boredom last winter'. But the memories did not worry her unduly because she was in good spirits. She had been given permission to use the upper floors of the Canonry in Bangor as a studio and looked forward to have a large space in which to work.

When she returned to Bangor, she cleared the studio and laid out all her Greek work. From these she selected twenty pieces, mainly collage, for her show in Aberystwyth and set aside a pile of ready-prepared collage fragments to use in three-dimensional constructions and new work which she wanted to exhibit in her spring exhibition.

After the Welsh Arts Council Literature Committee met in November 1969, Brenda heard that they were considering the prices of her manuscripts and that they were also interested in the Alun Lewis letters, and asked if she would consider selling them. Unfortunately, this query led to another confused period of correspondence between Brenda and the Welsh Arts Council. Brenda had already offered the letters to the National Library of Wales and she became puzzled when the Welsh Arts Council expressed an interest. She discovered that the National Library did not want to buy them and so offered them to the Welsh Arts Council for £500, the figure originally suggested by the National Library. The Welsh Arts Council was quick to respond and by the beginning of December Brenda had received an offer of £500 for the twenty-eight letters and £50 for the first draft of *The Water-Castle*. Brenda agreed, and on 19 December she received a cheque for £550. For the first time in months Brenda felt she did not have to worry about money. She could relax a little, enjoy the Christmas holiday and put her energy into her work.

[1] Brenda Chamberlain, letter to Alan Clodd, 12 November 1968, private collection.

[2] Brenda Chamberlain, letter to Alan Clodd, 14 January 1969, private collection.

[3] Brenda Chamberlain, letter to Meic Stephens, Welsh Arts Council, 22 April 1969. NLW MS 20809E, f. 21.

[4] John Petts, letter to the author, Sept. 1983.

[5] Alan Clodd, letter to Brenda Chamberlain, 25 March 1969, private collection.

[6] Ibid.

[7] Brenda Chamberlain, letter to Alan Clodd, 26 March 1969, private collection.

[8] John Barry, 'The plea of a political exile', *The Sunday Times*, 16 March 1969, p. 13.

[9] John Barry, art. cit., p. 13.

[10] Mikis Theodorakis, 'For three days I have lived with death at my side ... ', *The Sunday Times*, 19 April 1969, pp. 1, 4.

[11] NLW MS 21501E, f. 33.

[12] Ibid., f. 33.

[13] Ibid., f. 30.

[14] Ibid., f. 28.

[15] Brenda Chamberlain, letter to Alan Clodd, private collection.

[16] NLW MS 21501E, f. 27.

[17] Ibid., f. 27.

[18] Ibid., f. 33.

[19] Ibid., f. 34.

[20] Ibid., f. 34.

[21] Ibid., f. 31.

[22] Ibid., f. 29.

[23] Ibid., f. 29.

[24] Charles Dyer, *Staircase, or, Charlie always told Harry almost everything* (London: W.H. Allen, 1969).

[25] For 'Rose of Lima', together with a description of the making of the poem, see *TR*, pp. 182-83. A version of the poem appeared in her *Poems with Drawings* and in the 'Word & Image' exhibition, 1970, which toured to Bangor, Cardiff and Cwm-brân. See below pp. 394, 399, 406.

[26] *RV*, p. 115.

[27] *PD*, p. 22.

[28] Brenda Chamberlain, letter to Janette Read, 22 October 1969, private collection.

Chapter 14

Waiting for the Wingbeat 1970-71

Brenda's financial stability did not last long. After Christmas, the Department of Social Security officials, who had continued to support her since her breakdown, contacted her to say they had decided to treat the £550 from the Welsh Arts Council as income and would therefore stop their regular payments. This news upset Brenda and her mood changed rapidly. She lost her will to work, caught flu which developed into bronchitis, and became depressed. She consulted the Welsh Arts Council who told her that although the payment was not subject to tax, they could not prevent its being viewed as income by the Department of Social Security. This was not the response Brenda had hoped for but a few days later the Social Security contacted her again, to say that the money was not now to be assessed as income after all, although a sale of a painting would be. Brenda felt a great weight had been lifted off her.

Despite this improvement, other factors prevented her from settling to her work. She was taking medication but was still run down from her illness. Her concentration was not as good as it had previously been and she became increasingly vague about making and keeping arrangements. Isabel Hitchman from the Welsh Arts Council had to write to her twice for basic information about measurements of her paintings and details of poster design for the forthcoming exhibition. In Brenda's first reply, she had omitted to write down the necessary information. She sought constant reassurance about the quality of her work and became more reliant on the company of her friends.

As the *Word & Image* exhibition approached, Brenda was forced back to work, but found she had only limited energy. Sometimes she worked at the Canonry, but mostly she stayed in her new flat in Menai View Terrace, because she felt less isolated there. In between her bursts of activity Brenda would visit one or other of her friends She called most days at all the various friends she knew in the terrace – the Cookes, the Mundles, the Daniels, the Banks, Alan McPherson, and Vasilis Politis – and went to see Joan Rees, a friend and patron who also lived nearby.[1] Brenda had become a carrier of titbits of gossip from one household to another in Upper Bangor and it was a poor day for her if she did not have lunch in one or other of them.

Alan McPherson had been to Aberystwyth to collect the paintings from her previous show there, but Brenda decided not to include any of them in her spring exhibition. She was determined to present a completely different range of her Greek work and to exhibit it alongside the text of her Greek poems. She found it a challenge to combine her writing and her art and soon became engrossed in selecting poems and drawings which would complement each other. This was not easy to do because she wanted the words and the images to be of equal importance in the exhibition.

For a few weeks all the news Brenda received was good. She heard that Gottfried and Annette, two of Karl von Laer's children, were planning to spend four or five weeks of their holiday that summer in Bangor. This pleased Brenda, as she had known them since they were babies and was very fond of their company. Then two of her poems were accepted for publication in the spring edition of *Poetry Wales*: 'Nisi Leros' told of the restrictions in Greece caused by the Colonels' coup and 'At Mrs King's Water Castle' gave a nostalgic view of a stormy day at the Schloss in Germany.[2] In addition she was invited to give a talk about her work to the Literary Group at Wrexham. In March 1970, *Alun Lewis and the Making of the Caseg Broadsheets* was published by Enitharmon Press and Brenda stopped work on her exhibition to go to London to sign and number

ALUN LEWIS & THE MAKING
OF THE CASEG BROADSHEETS

WITH A LETTER FROM VERNON WATKINS AND
A CHECKLIST OF THE BROADSHEETS

ENITHARMON PRESS LONDON 1970

Title page, *Alun Lewis & the Making of the Caseg Broadsheets*, 1970 the three hundred copies of the limited edition. An additional set of thirty-five copies of the book were specially bound. She was relieved to see the book in print as she had found it such a struggle to prepare. Brenda had written an introductory account of how the broadsheets began and then added background notes between most of Alun Lewis's letters, which she had edited and arranged chronologically. Although it is a fascinating insight into the life of Alun Lewis during the years 1941-44, it is only a one-sided correspondence and there are no letters from Brenda and John to Alun. It also lacked the inclusion of letters which Alun had written to John. Brenda included two of her wood engravings and Broadsheets No. 1 and No. 2 were illustrated.

The book was greeted with great interest by scholars of Alun Lewis and sold steadily. At the time of publication it received few reviews and it was not until 1975 that a critical analysis of the book was written by Roland Mathias and published in the Alun Lewis Special Issue of *Poetry Wales*.[3] After reading Brenda's book, Mathias had been motivated to go to the National Library of Wales to read the original twenty-eight letters. He was curious to know what Brenda omitted and hoped there would be more to learn about Lewis by consulting the originals.

In his article 'The Caseg Letters: a commentary', Roland Mathias gives a full account of the content of Alun Lewis's letters and the way in which Brenda had edited and presented the extracts in her book. He was particularly surprised at the number of errors and alterations that Brenda had made when editing the letters and he drew attention to the frequent occasions when Brenda omitted phrases and words which significantly altered the sense of the letter. She had also changed words, such as Alun's 'cheeryble' to 'cheerful' and 'railway orifices' to 'railway offices'. But the worst errors appear in the way Brenda confused the dates of letters and moved paragraphs from one letter to another. Mathias cites one particular example:

On page 7 of her text Brenda Chamberlain printed a letter dated 25 April 1941. The holograph letter carries the date 25 August 1941, as clearly as Alun Lewis ever wrote his dates. As a result this letter appears much too early in the sequence, alleging among other things, that Allen and Unwin were using John Petts' engraving of Alun for the cover of *Raiders' Dawn* and that they might consider publishing the Broadsheets in book form, all of which clearly belongs, from the evidence of the other letters, to a period five months later. This error is compounded by the fact that the letter's postscript is printed on page 18 of the Chamberlain text, attached to the letter dated October 1941. The postscript which really belongs to this October letter is omitted altogether and the letter's text in the book, though editorially dated 'October', is introduced by a passage in which it is allocated to September. How errors of this sort should occur, and at what stage some of them happened, is almost a matter for creative fantasy.[4]

He also makes the observation that as Brenda's text progresses, the errors and omissions 'grow more frequent, as though increasing haste were a factor in the judgement'.[5] Brenda's work on the letters had been badly interrupted by other projects and ill health – indeed, the proofs were corrected while she was still convalescing in hospital. In one way it is not surprising that so many errors occurred, but it is still hard to explain how she managed to present

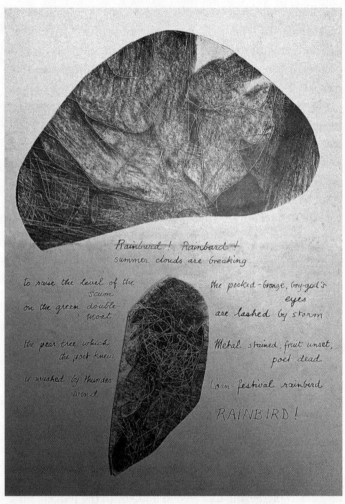

Rainbard, collage, used on poster for
Word & Image exhibition, 1970

the letters in such a muddled and misleading way. She had always upheld high standards in her work and in many ways it is a blessing that her confused presentation of the Alun Lewis letters was not brought to light during her lifetime, for she would undoubtedly have been deeply distressed by the exposure of her poor efforts. As it was, Brenda was oblivious of the errors when the book was published and she remained satisfied with her work.

Almost immediately after the publication of *Alun Lewis and the Making of the Caseg Broadsheets*, Brenda's exhibition, *Word & Image* opened in Cardiff. She had selected four collages, sixteen drawings and one three-dimensional construction and arranged them alongside sixteen framed, handwritten poems, which were enlarged to the same dimensions as the drawings and collages. While

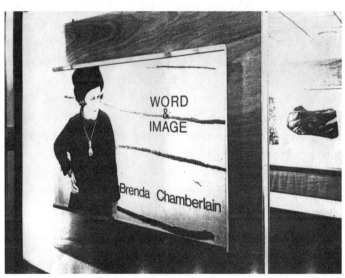

An installation photo from the *Word & Image Exhibition*, 1970

the drawings and collages were from the period 1965-66, the poems spanned a greater time, from the 1940s to the year of the exhibition. Some had been written on Bardsey and some in Greece. 'Poetry is too complex a process for me to pin down', explained Brenda, 'Its roots are too obscure. It really *is* a great mystery, involving railway stations, lonely shores, strong attachments to place; but out of time, in any strict sense. None of the poems can be dated, therefore'.[6] The private view on April 3 was a lively occasion. It was well attended and Brenda read some of her favourite poems. Both her books were on sale and although these sold well, there were few buyers for the drawings. Naturally, she was disappointed but hoped the exhibition would do better in Cwmbran and Anglesey, where it was to tour.

While she was in Cardiff, Brenda recorded a poem for the Welsh Arts Council's new 'Dial a Poem' scheme. By ringing a certain telephone number it was possible to hear a poem by an Anglo-Welsh or Welsh poet and for a year there was a poem a week. The recording lasted three minutes and began with a brief biography of the poet. Where the original poem was in the Welsh language, it was followed by an English translation. Brenda wrote a poem especially for the purpose. Part of it was taken from a prose fragment she had written in the 1950s, 'In Holstein I long for the Midi' which was also used as the beginning of her play 'A One-Legged man takes a walk'. The poem was called 'Why should it take so long to get out of these mountains' and is full of references to Bardsey and her driving trip through Europe in 1962. The overriding theme of this plaintive poem is one of being lost and out of control:

I fail to understand
why it should take so long
to reach nowhere

There you go, imagining things,
I can hear them say –
exaggerating as usual

We haven't moved for hours
either forward or back
we should have been there
a week ago, days past, anyway

For God's sake, not so fast!
Are you trying to kill us?[7]

There are constant references to being held back and
unable to move:

Look out of the window –
we're not moving, it's the same Rockplace

and

Ach! trapped here, between sweating rocks
and the lightning, we need reassurance
every step of the way, all day.

It ends:

STOP! somebody shouts
but I can't stop: I'm not driving

Who is in charge of this machine,
who is in charge of this machine?

Visual images from the poem emerged in a series of drawings which Brenda began in May in Bangor. She drew haunting, surreal images in black ink on a large sketchbook of thin paper. In all but a dozen of the series of around ninety drawings, there is the image of a body restrained by the surrounding objects. The subject is a young woman and although the features are not identical to Brenda's it is undoubtedly a self-image. The figures are trapped inside jugs4 and are straining to move, women's heads are imprisoned between piles of stones, immobile and forlorn. One set of drawings shows a woman's head and neck wrapped tightly in bandages, while another set traps the female body inside the form of a tree. The head emerging at the top strains to free the roots which are held down by the earth.

Jugs and Flowerpots, July 1970, ink on paper

Bandaged Heads, 23 October 1970, ink on paper

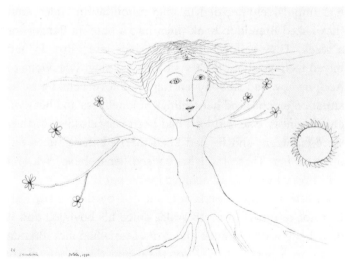

Apollo and Daphne, 1970, ink on paper

Some of the drawings show touches of whimsical humour in the floating bodies, birds with a woman's face and figures with webs as bodies, but the overriding mood is depressing. In a drawing of a boat, a female figurehead senses freedom on the sea but her head is pressed down by a heavy cloud sitting boulder-like on it. Once more movement has been restricted, the subject's freedom stopped by outside intervention. There is a feeling that no one is to blame. In each drawing, it is a natural element which is shown curtailing the action; a cloud, a pebble, a tree, but certainly not another person. This very personal series of drawings clearly reflected Brenda's state of mind at the time.

She stopped drawing in June when she spent a couple of days in London at the opening of an exhibition of the work of her Greek Cypriot friend, Marios Loizides, at the Institute of Contemporary Art. Then in mid-July, she heard from Karl von Laer that he and his third wife Grita Maria had impulsively decided to take a holiday in Wales, and they asked Brenda to book them into a hotel in Bangor for a week. They arrived just a few days later. Brenda had mixed feelings about their visit. She felt slightly envious of Karl; he now had a happy marriage and lovely children. His situation emphasised her feelings of loneliness and her own childlessness. She and Karl had been very close since they were eighteen, and he had been married three times but never to her. These thoughts caused her to look back and question what she had achieved with her life.

On the surface, Brenda was thrilled by their visit; Karl had not returned to north Wales since his boyhood and it was the first time Brenda and Grita Maria had met. Brenda arranged a busy itinerary for them and there were many trips to see the sights of north Wales. Karl wanted to see

Bardsey so Brenda took them down to the tip of the Llŷn peninsula where they would be able to see the island. But the weather was unkind, as she told Alan Clodd in a letter. The island was

> … in a winding sheet of thin seafog – when we returned to the village (Aberdaron), R.S. Thomas was just striding to church for the evening service, looking as though he might denounce onlookers like fiery Welsh parsons in the old days.[8]

Karl and Grita Maria returned to Germany at the end of July and a few days later, Karl's son and daughter Gottfried and Annette arrived. Brenda was very excited to see them. More visits from friends followed and Brenda regained her sense of fun and adventure, which had faded considerably in previous months. They went to beaches, to Snowdonia and to Parys Mountain on Anglesey where the vivid oranges, yellows and greens of the old copper mines enthralled Brenda. Before Gottfried and Annette left, Brenda joined them for a few days in London and showed them around the art galleries. She was sad to see them leave and decided to visit them in Germany at Christmas. This would give her something to look forward to.

Once all the visitors had left, Brenda began to think about her next show. She had received an invitation from Glyn Tegai Hughes to hold an exhibition at Gregynog, near Newtown in Montgomeryshire the following year, and to give a talk to the Montgomeryshire Literary Group. After discussing the exhibition with various friends, Brenda decided to show her new series of 'surrealist' drawings rather than use her Greek work, which had not proved to be very popular. She settled down to make some more drawings in the same style. Apart from working on these, Brenda still continued with her art classes at the hospital, even though she no longer found them stimulating. In mid-November she had a course of injections there and then went to London for a couple of days.

She was beginning to worry about money again, as her funds were getting dangerously low, when she suddenly received a cheque for £275 from the Welsh Arts Council. This was the hiring fee for her paintings and had been payable when the tour of *Word & Image* came to an end. She was also pleasantly surprised to receive a cheque for $15 from the *New York Times* as payment for reprinting her poem 'In Old Age'. An offer from Meic Stephens followed, with the promise of a £20 fee for writing an autobiographical essay for a book he was editing called *Artists in Wales*. In a sudden leap, Brenda's finances looked much healthier.

When she returned from London, she began writing the autobiographical essay, and in December went to Germany where she spent a few weeks with her old friends. It had been twelve years since her last visit and although her contemporaries had not changed a great deal, the children had all grown up and she found the atmosphere very different. Everyone seemed settled and happy with the rhythm of their lives and while Brenda felt secure and relaxed there, she knew that once she returned to Bangor her life would once more feel insecure and lonely.

As she had suspected, once back in Menai View Terrace, Brenda felt depressed. She had no inclination to paint and searched in vain for the inspiration to write. To occupy herself she spent most of her time visiting one friend after another in her daily tours of Upper Bangor.

Alan McPherson with Brenda playing the part of a Blind Woman
in the film made by the Film Society of the University College,
Bangor, April 1971

An abrupt improvement in her mood came at the end of
April 1971 when she took part in a film made by the
university's Film Society. Much of it was shot in her flat
and Brenda played the part of a blind woman. Being at the
centre of the project suited Brenda and she found it
refreshing to have her home full of lively students. She no
longer felt the urge to go out visiting and became more
relaxed. Working on the film gave her the idea of turning
her unfinished play 'A One-Legged man takes a walk' into
a film-script and she set to work on it enthusiastically. She
had begun the play in 1967 just before leaving Hydra and
over the years had made several attempts to complete it.
Now, deciding that it would work better as a film, Brenda

decided to set it in the copper mines of Parys Mountain. Recalling her recent visit with Gottfried and Annette, she felt it would be the perfect location. Apart from the unexpected range of colours in the hills of shale, the whole area had the desolate and rather surreal quality that Brenda wanted to create.

In the play the action revolves around four characters who are sitting in a wrecked car abandoned near a lake of rust-coloured water. Although the car has broken seats, no windscreen or steering wheel, the men, Antoniades, Paion, Bistas and Stamnos discuss their destination and continually question why they have not arrived. The characters believe they are moving although it is obvious they are not. The play extends the theme of being trapped and lost which Brenda had introduced in her poem recorded for 'Dial a Poem' in June. In the dialogue Antoniades questions:

'Why should it take so long to get out of these mountains? It's like drifting backwards when a springtide sets too strongly. I fail to understand why it should take so long to reach nowhere'.[9]

In the midst of the discussions in the car two women appear; Sissanis Phlotis is a prostitute who is troubled by fleas and the other is both a nun and a thorn tree.

Paion: Look there! She's got a butterfly net made of chain-mail. She's always trying to trap the reluctant passer-by.
Stamnos: But that isn't a woman; it's a thorn tree.
Paion: A woman wearing a butterfly-net.
Stanmos: A tree with bare branches.[10]

This recurrent preoccupation with metamorphosis relates quite clearly to Brenda's recent series of drawings where woman, trees and nets become interchangeable. A magazine cutting of a woman crouched behind the thorny branches of a bush is stuck in a sketchbook relating to the play.[11] Other cuttings and drawings in the book acted as reference points for the set and the other characters.

The next person to appear in the play is the King, who arrives in a hot-air balloon and is greeted by a battalion of soldiers/rams who suddenly emerge from a cave. The soldiers bleat like sheep, the balloon blows away, Antoniades throws himself off the edge of a chasm, the balloon returns, the King leaves and Bistas, the one-legged man, decides to take control. He throws away his crutches and his necktie, unscrews his wooden leg and crawls away talking about his mother and father.

The five extant drafts of the play vary a little from each other but all have the same surreal plot and disjointed dialogue. Neither the play nor the film-script of 'A One-Legged man takes a walk' was ever finished, but the texts reverberate with feelings of sadness, loneliness, confusion and despair:

Anton: Answer me; are we making for somewhere, or are we simply running away?[12]

Brenda was distracted once more by the need to organise the exhibition at Gregynog. She selected thirty-eight of her 'surreal' drawings which she then sent off to be framed. When they returned in dark grey frames Brenda thought they looked dreadful and depressing and wanted to change them, but there was insufficient time before they had to go to Gregynog.

On 29 April Brenda went to give her talk to the Montgomeryshire Literary Group and stayed on for the opening of the exhibition. The drawings were displayed in the Music Room and despite a few sales most people found them sad and disturbing. Although she needed the money from the sales, Brenda was much more concerned with the reaction of the critics and public to her work. She was disheartened and began to despair. For so many years her work had had a good reputation and had sold steadily, but now it all seemed such a struggle and people appeared not to like it any more. Short of ideas and inspiration, she continually looked back and tried to follow up old themes rather than be excited by new ones. In the past, the majority of her work had been inspired by the places in which she lived and the people around her. This had worked well in Llanllechid, Bardsey, Germany, France and on Hydra, but somehow Bangor did not give her the necessary stimulus, and as Anthony Conran points out, 'Bangor meant a great deal to her; and yet she never wrote about it, nor (as far as I know) did she paint its secrets'.[13]

In response to a request from the Welsh Arts Council for a second poem for their 'Dial a Poem' scheme she quickly wrote a new poem to be read out aloud. Entitled 'Why did you ring me?', it is a poem of negativity, of closed doors, of questions:

Why did you ring me?
are you sure it is the right number?
I have no merchandise
my possessions
would fill a small suitcase[14]

There are faint echoes of the themes of 'The Protagonists' in the following lines:

> If you need rubberstamps
> permits
> visas
> identity cards
> false noses
> tarot cards
> you are on the wrong line

And similarly in the lament of better times in the past:

> Out there, how does it feel?
> are there bars in front of your face?
> if so, you must try to remain calm
> remember Saturday afternoons by the sea
> and gardens given to silence
> young men sinuous-oiled as gods
>
> under sponge-clusters on the yards
> of a homeward ship
> If I could comfort you, then
> I would offer comfort
> but times are harder now
> than they were in my youth

Brenda was in need of that comfort, for she felt very lost. As she became more isolated and at a loss for inspiration, she turned increasingly to her friends, perhaps calling into one household three or four times in the course of a morning. Inevitably, her frequent tiptoeing into and out of

411

their kitchens and living rooms no longer received much attention. Even the children who had always adored Brenda's company, now sought to hide from her. One friend later recalled that during one outing to a nearby beach, one of the children was heard to say, 'Yes, come on, let's go right away – but don't tell Brenda'. She needed to be sustained by constant interest in her and it was difficult for her friends to fulfil this constant demand. Since returning to Bangor Brenda had not had a place where she felt she could really settle and when she learnt that 10 Menai View Terrace was going to be sold, she felt distressed at the thought of having to move yet again. Although she had finally accepted she could not return to Greece because of the new military regime, it was where she wanted to be and she found that very depressing. She felt desperately lonely and was finding it a struggle to create new work.

Pushed to the extreme, Brenda took an overdose of barbiturates on the morning of 8 July 1971. At about 10 o'clock that morning she had called round to see her friend and neighbour, Ann Cooke, as she often did, and stayed a few minutes. Everything seemed quite normal and then, apparently, Brenda returned a few minutes later but Ann did not see her. At about ten past eleven Brenda went to the house again and this time she was very distressed and said she had taken eighteen tablets. While Ann rang the hospital, Brenda stayed with Maurice Cooke whom she told, 'I have done a very foolish thing. This is a cri de coeur'.[15] At the hospital Brenda was treated immediately and although the concentration of barbiturate was reduced, the overdose had caused changes in the brain and Brenda died three days later. An inquest was called and the pathologist, Dr O.G. Jones, said that the cause of death was due to a combination of hypoxia, brain haemorrhage and the overdose. The verdict of the inquest was accidental death.

On 15 July 1971 there was a service at St. David's church, Bangor and the burial took place at Glanadda Cemetery. Obituaries and tributes appeared in several newspapers and periodicals. Because Brenda's death had come so suddenly, many of her friends did not hear the news until long after the funeral. For some, it came as a surprise, but for others, it was seen as the inevitable conclusion to one who had become so sad, so lonely and so drained of inspiration since her return from Greece.

Brenda left a will made five months earlier:

LAST WILL AND TESTAMENT OF BRENDA IRENE CHAMBERLAIN (PETTS) – FEBRUARY 1971

I give and bequeath unto Gottfried von Hoppfgarten von Laer; my German notebooks of which 2 are dated December 1953, July 1954; one is dated Xmas 1954, one is dated September 1954, one is dated July 1954, one is dated March 1955, one is dated January 1956 and the last is dated March 1958. Also, my sketchbooks and paintings of mine which are still in my possession to go to him if he so desires. If I should die before he reaches the age of 21, these things are to go to his father, Karl von Hoppfgarten von Laer.

WITNESSES: Joan Rees, March 19th 1971
                           Maurice Cooke, 8 Menai View Terrace[16]

However, the will was declared not valid since the signatures had not been properly witnessed, and consequently Brenda was regarded as having died intestate, which meant that her belongings were automatically bequeathed to her mother. Mrs Chamberlain spent some weeks deciding what to do about Brenda's work. She gathered her notebooks together, put them in order and separated out the journals relating to her trips to Germany, which had been the ones listed in Brenda's will. She felt that these belonged with Karl von Laer and his family in Germany as Brenda had requested. She sorted out sketchbooks and drawings of the German children and landscapes and put these on one side too. Gottfried later went to north Wales to collect these things and take them back to Germany.

There were still a large number of paintings and drawings, and Mrs Chamberlain appointed the artist Kyffin Williams as executor of Brenda's art work. All the art work was gathered together and Mrs Chamberlain invited each of Brenda's friends to choose a painting they would like. Then each of the major art galleries in Wales was contacted and given the opportunity to choose a painting for its collection.

A great deal of Brenda's work still remained, both art and writings, which Mrs Chamberlain chose to keep. When she herself died in August 1972, her estate passed to her son, Neville, who was living in the Midlands. In 1973 he decided to organise and exhibition and sale of Brenda's paintings and drawings in the Tegfryn Gallery in Menai Bridge on Anglesey. The exhibition included work from Bardsey, Hydra and her last series of 'surreal' drawings which had by then become known as the Gregynog Drawings. It allowed many of the people who had known Brenda to buy something of her work and in fact much of the exhibition sold. The many manuscripts, sketchbooks and files of letters had been offered to the National Library of Wales which purchased them in 1972, and in 1973 several manuscripts donated by Joan Rees were added to this collection.[17]

In 1973 a Memorial Exhibition of Brenda Chamberlain's work was organised by the National Museum of Wales and the Welsh Arts Council. Maurice Cooke selected the paintings and prepared the catalogue and the exhibition opened in Cardiff in July before touring to Aberystwyth and Bangor. It was a carefully selected exhibition of Brenda's work spanning the years 1938 to 1971 and included many of her finest paintings. Writing in his foreword to the catalogue, Rollo Charles, Keeper of Art at the National Museum of Wales, stressed that the life and work of Brenda Chamberlain fully deserved to be recognised and remembered:

> An exhibition like this can be little more than a public salute at an art which was essentially personal. But it is right that Wales should pay tribute to the talents which she nurtured.

But perhaps her true epitaph can be found in her own writing:

> THERE IS NEVER an end.
> Nothing ever finishes, we flow like wine,
>
> generation into generation, not dying;
>
> we flow and break new shapes,
> new forms out of archaic moulds.

I love he loves she loves they love
I die he dies she dies they die, but it is
not death; it is flower in the rock,
the bird on the winter sea.[18]

[1] Joan Rees, who was married to the Welsh writer and academic, Brinley R. Rees, bought many of her paintings, drawings and manuscripts from the 1930s onwards, to help Brenda survive financially. Joan Rees presented some of these items to the National Library of Wales in 1973, and after she died in 2001 the residue of her collection was also given to the National Library.

[2] *Poetry Wales* v.iii (Spring 1970), 12.

[3] Roland Mathias, 'The Caseg letters – A Commentary', *Poetry Wales* 10.iii (Winter 1973-74), 47-77.

[4] Ibid., p. 57.

[5] Ibid., p. 54.

[6] Catalogue essay, *Word & Image* exhibition, 1970.

[7] 'In Holstein I long for the Midi', NLW MS 21501E, ff. 59-61; 'A One Legged man takes a walk', NLW MS 21495C, featured in 'Dial-a-Poem' for Welsh Arts Council, recorded Cardiff, April 1970.

[8] Brenda Chamberlain, letter to Alan Clodd, 2 Aug. 1970, private collection.

[9] Third draft, NLW MS 21497E, f. 5.

[10] Ibid., f. 11.

[11] Third draft, NLW MS 21496E, f. 11.

[12] Third draft, NLW MS 21497E, f. 11.

[13] Anthony Conran, 'The Writing of Brenda Chamberlain', *Anglo Welsh Review*, 20.xlvi (Spring 1972), 19-23 (p. 19); a revised and slightly extended version of this essay was later published Anthony Conran, *The Cost of Strangeness* (Llandysul: Gomer, 1982), pp. 202-211 (pp. 202-203).

[14] The poem was recorded in April 1970 for the Welsh Arts

Council's 'Dial a Poem' project and received 1036 calls. It also featured in 'The Protagonists'.

[15] Maurice Cooke in conversation with the author, 19 April 1973.

[16] Transcribed by the author from the original document in a private collection. The full form of the von Laer family's surname was von Hoppfgarten-Laer.

[17] See note 1 above.

[18] Acting script of 'The Protagonists', as performed 1968, p. 36; *PD*, p. 7.

Select Bibliography

The main archive of material relating to Brenda Chamberlain is held at the National Library of Wales, Aberystwyth. It includes notebooks, journals, drafts of published and unpublished poetry and prose and correspondence, together with photographs, sketches, drawings and other original works of art.

Detailed references to primary and secondary sources cited, including individual poems and short prose works and uncollected works, may be found in the notes to each chapter, and accessed via the Index.

PUBLISHED WORKS BY BRENDA CHAMBERLAIN

[With John Petts], 'From Other Hills (Letters from the Western highlands, with Wood-engravings by the Writers)', *The Welsh Review*, 2.4 (Nov. 1939), pp. 197-205.

The Green Heart (London: Oxford University Press, 1958) [*GH*].

Tide-race (London: Hodder & Stoughton, 1962) [*TR*].

The Water-Castle (London: Hodder & Stoughton, 1964)
[*WC*].

A Rope of Vines (London: Hodder & Stoughton, 1965)
[*RV*].

Poems with Drawings (London: Enitharmon Press, 1969)
[*PD*].

Alun Lewis and the Making of the Caseg Broadsheets
(London: Enitharmon Press, 1970) [*ALCB*].

'Brenda Chamberlain', in Meic Stephens (ed.), *Artists in
Wales* (Llandysul: Gomer, 1971) [*AW*].

CATALOGUE ESSAYS:
Two Painters: Brenda Chamberlain and Ernest Zobole
(Welsh Committee of the Arts Council of Great Britain,
1963).

Word & Image (Welsh Arts Council, 1970).

OTHER PUBLISHED SOURCES
[Anon.], 'Bust of the Age of Praxiteles', *The Times*, 5 Nov.
1953, p. 8.

— 'Brenda Chamberlain's Bardsey', *House and Garden*
(April 1959), p. 71.

— 'An Island Painter: One woman realises her dreams',
The Lady, 16 April 1953, p. 480.

Barry, John, 'The plea of a political exile', *The Sunday
Times*, 16 March 1969, p. 13.

Conran, Anthony, 'The Writing of Brenda Chamberlain', *Anglo-Welsh Review*, 20 (1972), 19-23; revised version in Anthony Conran, *The Cost of Strangeness* (Llandysul: Gomer, 1982), pp. 202-211.

Cooke, Maurice, 'The Painting of Brenda Chamberlain', *Anglo-Welsh Review*, 20 (1972), 3-16.

Dyer, Charles, *Staircase, or, Charlie always told Harry almost everything* (London: W.H. Allen, 1969).

Firbank, Thomas, *I bought a mountain* (London: Harrap, 1940).

Garlick, Raymond, in Meic Stephens (ed.), *Artists in Wales 2*, (Llandysul: Gomer, 1973), pp. 83-97.

Garlick, Raymond, 'Some Painters', *Planet* 108 (Dec. 1994-Jan. 1995), 67-73.

Jones, Peter (ed.), *Imagist Poetry*, (Harmondsworth: Penguin, 1972).

Lewis, Alun, 'The Wanderers', *The Welsh Review* 2.4 (Nov. 1939), 128-39.

McPherson, Alan, interview with Brenda Chamberlain, *Forecast* (UCNW Bangor, April/May 1968), 18-19.

Mathias, Roland, 'The Caseg letters – A Commentary', *Poetry Wales* 10.iii (Winter 1973-74), 47-77.

Petts, John, *Welsh Horizons* (1983 Radio Wales Lecture, London: BBC Publications, 1984).

Rilke, Rainer Maria, *Selected Letters of Rainer Maria Rilke 1902-1926*, ed. & trans. R.F.C. Hull (London: Macmillan, 1946).

Smith, Alison, *John Petts and the Caseg Press* (Aldershot: Ashgate, 2000).

Theodorakis, Mikis, 'For three days I have lived with death at my side ... ', *The Sunday Times*, 19 April 1969, pp. 1, 4.

UNPUBLISHED SOURCES
Holman, Kate, 'The literary achievement of Brenda Chamberlain', (MA thesis, University of Swansea, 1976).

Index

Page references in **bold** print are to the black and white illustrations within the text. References to colour plates are in **_bold italics_**.

426

428

Acknowledgements

The author would like to thank the Estate of Brenda Chamberlain for permission to reproduce the work of Brenda Chamberlain.

ILLUSTRATIONS
Colour plates:

Frontispiece, 6	National Museum Wales
1, 2, 3, 4, 8, 11, 12, 15, 16	Private collections
5	Formerly in the collection of Merthyr Tydfil Education Authority, currently untraced
7	Glynn Vivian Art Gallery, Swansea
9	Mural in Carreg, Bardsey Island, now painted over
10	Amgueddfa ac Oriel Gwynedd, Bangor/Gwynedd Museum & Art Gallery, Bangor
13, 14	The Estate of Brenda Chamberlain

Illustrations in the text, listed by page number, are reproduced with kind permission of:
Amgueddfa ac Oriel Gwynedd, Bangor/Gwynedd Museum & Art Gallery, Bangor, 189, 201
Bangor University, 181, 188
Kitty Crapster, front dust jacket, 341
Cyfarthfa Castle Museum & Art Gallery, Merthyr Tydfil, 183
Enitharmon Press, 387
The Estate of E.E. Pritchard, back dust jacket, 193
Douglas B. Hague, maps on 9, 66, 52, 200, 270, 282
Gwynedd Archives, 85
P.S. Hughes, 58
Peter Jones, 384
Llyfrgell Genedlaethol Cymru/The National Library of Wales, 20 (NLW Facs 974), 175 (photo by Geoff Charles), 254 (photo by Geoff Charles), 309 (NLW MS 21518C), 317 (NLW MS 21520B), 366, 403 (W1A6NL 003381769).
Frances & Nicholas McDowell, 174
Mrs Anna Petts, 44
Jill Piercy, 229, 285, 329, 330, 372

All other works are in private collections.

QUOTATIONS
Permission to reproduce correspondence between Alan Clodd and Brenda Chamberlain has been granted by Alan Clodd's family.
Other quotations from:
Roland Mathias © The Estate of Roland Mathias
Interview in *Forecast* by permission of Alan McPherson